New Hampshire

JEFF BINDER

Photography by Thomas Mark Szelog

COMPASS AMERICAN GUIDES
An Imprint of Fodor's Travel Publications

New Hampshire

Copyright © 2002 Fodors LLC
Maps copyright © 2002 Fodors LLC

Compass American Guides is a registered trademark of Random House, Inc.
Fodor's is a registered trademark of Random House, Inc.

First Edition

ISBN 0-676-90151-4
ISSN 1539-249X

Editors: Daniel Mangin, Chris Culwell, Kit Duane
Designer: Christopher Burt
Photo Editors: Christopher Burt, Melanie Marin
Map Design: Mark Stroud, Moon Street Cartography
Production House: Twin Age Ltd., Hong Kong

Compass American Guides, 280 Park Avenue, New York, NY 10017
Printed in China
10 9 8 7 6 5 4 3 2 1

To Joe Binder, Dave Eakin, and Debi, forever—J.B.

To my mother, Josephine Vyrros, thank you for the love and direction—T.M.S.

C O N T E N T S

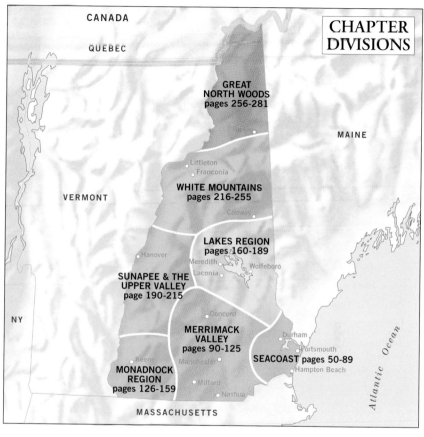

CANADA

QUEBEC

CHAPTER DIVISIONS

GREAT
NORTH WOODS
pages 256-281

MAINE

Littleton
Franconia

WHITE MOUNTAINS
pages 216-255

VERMONT

Conway

LAKES REGION
pages 160-189

Hanover

Meredith   Wolfeboro

SUNAPEE & THE   Laconia
UPPER VALLEY
page 190-215

NY

Concord

MERRIMACK
VALLEY   Durham
pages 90-125   Portsmouth

Keene   Manchester   SEACOAST pages 50-89
MONADNOCK   Hampton Beach
REGION   Milford
pages 126-159   Nashua

MASSACHUSETTS

Atlantic Ocean

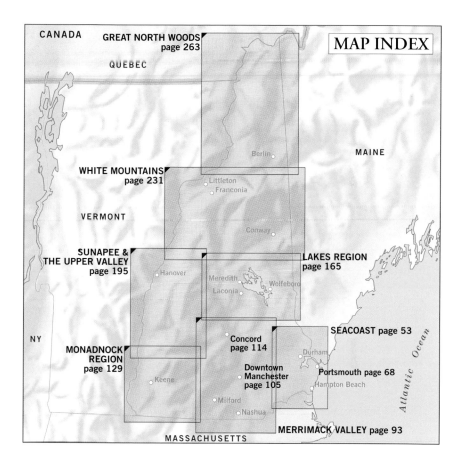

MAP INDEX

CANADA

GREAT NORTH WOODS
page 263

QUEBEC

Berlin

MAINE

WHITE MOUNTAINS
page 231

Littleton
Franconia

VERMONT

Conway

SUNAPEE &
THE UPPER VALLEY
page 195

Hanover

Meredith
Laconia

Wolfeboro

LAKES REGION
page 165

SEACOAST page 53

NY

MONADNOCK
REGION
page 129

Keene

Concord
page 114

Durham

Downtown
Manchester
page 105

Portsmouth page 68

Hampton Beach

Milford

Nashua

MERRIMACK VALLEY page 93

Atlantic Ocean

MASSACHUSETTS

Maps

Literary Extracts

Topical Essays

BORDERS

BORDERS
BOOKS MUSIC AND CAFE
1 Crossgates Mall Road, Space L210
Albany, NY 12203
518-452-1054

```
STORE: 0471    REG: 02/12  TRAN#: 0358
SALE           09/01/2006  EMP:  00401

COMPASS AMER GD NH
      6800721    QP T          21.95

            Subtotal           21.95
BR: 8262449294     S

            Subtotal           21.95
            NEW YORK 8%         1.76
 1   Item   Total              23.71
            MASTERCARD         23.71
ACCT # /S XXXXXXXXXXXX2410
            AUTH:   708136
NAME: WEINBERG        /NORMA A
```

CUSTOMER COPY

09/01/2006 08:31PM

T·Mobile
HotSpot

BORDERS.   VISA

BORDERS.

T··Mobile·
HotSpot

Borders is a T-Mobile HotSpot. Enjoy wireless
broadband Internet service for your laptop or PDA.

```
************************************
      BORDERS REWARDS
       MEMBERS ONLY

       SAVE 20% OFF
        List Price of
      Any One Item
   WHEN YOU SPEND $10 OR MORE
```

Valid at Borders, 9/7 - 9/10/2006

159014480000000000

POS: This is a programmed coupon.
If the purchase is $10 or more, scan
the barcode.

One coupon per customer per day.
Discount on electronics and video
games is 10%. Excludes online & prior
purchases, non-stock special orders,
gift cards, periodicals, comics,
and Seattle's Best Coffee products.
Cannot be used with with other
coupons, sale pricing or standard
group discounts. Cash value .01 cent.
Not redeemable for cash. No copies
allowed. Other uses constitute fraud.
```
X                                    X
STORE: 0471   REG: 02/12  TRAN#: 0358
SALE          09/01/2006  EMP:  00401
************************************
```

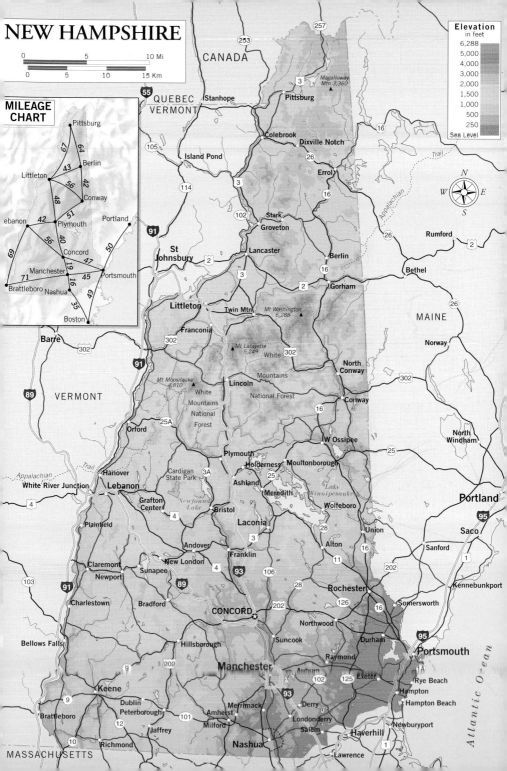

NEW HAMPSHIRE

0   5   10 Mi
0   5   10   15 Km

MILEAGE CHART

Pittsburg
67
64
43 Berlin
Littleton 56 42
48 Conway
51
ebanon 42 Plymouth Portland
56 40
69 Concord 50
19 47
Manchester 16 45
71 Nashua 49 Portsmouth
Brattleboro 35
Boston

CANADA

QUEBEC
VERMONT

Stanhope
Pittsburg
Magalloway
Mtn 3,360

Island Pond
Colebrook
Dixville Notch

Errol

Stark
Groveton
Lancaster
Berlin

Gorham

MAINE

Rumford

Bethel

St
Johnsbury

Littleton
Twin Mtn
Mt Washington
6,288

Franconia
Mt Lafayette
5,249
White

North
Conway

Mt Moosilauke
4,810
Lincoln
White
Mountains
National
Forest

Conway

Norway

North
Windham

VERMONT

Orford

Hanover
White River Junction
Lebanon

Cardigan
State Park

Plymouth
Holderness
Moultonborough
Ashland
Meredith

Lake
Winnipesaukee

Wolfeboro

Portland

Saco

Barre

White
Mountains
National
Forest

W Ossipee

Plainfield

Grafton
Center

Newfound
Lake

Bristol
Laconia

Union

Alton

Sanford

Kennebunkport

Claremont
Newport
Sunapee

Andover
New London
Franklin

28

11

202

Rochester

16

Somersworth

Charlestown
Bradford

CONCORD

202

28

126

Durham

Portsmouth

Bellows Falls

Hillsborough

Suncook
Northwood

Raymond

Keene

Dublin
Peterborough

Manchester
Auburn

102 125 Exeter

Rye Beach
Hampton
Hampton Beach

Brattleboro

Jaffrey

Merrimack
Amherst
Milford

Derry
Londonderry
Salem

Newburyport

Richmond

Nashua

Haverhill

Lawrence

MASSACHUSETTS

Atlantic O-ean

Elevation
in feet

6,288
5,000
4,000
3,000
2,000
1,500
1,000
500
250
Sea Level

O V E R V I E W

SEACOAST AND THE
PISCATAQUA BASIN *pages 50–89*

New Hampshire's shoreline is a mere slip of land, only 18 miles in length, but what the coast lacks in size it more than makes up for with abundant sun and gardens, sandy beaches and salt marshes, lobster shacks and clam bakes, and unforgettable drives that skirt colonial forts and bucolic seaside settlements. Farther inland, along the Piscataqua Estuary, picturesque New England towns, with many 18th- and 19th-century estates, dot the landscape.

MERRIMACK VALLEY
pages 90–125

The wide central valley that straddles the Merrimack River is a geographical and cultural gold mine. Manchester's textile mill, once the world's largest, has been converted into an impressive museum devoted to the mills, and the city's cultural life includes a superb regional art museum, the Currier. You can poke around antiques shops in historic Milford, visit an 18th-century Shaker village or a modern planetarium, or tour the home where Robert Frost wrote some of his most enduring poetry. The best way to experience the Merrimack is on the river itself—by canoe, kayak, or tour boat.

MONADNOCK REGION
pages 126–159

Hikers flock to Grand Monadnock mountain, but there is more to do in this region than scale peaks. The wild Contoocook River and Sheiling State Forest, with walking trails, a wildflower preserve, and 45 acres of woods, lure nature lovers, just as surely as Peterborough, which inspired Thornton Wilder's play *Our Town*, draws culture buffs. The arts

flourish here, in galleries and performance venues and at the MacDowell Colony artists retreat. Nestled in wooded hills, busy Jaffrey and Keene and the sleepy hamlets of Dublin, Fitzwilliam, and Hancock are what many see when they close their eyes and think of New England.

LAKES REGION   *pages 160–189*

Roads in the Lakes region meander around sun-dappled water, exposing jaw-dropping vistas of mysterious coves and rocky cliffs. Lake Winnipesaukee beckons with its sparkling water and undulating shoreline, and forests of oaks, maples, and birches attract hikers and picnickers. Busy Weirs Beach has something for everyone, from penny arcades to a scenic railroad. Nearby Wolfeboro provides the upscale sheen with Brewster Academy and fine restaurants.

SUNAPEE & THE UPPER VALLEY *pages 190–215*

The site of border disputes and Indian raids, the Lake Sunapee and Upper Connecticut River valley region is an undiscovered pocket of tranquillity sprinkled with idyllic farms and stunning views. Colonial-era forts, creaking covered bridges, kayak and canoe runs, ski areas, a national wildlife refuge, and plenty of top-flight inns make this an ideal summer or winter retreat. Big Lake Sunapee occupies the center of the region, with water-skiing, cruises, and the stunning gardens of an old estate. The retreat of a world-famous sculptor and Dartmouth College, with the stellar Hood Museum of Art and other cultural venues, are a short hop up Interstate 93 from the lake.

WHITE MOUNTAINS *pages 216–255*

The first heavily touristed wilderness in America, the White Mountains are a magnet for writers, artists, poets, hikers, and all who crave fresh mountain air. Roads and trails wind through spectacular mountain passes, or "notches," under outcroppings thousands of feet above. The narrow Flume Gorge, carved through granite cliffs by Flume Creek, and vertiginous Crawford Notch are no less thrilling. You can tour the cottage where Robert Frost lived while he taught at what is now Plymouth State College, or learn the story of skiing at the New England Ski Museum.

GREAT NORTH WOODS *pages 256–281*

Seven months of winter and up to 60 days of subzero temperatures make this one of the more forbidding regions in the United States. But desolation wilderness has its rewards—the sights of fat trout rising to take a fly and black bears, moose, and coyotes, the smell of fresh pine in the air, and the sound of ruffed grouse and loons breaking the forest silence.

UNIQUELY NEW HAMPSHIRE

I TOLD AN OUT-OF-STATE FRIEND—"from away," as they'd say up north in Coos County—that I was writing a book about New Hampshire. "Oh, that won't take long," she responded, winking slyly. "It's such a tiny state." New Hampshire is smaller than most states, but just try to write a book about it. After more than two decades in the Merrimack Valley, I've come to understand that the Granite State—so named for the abundance of that coarse-grained igneous rock—is hardly small, and as I rediscover almost every day, anything but predictable.

Local history can be full of insignificant facts—*first this, largest that.* We may be surprised to hear that the first potato grown in North America was planted in Londonderry, or that New Hampshire is larger in land miles than Massachusetts, its neighbor to the south. But such minutiae hardly render a complete portrait.

Endowed with rich natural resources and a quirky, self-reliant citizenry, New Hampshire itself is the revelation. Its beauty has attracted writers like Thoreau, Hawthorne, and Cather; the painters Homer, Cole, and Stella; and the poets Frost, cummings, and Simic. The potential for inspiration endures, whether you're viewing the graceful, sloping lawn of the Cornish estate where the sculptor Augustus Saint-Gaudens lived and worked or standing on the shore of First Connecticut Lake at twilight as the loons begin to cry. Now *these* are experiences you can wrap a trip around.

■ TOPOGRAPHY

New Hampshire spreads out to the north and west from the blue Atlantic like a lopsided wedge of pie, encompassing an extremely varied topography: distant mountains and intimate seacoast, serene lakes and mad rushing rivers, floating bogs and boreal forests. And incredible mountains! Mount Washington, at 6,289 feet the tallest mountain in the Northeast, can be found here, along with Grand Monadnock, the most-climbed peak in North America. *Well, okay*—it takes most people less than two hours to hike Monadnock's 3,165 feet.

Dense forest cloaks most of the state's mountains, so stupendous views don't come easy—you must climb to the top, where your reward will be eye-popping perspectives on lakes, farmlands, and distant rivers. New Hampshire has been called

Steeple of the Congregational Meetinghouse in Fitzwilliam.

the "Mother of Rivers" for the major waterways that begin in its uplands. A brook at the Canadian border is the headwater of New England's largest river, the Connecticut. The Merrimack, which begins in the foothills of the White Mountains, once powered more woolen and cotton spindles than any other river in the world. Two old log-driving rivers, the Saco and the Androscoggin, originate in the north country before heading east to the Gulf of Maine. On at least 26 others you can go boating, kayaking, canoeing, or rafting.

■ CITIES

New Hampshire's cities are as diverse as its landscape, from the seacoast town of Portsmouth, to the manufacturing centers of Manchester and Nashua, to the bucolic college towns of Durham, Plymouth, and Hanover. Many towns are classic New England, with a white church and meeting hall and tidy homes arranged around a green space called a common. Industrialized New Hampshire cities reflect the tastes of later immigrant groups who came to work in the mills. Such a place is the paper mill town of Berlin, with its onion-domed Russian Orthodox church, wangan (lumberjack store), and French-Canadian cathedrals.

■ LANDSCAPE OF TREES

When I think of New Hampshire, I think of trees. This is, after all, the second-most forested state after Maine. I think of painter Maxfield Parrish's Cornish estate, the Oaks, and the farm in Amherst that inspired Robert Frost's "Birches," a poem my father-in-law would recite so expressively, often without prompting. I think also of the great white pines (*Pinus strobus*) that grow so straight and tall. Centuries ago, surveyors sent by the king of England marked them to be cut and shaped into masts for the royal navy.

A white ash tree outside our house in Bow stood more than 100 feet tall, ringed at its base by an iron wagon wheel, thus dating both tree and wheel. We watched in amazement one moonlit winter night as five moose passed in a ghostly procession under its bare branches. Across South Bow Road, a birch rose out of dark pines like a white angel fringed in pale green.

(following pages) Fall reflections on Norway Pond in Hancock.

New Hampshire birches. (Claudia Rippee)

> ...Earth's the right place for love:
> I don't know where it's likely to go better.
> I'd like to go by climbing a birch tree,
> And climb black branches up a snow-white trunk
> Toward heaven, till the tree could bear no more,
> But dipped its top and set me down again.
> That would be good both going and coming back.
> One could do worse than be a swinger of birches.
>
> —Robert Frost, excerpted from "Birches," 1916

Here's a startling statistic about New Hampshire's forests. Three decades before the Civil War, 60 percent of the state had been cleared for farming (the seacoast was more than 80 percent logged by the 1830s). Today, nearly 84 percent of the state is forested. The efforts of early conservation groups like the Appalachian Mountain Club and the Society for the Protection of New Hampshire Forests helped alert the public to the devastation caused by lumber barons George Van Dyke and J.E. Henry and the need for forest protection. In 1911, the threatened forests of the White Mountains were protected by an act of Congress. The Weeks Act created 50 national forests east of the Mississippi, the first of which was the White Mountain National Forest.

New Hampshire, it's been said, has a greater variety of trees than all of Europe: oak, hickory, spruce, fir, and birch, to name a few. "Too damn many trees," mutters my friend Rich, on a visit from Chicago, unwittingly alluding to a major debate in this state. Many foresters argue that a monolithic single-aged forest carpets New Hampshire, the result of massive clear-cutting during the 19th century. The thicket's uniformity limits the diversity of plant and other life, species like deer and grouse, for instance, that thrive at the edges of forests. One proposed solution is selective cutting, but many people viscerally oppose logging, even if done in accordance with modern concepts of forest management.

■ PEOPLE AND THEIR PURPOSES

Fishermen began coming to the Isles of Shoals, several miles off the New Hampshire coast, perhaps as early as the 1500s (unlike explorers, fishermen generally don't publicize their discoveries). The first Europeans to settle in New England, the Pilgrims who arrived in Massachusetts at Plymouth Bay in 1620, came seeking religious freedom. New Hampshire's first settlers, who arrived in 1623, came for fur, fish, and timber. If one thing distinguishes the Massachusetts settlers from those of New Hampshire's Piscataqua River basin it's this: the Pilgrims were fleeing England, but the first Graniteers were sent by its king to explore the area's economic potential.

Unabashed exploitation of raw materials continued for three centuries. Fortunes were made first in natural assets like fish, timber, isinglass, and clay (for brick), and later from manufacturing goods in mills that utilized New Hampshire's considerable water resources.

Trade and waterpower changed the face of the state, bringing farmworkers to the cities and creating a thriving manufacturing economy. A hundred years later, with the collapse of the mills during the Great Depression, the economy faltered. Recovery proceeded only incrementally until New Hampshire developed into a center for high-tech industry in the late 20th century.

■ THAT NEW HAMPSHIRE ATTITUDE

Many Americans believe the Revolutionary War began in 1775 at the Massachusetts towns of Lexington and Concord, heralded by Paul Revere's famous ride. But any Graniteer will tell you that it all started in 1774 with another Revere ride, to Portsmouth. Revere roused the New Hampshire militia to storm Castle William and Mary. The munitions the militiamen stole were used in 1775 at the battle of Bunker Hill, which saw more soldiers engaged in battle from New Hampshire than from any other state.

New Hampshire was the first American colony to declare its independence from England and the first to adopt a state constitution, a document that admonishes citizens to revolt if we are dissatisfied with our government. We the people have taken this advice seriously, often threatening to leave the state—with part of it in tow. In the far northern reaches of New Hampshire, residents unhappy with the state government formed the Indian Stream Republic in the 1832 and operated autonomously until 1835. In the late 20th century, disgruntled taxpayers on the seacoast threatened to secede over what they interpreted as unfair and excessive taxation for school funding.

And the border disputes! Maybe New Hampshire's feisty attitude comes from the fact that each of its borders has involved a bloody dispute, rebellion, secession, or a lengthy court battle. Over the past four centuries, Massachusetts, Vermont, Canada, and Maine have looked to add to their territory at New Hampshire's expense. In 2001, the U.S. Supreme Court settled the latest tiff when it ruled that the Portsmouth Naval Shipyard belongs to Maine, not New Hampshire.

"New Hampshire is full of woodchucks and wing nuts," my friend "from away" confided to me. "You've got to be careful." You can't blame people for getting the wrong impression. For one thing, there's the blunt message on our license plate

Jesse Jackson works the crowd during the 1984 New Hampshire primary campaign.

PRESIDENTIAL PREROGATIVE

In each presidential election since 1920, New Hampshire has hosted the nation's first primary, making the state a crucial stop for candidates aspiring to occupy the White House. Local politicians have successfully fended off numerous challenges to the state's premier status over the years, though it was practicality and frugality, not finagling and finesse, that initially earned New Hampshire the number one slot.

In 1916, the first year a majority of the nation's states held presidential primaries, voters in New Hampshire and Minnesota headed to the polls in May, a week after their counterparts in Indiana. But casting ballots in late spring conflicted with farm tasks like plowing fields, so rural voters lobbied for an earlier election. And if they were going to bother making it earlier, why not combine it with the annual town meeting so as not to incur the cost of lighting town hall twice in one month? State officials scheduled the 1920 primary for the second Tuesday in March, establishing it as the nation's first.

The primary is arguably as significant to New Hampshire for its economic impact and the worldwide attention it garners as for any contribution it makes to the American political process. But one of its vocal advocates, former Gov. Hugh Gregg, defends it as "the quickest, easiest, least expensive, and most effective place" for a relative unknown to kick-start a campaign. Strong showings by southern Democratic governors Jimmy Carter, who won the party primary in 1976, and Bill Clinton, who placed a convincing second in the 1992 primary a few weeks after tabloids revealed an extramarital affair he'd had, supplied them instant credibility and convinced big-time financial contributors that these were viable candidates.

The primary's "giant-killer" reputation has been confirmed numerous times; incumbent presidents Harry Truman (1952) and Lyndon Johnson (1968) declined to seek reelection in the face of disappointing results. And until recently, New Hampshirites proved exceptionally adept at predicting future presidents. Only Bill Clinton (1992) and George W. Bush (2000) failed to win their party's presidential primary here and still attained the office.

So strong is the identification of New Hampshirites with their primary's primacy that the state legislature passed a bill in 1977 mandating that the election always be the nation's first. Enforcing the statute hasn't always been easy, though. More than a few states have attempted to derail New Hampshire by scheduling earlier primaries. But according to Trina Purcell, the assistant director of the New Hampshire Political Library, "Our secretary of state looks around and sees who is holding primaries when, and whenever the earliest date is, we set ours a week before." The 2000 primary took place in mid-February; the 2004 primary may take place in January.

Not everyone subscribes to the notion that New Hampshire residents should have the first electoral say. Some opponents assert that the state's largely white, middle-class population poorly reflects the diverse American public. Nevertheless, locals defend their institution and decry recent proposals for a larger, regional primary. Charles Brereton, a writer who specializes in New Hampshire politics, warns that such a plan could have a negative impact. If the alternative to New Hampshire's primary is "a bunch of states lumped together," he asks, "who would get a fair hearing then?"

—*Lisa Oppenheimer*

Live Free or Die. It's certainly a far cry from the feel-good slogans of two of our neighbors: Spirit of America (Massachusetts) and Vacationland (Maine). Live Free or Die, also the state motto, comes to us from the patriot Gen. John Stark, who held the left wing at Bunker Hill, the right at Trenton, and at the Battle of Bennington was instrumental in slowing British General Burgoyne's advance through Vermont.

Stark wrote his words in a letter to veterans of the Battle of Bennington, suggesting it as a toast: "Live free or die. Death is not the worst of evils." Those who live here long enough come to view these words—blunt, concise, unapologetic— as a legitimate expression of who we are and what we stand for: self-determination, small government, low taxes.

Yet this state that appears to be so conservative and old-time Yankee recently elected a woman as Democratic governor, twice. More than 60 languages and dialects are spoken in the schools of Manchester, the state's largest city, reflecting an ability to accommodate new people and ideas. Keeping government small is considered crucial, but people participate in the process of governance to an exceptional degree. In a survey of 40 regions in the United States, New Hampshire scored highest in the category of "civic equality." Wrote the Harvard University political scientist Robert Putnam, "In New Hampshire, the bank janitor and the bank teller take part in community activities along with the bank president."

New Hampshire voters are exceptionally well prepared and prove it every four years during the first presidential primary election in the nation. It's an oddly intimate experience for us to needle a candidate about foreign policy in a neighbor's home over bad hors d'oeuvres and white zinfandel. But it's democracy at its best. This is, as my friend asserts, a small state. Its size allows every candidate to make the most of limited campaign dollars.

As British political scientist Niall Palmer observes in *The New Hampshire Primary and the American Electoral Process,* "Opinion surveys since the 1970s suggest that, despite the Republican monopoly and New Hampshire's conservative reputation, voter attitudes remain surprisingly flexible."

That's what's great about New Hampshire. It won't stay put, and it won't be pinned down. Just when you think you've got it pegged, it shows you another side of itself.

Icicles form on the Balsams Grand Resort in the Great North Woods.

■ THE SEASONS

◆ WINTER

Here's an old joke about the seasons in New Hampshire. When God created the state, he gave it five: Not Winter, Nearly Winter, Winter, Still Winter, and Construction. Though not exactly true, it might as well be. If you live in New Hampshire, you've got to make an accommodation to the north wind.

When purple shadows lengthen across the blue drifts, you'll find my friend Rob hunkered over his camp stove, settling in for a chilly night of winter camping. The average winter temperature is 19 degrees Fahrenheit, but don't count on it being that warm north of the White Mountains. He'll snowshoe into some remote site and spend the weekend. For fun. The slightly less adventurous enjoy New Hampshire's 18 alpine and countless nordic ski areas. Few experiences are finer than sitting in front of a snug inn's crackling fire at the end of a frosty day outdoors.

Spring flowers in the gardens at Canterbury Shaker Village.

◆ SPRING

Spring in New Hampshire can be achingly beautiful, possibly because we've waited so long for it to arrive. Explosions of yellow forsythia and brilliant red maple buds seem to encourage the pale green of baby birch leaves. It's a green so pale it's like a dream of green, Copland's oboe in *Appalachian Spring* floating high above the heavy symphony of dark firs and spruces that stoically weathered the severe winter.

But the old joke about New Hampshire's seasons leaves out black fly season. For a few weeks every May, the buffalo gnat (*Diptera simuliidae*) rules the woods. Inflicting painful bites, these pests cannot be brushed away like mosquitoes. They'll dodge your swats, then invade eyes, hair, nostrils, and ears—even zoom up pant legs. It's been said that in the deep woods they drive horses mad and moose into wallow. A standing joke in Bow is that during a nor'easter, the black dots between the snowflakes are black flies, looking for blood.

◆ SUMMER

Every July, my wife, Debi, and I take a river canoe trip, camping out on sandbars in the upper reaches of the Merrimack, letting Chloe the dog get her fill of swimming until she collapses in tongue-lolling exhaustion. In summertime the cool waters of New Hampshire provide pure pleasure, whether you're swimming off a crowded seaside beach, sailing across a sparkling lake, or walking barefoot in a cool mountain stream. We've found few better things to do during the hot months than head north.

◆ AUTUMN

A day comes in late September when the temperature drops even while the sun blazes away. Humidity disappears, and the inevitability of the climatic cycle becomes obvious. Fall draws thousands to the state, and in a dry year, there's no finer time to visit. A hike near Waterville Valley around the twin peaks of Welch and Dickey takes you on a pretty three-hour loop around a vaulting ledge at the rim of a spectacular bowl of autumn colors. Every shade of green, yellow, orange, red, and even hot pink seems on display on a sunny day in late September. You catch the musty scent of leaves on the ground, see the last sunset of summer captured in the neon-bright leaves, and know that the yearly wheel's come round again.

New Hampshire glows with warm colors in autumn.

H I S T O R Y

ABOUT 10,000 YEARS AGO, AT THE END of the last ice age, the first people came to hunt and fish in what is now New Hampshire. The first Europeans arrived in the 16th century. Genoese explorers representing French and English interests sailed the coast of New England in the 17th century, followed by settlers determined to exploit the land's resources. British royal governors led these efforts, all the while fending off French and Indian threats to the region's security. New Hampshire, initially part of the Massachusetts Bay Colony, became a separate royal colony in 1741, joined the fight for independence, and attained statehood in 1778.

New Hampshire developed into a vibrant mercantile center during the 17th and 18th centuries, the early products being furs, fish, and timber. During this period, Portsmouth rivaled Boston as a shipping hub. New Hampshire became a manufacturing center in the 19th century, its rivers powering a network of mills. Today, most of the mills are closed, replaced in the state's southern cities by high-tech enterprises. Tourism is another major moneymaker.

Below are a historical timeline and the stories of some of the state's most important figures.

This 17th-century watercolor depicts two members of the Abenaki tribe, which inhabited eastern New Hampshire near the Piscataqua River.

NEW HAMPSHIRE TIMELINE

PRE-HISTORY

8,000 B.C.E. Paleo-Indians arrive in region.

A.D. 1500s Abenaki Indians, an Algonquin people, inhabit New Hampshire. English fishermen begin visiting the coast of North America and fishing off the Isles of Shoals.

Algonquins descend a trail to the water.

EXPLORATION

1524 Italian explorer Giovanni da Verrazzano, sailing under French flag, explores the Northeast coast and trades with Maine Abenakis. He notes in his log that he has seen the White Mountains.

1603 English Capt. Martin Pring reaches the Piscataqua River near Portsmouth.

1605 Samuel de Champlain explores Piscataqua Bay for his native France.

1614 English Capt. John Smith maps the area from Penobscot to Cape Cod. Prince Charles, son of King James I of England, calls the area New England.

1621–1623 Capt. John Mason, governor of Newfoundland, joins with English aristocrat Sir Ferdinando Gorges to finance the "Mason Grants." The new area is named New Hampshire for Mason's home county of Hampshire. Overlapping grants are made, leading to generations of confusion about which parcel belongs to which colony.

John Smith

SETTLEMENTS ESTABLISHED

1623 First settlement established by English at Odiorne Point near Portsmouth.

1629 Colonists sign treaty with Indian leader Passaconaway for rights to the land from shore to the Merrimack River.

1641 New Hampshire province's 1,000 inhabitants ask to be put under the control of Massachusetts.

1642 With the help of Indian guides, colonist Darby Field ascends Mount Washington, first European to do so.

1673 Nashua becomes first town established in state's interior.

1675 First organized Indian rebellion, known as King Philip's War, begins.

1679 England's King Charles II proclaims New Hampshire a royal province.

1693 Taxes are levied to support a schoolteacher and a schoolhouse for every town in New Hampshire.

1724 John Wentworth is appointed lieutenant governor of Massachusetts, with jurisdiction over the province of New Hampshire.

1741 New Hampshire becomes independent of Massachusetts, and the boundary between the two provinces is set. Benning Wentworth, son of John, becomes New Hampshire's first royal governor.

1756 First newspaper, the *New Hampshire Gazette*, is established in Portsmouth.

1763 French and Indian War ends. Settlement of the New Hampshire frontier accelerates.

1767 Benning Wentworth's nephew John succeeds him as royal governor.

1769 Dartmouth College founded in Hanover.

New Hampshire Gazette.

REVOLUTION IN THE AIR

1774   First military action of the Revolutionary War takes place when American colonists capture British supplies from Castle William and Mary.

1777   New Hampshire–born Gen. John Stark wins the dramatic Battle of Bennington.

John Stark

1778   New Hampshire becomes a state and Ethan Allen founds Vermont. Over the next three years, 16 towns on the Connecticut River's east bank declare themselves part of Vermont. George Washington issues a stern reprimand, and the towns remain part of New Hampshire.

RELIGION AND COMMERCE

1792   The Shakers, a Protestant sect, establish a community in Canterbury.

1800   Nation's first federal shipyard is created in Portsmouth.

1803   First hotel in White Mountains opens.

1804   First cotton mill is established in New Ipswich.

1810   Amoskeag Mill, whose workers produce textiles, opens in Manchester.

1813–17 Daniel Webster represents New Hampshire in Congress.

1819   State capitol is completed.

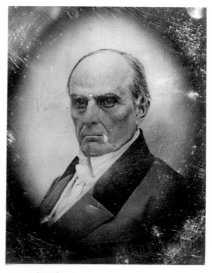

Daniel Webster

COMMERCE AND POLITICAL POWER

1827 First Concord coach is manufactured. Popularly known as a stagecoach, the conveyance is used extensively in the West for transportation.

1832 Residents near Canadian border establish Indian Stream Republic and secede from New Hampshire.

1835 State militia marches into northern New Hampshire and puts an end to the Indian Stream Republic.

1853 Hillsborough native Franklin Pierce is inaugurated 14th U.S. president.

1853 State Republican party founded in Exeter on antislavery platform.

1857 Residents of African descent granted full citizenship; adult males given right to vote.

1869 Enos M. Powell invents first automobile. Government of Sunapee bans the contraption: it's too noisy.

1869 Mount Washington Cog Railway begins service to summit.

1885 Sculptor Augustus Saint-Gaudens moves to Cornish.

1886 Poet Robert Frost moves to state.

Mount Washington Cog Railway.

1905 Treaty ending Russo-Japanese War signed in Portsmouth.

1929 Currier Gallery of Art opens in Manchester.

1934 On April 12, the wind gusts 231 mph on Mount Washington summit. This remains the highest recorded wind velocity on earth.

1936 Amoskeag Mill, in its late-19th-century heyday the world's largest textile mill, goes bankrupt and closes.

Machine shop, Amoskeag Mill.

1944 International Monetary Fund established at Bretton Woods Conference, held in White Mountains.

1963 New Hampshire's legislature becomes first in 20th century to authorize a state-run lottery.

1976 Boundary dispute with Maine settled by Supreme Court. Maine given rights to much of coastal waters.

Christa McAuliffe

1985–6 Teacher Christa McAuliffe of Concord selected to be the first civilian in space. She perishes with six other astronauts when space shuttle *Challenger* explodes on takeoff from Cape Canaveral, Florida.

1990 Seabrook Station nuclear power plant opens, last such facility in nation to be licensed during 20th century.

1995 Museum of New Hampshire History opens in Concord.

2000 The Millyard Museum, chronicling the history and heritage of the Amoskeag Mill, opens.

2001 U.S. Supreme Court rules Portsmouth Naval Shipyard belongs to Maine. Justice David Souter, born and raised in New Hampshire, abstains.

2001 Manchester-area inventor Dean Kamen debuts his Segway Human Transporter, a battery-powered sidewalk cruiser.

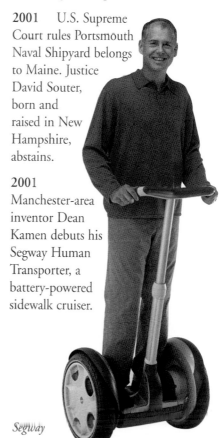

Segway transporter.

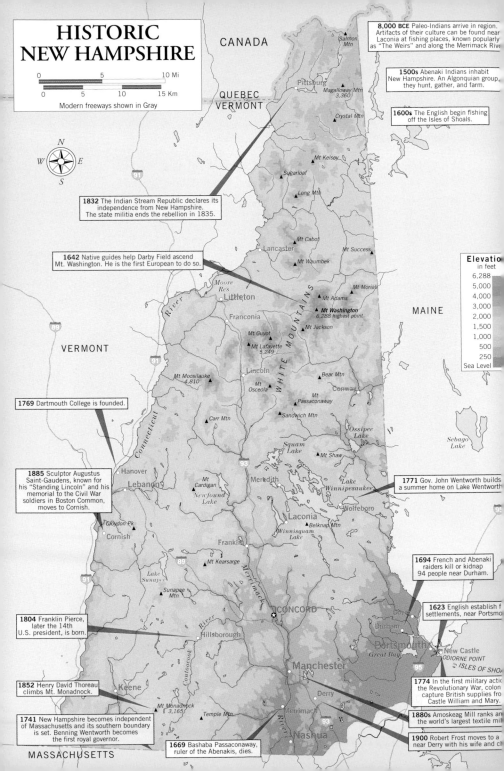

■ New Hampshire Eras and Leaders

◆ Pre-Columbian New Hampshire

When the first European explorers reached the shores of what is now New Hampshire, about 4,000 members of an Algonquin group known as the Abenakis, or "people of the dawnland," inhabited it. Though they lived as hunters and gatherers, they also maintained communal gardens and villages. The English settlers named the various native bands after the rivers or lands where the settlers first encountered them (Winnipesaukee, Penacook, Souhegan). They perceived of the groups as "tribes" led by "chiefs," but the native peoples thought of themselves as members of this or that kinship group, whose leader was a sachem, or chief. Out of these loosely organized groups, which nevertheless had strong blood ties, leaders of outstanding persuasive powers would emerge. These leaders, who ruled over larger confederations of local bands, were known as sagamores ("great chieftains" to the settlers), or in the case of Passaconaway, a key participant in New Hampshire history, *bashaba* (akin to an emperor).

Passaconaway (1562–1669)
Indian Ruler
b. Merrimack Valley, New Hampshire

Bashaba Passaconaway was a man of great dignity. A spiritual and political leader, he guided the Abenaki group the settlers called the Penacooks. His name—Papisseconewa, as he pronounced it—means "the child of the bear." Tall and athletic, he outshone his peers "in sagacity, duplicity and moderation," wrote the 18th-century clergyman and regional historian Jeremy Belknap. But Passaconaway's stature among the native people who lived between the Connecticut River and the ocean also derived from his supposed mastery of nature. Wrote Belknap, "They believed that it was in his power to make water burn, trees dance, and to metamorphose himself into flame; that in winter he could raise a green leaf from the ashes of a dry one, and a living serpent from the skin of one that was dead."

Passaconaway, who witnessed the Pilgrims landing at Plymouth, practiced incantations to drive them away, but he recognized early on that the English settlers would eventually control the area. He and three chieftains signed a treaty in 1629 for rights to the land from the Piscataqua River to the Merrimack River.

Though Passaconaway distrusted the English, he advocated coexistence with them, hoping they would act as a buffer against the Mohawks, whom he feared even more. His plan backfired, as C.E. Potter notes in his 1856 history of Manchester: "In less than 20 years from the time that Passaconaway submitted himself to the colonists, and put himself under their protection, he and his tribe were literally reduced to beggary." In 1662, Passaconaway, the bashaba of the Merrimack Valley, "and the rightful owner of all its broad lands," petitioned Gov. John Endicott and the Great and General Court in

This print illustrates one of the many misunderstandings that occurred during negotiations between colonists and native people.

Boston for land upon which he could die in peace. He was granted a mere three square miles around his beloved Natticook in Merrimack.

After Passaconaway died (he reputedly lived 107 years) his son Wonalancet sheltered his people from the annihilation of King Philip's War by staying out of the conflict. Nonetheless, by the early 1700s these local peoples had either died of disease or been chased away.

◆ ENGLISH ROYAL COLONIES

The first English to come to live and work along New Hampshire's shores were fishermen, followed by settlers hoping to farm, hunt, and cut timber for sale to the British navy. In 1641, the people of Portsmouth and nearby towns asked to be taken under the wing of Massachusetts—and then spent much of the ensuing century trying to revoke the arrangement. English governors established trade, built roads, and raised militias to defend their settlements against raids by native peoples and their French allies. The most important family in this early struggle for self-definition was the Wentworths of Portsmouth.

THE WENTWORTH DYNASTY

The Wentworth family dynasty of John, his son Benning, and Benning's nephew John, engineered the transformation of New Hampshire from a Massachusetts backwater to thriving independent province.

John Wentworth (1671–1730)
Lieutenant Governor of
Massachusetts, including
New Hampshire (1724–1728)
b. Portsmouth, New Hampshire

In the 1720s, Lt. Gov. John Wentworth, the first of three generations of Wentworth governors, began to grant towns in the Merrimack Valley and to settle vying claims among John Mason's descendants and others. To the British Crown, Wentworth cannily portrayed the territorial conflict

Joseph Blackburn painted this portrait of Lt. Gov. John Wentworth circa 1760.

between New Hampshire and its neighbor to the south as the struggle of "a poor little province" against a "rapacious and arrogant Massachusetts."

Benning Wentworth (1696–1776)
Royal Governor of New Hampshire (1741–1766)
b. Portsmouth, New Hampshire

In 1741 King George II declared New Hampshire an independent province. The first royal governor of New Hampshire, Benning Wentworth, ruled longer than any other royal governor in the colonies and was well liked by his subjects despite his excesses. Popularly known as "Uncle Benning," he granted his supporters huge tracts west of the Connecticut River in what would later become Vermont. Benning amassed a large fortune from the fees and property rights associated with his grants, married his chambermaid, Martha Hilton, in 1760, and retired to his magnificent home in Little Harbor in 1766.

John Wentworth (1737–1820)
Royal Governor of New Hampshire (1767–1775)
b. Portsmouth, New Hampshire

John Wentworth succeeded his uncle in 1767, mostly because of John's friendship with the Marquis of Rockingham, a distant relative whom he had met in England while betting on the nobleman's horses. Despite being a staunch loyalist, John ruled New Hampshire benignly, balancing his duties as a royal representative with his desire to improve his subjects' welfare. He strongly opposed the Stamp Act, which levied a tax on legal and commercial documents and much printed material (which had to carry a special stamp, hence the act's name). John called it "totally obnoxious" and accused the British of being "ignorant of the Colonies."

Like his uncle, though far different in demeanor, John was a popular governor, perhaps the most beloved of any royal governor in America. At the outbreak of revolution, he went into exile and never returned to the United States. In 1778 John Adams, a former classmate at Harvard, ran into him at a Paris theater. Adams later wrote, "At first I was somewhat embarrassed, and knew not how to behave towards him. As my classmate and friend at college and ever since I could have pressed him to my bosom with the most cordial affection. But we now belonged to two different nations…at war with each other and consequently we were enemies." Several days later Adams was relieved to write, "Not an indelicate expression to us or our country or our ally escaped him. His whole behaviour was that of an accomplished gentleman."

◆ FRENCH AND INDIAN WARS

From 1689 to 1763, France and England clashed four separate times in Europe and the colonies. Each time, France allied with the Hurons and the Abenakis, and England partnered with the Iroquois.

The first three disputes concerned royal succession in Europe, but the fourth, known in Europe as the Seven Years War and in the colonies as the French and Indian War (1755-63), was different. This one, writes Fred Anderson in his excellent book *Crucible of War,* "was about the control of territory, not thrones; it created a seismic shift in Europe's alliance system and balance of power; and its first shots were fired not on a European, but an American, frontier." During the several generations of conflict, about 1,600 New England settlers were abducted to Canada for ransom or enslavement. New Hampshire's farms and villages were important targets for the French, who sought to disrupt English settlement of the frontier.

During the French and Indian War, American colonists got a close look at the tactics of their allies in the British army. The British regulars fought in lock-step formation, which seemed like madness to those who had been fighting Native Americans for years. But the British sneered at the colonist volunteers, one officer calling the ragtag New Hampshire volunteers "Yankee Doodles." Among the standout doodles-in-arms was Robert Rogers.

Robert Rogers (1731–1795)
Major in the French and Indian Wars
b. Methuen, Massachusetts

For Robert Rogers, it was either become a famous guerrilla fighter or be hung. A Massachusetts native who grew up in Goffstown, New Hampshire, Rogers was caught passing counterfeit currency in 1738. A conviction would have brought a long prison term or death. So he offered to Benning Wentworth a regiment he had assembled for a Boston underwriter. The governor, ever eager to nurture military talent—and embarrass Massachusetts—took Rogers on.

Robert Rogers

Rogers is best known for the exploits of his Rogers' Rangers—units that roamed the Lake Champlain region, attacking the French and their Native American allies. In 1759, he destroyed St. Francis, a staging point on the St. Lawrence River for many raids against settlers, an event depicted in Kenneth Roberts's best-selling novel *Northwest Passage*. Rogers was wildly popular in London for a series of autobiographical chapbooks—and so hated by the Hurons that they dug up the fresh grave of his brother to take the scalp. In the end, the American colonists weren't too thrilled with Rogers, either. He chose the losing side during the Revolutionary War and died penniless in England.

◆ REVOLUTIONARY ERA

New Hampshire stakes a claim to the first battle of the Revolutionary War, the raid in 1774 on Castle William and Mary. Three signers of the Declaration of Independence—Matthew Thornton, Josiah Bartlett, and William Whipple—were born in the state or lived here. Two New Hampshirites who contributed greatly to the war effort were John Stark and John Langdon.

John Stark (1728–1822)
Soldier in the French and Indian War, general in the Continental Army
b. Londonderry, New Hampshire

As a young member of Rogers' Rangers, John Stark was abducted by the Abenakis. He earned their respect by running the gauntlet bravely, shouting, "I'll kiss all your women!" Stark is better known, though, for coining New Hampshire's motto, "Live Free or Die," and for his exhortation to his men (several versions of which have come down through history) during the Battle of Bennington: "Yonder are the redcoats. We will defeat them or Molly Stark will sleep a widow tonight!"

John Stark rallies his troops before the Battle of Bennington.

Stark, who also fought at Bunker Hill and in George Washington's New Jersey campaign of 1776–77, defeated the British at Bennington, Vermont, on August 16, 1777, helping to foil their plan to split New England from the rest of the colonies by driving down from Lake Champlain to the sea. The story has often been repeated that he defeated Gen. John Burgoyne. Bennington was a vital battle that denied supplies to Burgoyne when he needed them most and set up his defeat at Saratoga, New York, but Burgoyne wasn't at Bennington. The general had sent Friedrich Baum, a Hessian mercenary, on a foraging expedition with Tories, Native Americans, and unmounted cavalrymen. Stark's forces, outnumbering them two to one, pounced. Of the invaders, 200 were killed and 700 wounded. The casualties on Stark's side were 40 men dead and 30 wounded.

John Langdon (1741–1819)
Merchant and politician
b. Portsmouth, New Hampshire

Few men were as active in the fight for independence as John Langdon, who on December 14, 1774, led the 400 local militiamen who stormed Castle William and Mary. Langdon oversaw the construction in Portsmouth of three fighting ships, the

PAPERS AND POLITICS

New Hampshire's newspapers have long played a colorful role in state politics. The high-profile *Manchester Union Leader*, acquired by the ultraconservative William Loeb in 1946, provided him with a bully pulpit for decades. The publisher savaged anyone who vexed him, from Democrats like Edmund Muskie, the senator from Maine whose 1972 presidential bid withered under Loeb's incessant attacks, to fellow Republicans who wavered from his narrowly defined program.

Loeb was by no means the first activist editor, however. Isaac Hill, a Jacksonian Democrat and the editor of the Concord-based *Patriot*, preceded him by more than a century. A sour-faced man who dressed in black printer's garb even after he no longer needed to hide the ink stains from his presses, he distrusted denizens of both the seacoast and the Connecticut River Valley and was always lashing out at someone.

In their book *New Hampshire: Crosscurrents in Its Development*, Nancy Coffee Heffernan and Ann Page Stecker examine the similarities between Loeb and Hill and conclude that the men ran their papers more or less the same way, "full of flamboyance, invective, and political bias." The two publishers had nearly the same agenda, namely "low taxes, small government, concern for the common man." The only difference was that in Hill's time liberals supported these notions and in Loeb's conservatives did.

Other shapers of public opinion included William E. Chandler, the publisher of the *Independent Statesman*, who in 1881 presented three bills to the New Hampshire legislature in an attempt to curb growing power of the railroads. For the next 36 years, he editorialized against the them in his paper. Henry Putney, the editor of the *Manchester Mirror*, who was firmly in the pocket of the Boston & Maine Railroad, took a pro-railroad stance.

Loeb was probably the most caustic of all the newspaper people, though. When he died in 1981, his wife, Nackey, presided over the paper in much the same spirit as her husband. Months before Nackey Loeb's death in 2000, Joseph McQuaid became the *Union Leader*'s publisher. Though he has been described as curmudgeonly, he has toned down the paper, which remains the state's largest, a bit. But he too knows how to wield the knife. In the 2000 presidential primary, he saucily derided all the Democratic candidates and the Republicans as well, flouting political correctness by declaring that Elizabeth Dole brought nothing to the race "besides an X chromosome."

Raleigh, the *Ranger,* and the *America.* He outfitted seven privateers to raid English shipping and made a fortune as prize agent, converting liberated goods and ships into currency. Some contemporaries criticized Langdon for becoming wealthy while others were sacrificing so much for the cause.

From 1776 to 1782, Langdon was speaker of the New Hampshire State House of Representatives, where he was an advocate for the mercantile interests of Portsmouth over those of interior towns. After serving at the Constitutional Convention in Philadelphia, he returned to New Hampshire and lobbied for the ratification of the U.S. Constitution, which the state legislature did on June 21, 1788. The next year he became president of the United States Senate and in that post administered the oath of office to George Washington. He served as a senator until 1801, then returned home to serve as state senator, speaker of the house, and governor. He died in his mansion on Pleasant Street in Portsmouth.

◆ ABOLITIONISTS, UNIONISTS, AND THE CIVIL WAR

The national debate over the institution of slavery overshadowed the careers of men who came of age in the mid-19th century. The abolitionist movement began in New England, and it was from New England that the South wished to secede, sundering a Union just 75 years old. The fates of four important New Hampshire native sons were tied to this issue: Daniel Webster, Salmon P. Chase, Horace Greeley, and Franklin Pierce.

Daniel Webster (1782–1852)
Lawyer, politician, statesman
b. Salisbury, New Hampshire

The man known as the "fiery orator" and (for his dark moods) "Black Daniel" practiced law in Boscawen and Portsmouth after graduating from Dartmouth College. He served as a member of the U.S. House of Representatives from New Hampshire from 1813 to 1817, later represented Massachusetts in the House and Senate, and was the secretary of state for Presidents Harrison, Tyler, and Fillmore. In 1842 he negotiated the Webster-Ashburton Treaty, which settled the dispute with Great Britain over the U.S.-Canadian border. The long-simmering feud had given rise to the Indian Stream Republic in 1832.

Webster is famous for his many speeches, among them his defense of Dartmouth

A portrait of Salmon P. Chase appears on the $10,000 bill.

against the State of New Hampshire, which wanted to take over the college, and his justification of the Fugitive Slave Law. Yet another popular oration explained "The Dignity and Importance of History."

Salmon P. Chase (1808–1873)
Secretary of the Treasury, Chief Justice of the United States
b. Cornish Township, New Hampshire

The man who invented the greenback gazes imperiously from the $10,000 bill. As Abraham Lincoln's secretary of the treasury, Salmon P. Chase also initiated the first federal income tax, to help the Union cover the cost of fighting the Civil War.

Chase was born in New Hampshire and moved to Ohio, where he rose to political power. An ambitious man with presidential aspirations, he was a radical abolitionist whose views brought him into constant conflict with Lincoln. The president accepted Chase's fourth, petulant offer of resignation, much to Chase's surprise and chagrin. As a consolation, Lincoln appointed him to the Supreme Court, where as chief justice he presided over the Senate impeachment trial of Lincoln's successor, President Andrew Johnson.

Horace Greeley (1811–1872)
Journalist and political leader
b. Amherst, New Hampshire

The founder of the *New York Tribune* is most famous for something he never said: "Go west, young man." The sentiment is his, but the words first appeared in an editorial in an Indiana newspaper. Greeley's own editorial, written in 1841, reads, "Do not lounge in the cities! There is room and health in the country, away from the crowds of idlers and imbeciles. Go West, before you are fitted for no life but that of the factory." Droves of young men took his advice later in the decade when gold was found at Sutter's Mill in northern California.

Born on a farm near Amherst, New Hampshire, Greeley was apprenticed to a Vermont printer at the age of 15. As the editor of the *Tribune*, he shaped public opinion during the Civil War as few others could, vacillating between pacifism ("Sign anything, ratify anything, pay anything...there never was a good war or a bad peace.") and bellicosity: "On to Richmond! Crush the rebels in blood and fire!" Greeley ran for president against Ulysses S. Grant in 1872 and died soon after losing.

Franklin Pierce (1804–1869)
14th President of the United States
(1853–1857)
b. Hillsborough, New Hampshire

The only president from New Hampshire was the son of a state governor who raised his children to revere Jeffersonian Ideals and serve their country. A popular congressman and

GREELEYISMS

"Common sense is very uncommon."

"Abstaining is favorable both to the head and the pocket."

"Journalism will kill you, but it will keep you alive while you're at it."

"Fame usually comes to those who are thinking of something else."

"Fame is vapor, popularity an accident, riches take wings. Only one thing endures and that is character."

Matthew Brady daguerreotype of Horace Greeley taken circa 1850. (Library of Congress)

Franklin Pierce

senator, Pierce joined the military in 1846 and served as an officer in the Mexican War.

During the presidential campaign of 1852, the Democratic party selected Pierce as its candidate on the 49th ballot. He defeated the Republican candidate, his former commander Winfield Scott, becoming the youngest president to that point in U.S. history. On the way to the inauguration, his son Benny was decapitated before his parents' eyes in a train wreck. Pierce's wife, Jane, was so grief-stricken she never moved into the White House.

Slavery and his stand on the issue clouded the presidency of the genial Pierce, a man of compromise at a time when being one meant taking a dubious moral stand. He believed the North should make concessions to the South about slavery rather than risk dissolution of the Union and signed the controversial Kansas-Nebraska Act, which allowed settlers of the new territories to decide the issue of slavery for themselves. Pierce's inability to stem the South's drift toward secession diminished his legacy. He left office a discredited man, and when his best friend, Nathaniel Hawthorne, passed away, Pierce was not even asked to be a pallbearer.

◆ INDUSTRY, ART, RELIGION, AND OUTER SPACE

As the 19th century gave way to the 20th, New Hampshire was enjoying prominence in industry and the arts, and a native daughter was establishing a popular religion. Mills churned out goods along its rivers, and painters and writers came to enjoy its mountains. Robert Frost spent many years in New Hampshire, and his poems connect his inner experience to the state's landscape. Heavy industry began to diminish by the middle of the 20th century, but as the new millennium dawned the state went high-tech. Along the way, New Hampshire residents participated in two of the country's most dramatic moments in space, one a triumph, the other a tragedy.

Mary Baker Eddy (1821–1910)
Founder of Christian Science
b. Bow, New Hampshire

Mary Baker Eddy had been an invalid until 1870, when a religious experience restored her health. Perceiving an important connection between mind and body, she developed the belief system propounded in her book *Science and Health with Key to the Scriptures,* published in 1875. More than nine million copies of this founding document of the Church of Christ Scientist, or Christian Science, have been sold. In 1908, Eddy founded the respected newspaper the *Christian Science Monitor.*

Mary Baker Eddy

Robert Frost (1874–1963)
Poet
b. San Francisco, California
Frost's poems honor the plainspoken flinty language of northern New England. The writer did not live in New Hampshire until he was 12, but he came to identify strongly with his adopted home. His mother, Belle, taught school in Salem, and young Robert enjoyed afternoons of berry picking on his Uncle Messer's farm in Amherst, where the author of "Birches" swung his first birch. He spent a term at Dartmouth, an idyllic summer honeymoon in Allenstown, a summer in Bethlehem, four years teaching at Pinkerton Academy and another year at what is now Plymouth State College.

The town that holds the strongest claim to young Robert Frost is Derry, where he gave up poetry for a time to farm and sell eggs before finding his literary voice. The Robert Frost Homestead in Derry is now a museum devoted to his life and works.

Alan B. Shepard, Jr.
(1923–1998)
Astronaut
b. East Derry,
New Hampshire

One of the seven original American astronauts and the first American to fly in space, Alan B. Shepard, Jr. served on a destroyer during World War II and became a test pilot after

Robert Frost, circa 1950. (Dartmouth College Library)

the war. On May 5, 1961, he boarded the *Freedom 7* Mercury capsule for his 15-minute historic flight. This triumph was followed by 10 years of disappointment. But for an inner ear disorder he might have commanded the first Gemini mission, and he was assigned to command the fateful *Apollo 13* mission but was held back for more training.

Finally, in 1971, Shepard flew to the moon on *Apollo 14*. As the fifth person to walk on the moon, he is remembered for hitting a few golf balls over the lunar surface. Shepard retired from NASA and the navy in 1974 and went into business developing commercial property. For a time after his famous flight, his hometown of Derry was known as Spacetown.

Alan B. Shepard, Jr.

Christa McAuliffe (1948–1986)
Teacher, astronaut
b. Framingham, Massachusetts

Sharon Christa McAuliffe, a social studies teacher at Concord High School, was to have been the first teacher and civilian in space, but she died in an explosion onboard the space shuttle *Challenger* during launch.

The eldest of Edward and Grace Corrigan's five children, McAuliffe attended Framingham State College, majored in history, and in 1970 married her high school sweetheart, Steve. A teacher with an active community life, she began her training at NASA's facility in Houston in September 1985. On January 28, 1986, just 73 seconds after liftoff, the space shuttle exploded, killing McAuliffe and six other astronauts. In 1988, the New Hampshire legislature appropriated funds to build a planetarium in Concord to honor her life and career.

THE SEACOAST
& PISCATAQUA BASIN

■ **Highlights**

	page
Mansions at Little Boar's Head	55
Fuller Gardens	57
Isles of Shoals	57
Odiorne Point State Park	62
Portsmouth	68
Strawbery Banke Museum	70
Exeter	80

Map page 53

Portsmouth

Exeter   Rye

■ **Area Overview**

The New Hampshire seacoast is one of the state's great treasures, all the more so for being so minuscule. But what it lacks in size, the 18-mile shoreline more than makes up for in visual contrast: broad sandy beaches opposite sun-bleached salt marshes, brilliant gardens in shady coves, dreamlike drives that skirt sedate mansions, colonial forts, and three of America's oldest seaside settlements. Inland along the Piscataqua Estuary are historic New England towns well worth a leisurely visit. You can tour the old neighborhoods and mansions of Portsmouth and explore New Hampshire's Revolutionary-era capital, Exeter.

Weather: Summer temperatures average 69 degrees F, winter 23 degrees, with extremes of 103 and -35. The moderating influence of the Atlantic Ocean often makes Portsmouth a pleasant place to linger on a blistering summer day; take a sweater and windbreaker out on the water. In winter, the seacoast is the best place to experience a nor'easter, a type of blizzard unique to the New England coast, during which moisture-laden air sweeps in from the Atlantic, dumping a wet, heavy snow that reflects a blue-green light if you stick a shovel in it.

■ HISTORY

The European history of New Hampshire's coastal region begins with the exploitation of the vast inland waterway called the Piscataqua Basin and the fertile fishing grounds offshore. Four towns surrounding this basin came to dominate the region—Hampton and Portsmouth on the seacoast; Exeter on the Squamscott River, 15 miles west of Hampton; and Dover, 8 miles upstream from Portsmouth.

Before there were towns, there were crude plantations settled after King James I awarded a royal grant to Capt. John Mason and Sir Ferdinando Gorges. The first, South Plantation, which the native peoples called "Pannaway," was founded in 1623 at present-day Odiorne Point. Here, Mason's men, led by David Thomson and son Amias, built a fortified communal dwelling. Several years later, the Hilton brothers, transplanted London fishmongers, left Pannaway to settle on a neck of land 8 miles up the Piscataqua they called "North Plantation." It later became Dover. In 1630, English settlers and eight Danish workmen founded Portsmouth, or "Strawbery Banke" as it was known then.

Unlike the Puritans to the south, who burned with religious fervor, the first New Hampshire settlers were interested in wealth and proposed to earn it by meeting Europe's most basic needs: fish for food, fur for clothing, and timber for shelter and ships. New Hampshire's tall, straight white pines were highly valued in Europe as a building material and by the British navy, which was eager to build more ships and dominate the seas. Waterways like the Piscataqua and the Merrimack facilitated the transport of these timbers from the interior forests to mast depots, shipyards, and cooperages on the seacoast. Families like the Waldrons and the Vaughans made fortunes in the masting trade. The Wentworths, as mast agents for the king, amassed wealth that supported a governing dynasty of three generations.

The Puritans of Massachusetts were as intolerant of dissent as the Anglicans they had fled. They regularly purged themselves of antinomians, who wished to move beyond strict observance of Old Testament law to achieve a more emotional relationship with God. Among the antinomians were Roger Williams, Anne Hutchinson, and her brother-in-law John Wheelwright. In 1638, Wheelwright moved north to found Exeter, 15 miles inland, far from the high-living Anglicans on the seacoast and the prying Puritans of the Massachusetts Bay Colony.

Some Puritans had already crossed over the Merrimack River into New Hampshire to found Hampton; others purchased the grant of the Hilton brothers to establish

Dover. In time these transplants would displace the rough-and-tumble fishermen and the Anglican hierarchy to forge a new dynamic more in tune with the ambitions of the Bay Colony. In 1641, the four towns voted to become a part of Massachusetts.

During the reign of the Bay Colony, New Hampshire experienced its own witch trials, almost 40 years before the more famous ones in Salem, Massachusetts. Eunice "Goody" (short for Goodwife) Cole was convicted of cursing cattle in the town of Hampton in 1656 and sent to prison in Boston. In 1657, tolerant Portsmouth acquitted Jane Wolford of witchcraft, and she later won a suit of slander against her accuser.

Successive British kings separated, united, and re-separated the scrapping colonies, as much to keep the Puritans in check as to establish efficient governance. After a century of legal wrangling between the heirs to Capt. John Mason's land grant and powerful Puritan families like the Cutts, Vaughans, and Waldrons (the Wentworths were Anglican royalists), documents recording previous decisions favorable to the Mason heirs suddenly disappeared. Then a "treaty" that appeared to give land ownership to the Puritans surfaced. It took 200 years for the forgery—and the complicity of two of Portsmouth's leading Puritan families—to come to light.

Mason's frustrated heirs eventually sold their claim to the London solicitors of Benning Wentworth, who in 1741 became the first governor of the independent colony of New Hampshire. Finally, 120 years after Capt. John Mason named the region for his homeland in England, the four towns had established a common identity, separate from the Bay Colony.

Thus, locked in a self-perpetuating struggle with its ambitious sister to the south, and scarcely unified within its own shifting borders, New Hampshire was born.

■ HAMPTON BEACH *map page 53, C-5*

Touring ←🚗→ *Route 1A takes you from the honky-tonk Massachusetts town of Salisbury Beach across the state line to the tattered three-decker houses of Seabrook. North of the bridge over Hampton Harbor, on your left you'll see a crowded strip of hotels, juke joints, trinket shops, and B&Bs. On your right is a low sea wall, and beyond it, a vast inviting beach. You're in the "resort" town of Hampton Beach.*

Sophisticates hate to admit it, but Hampton Beach is fun. This broad white strand with a strip of fried-food purveyors and sellers of summer sundries unabashedly delivers sensual pleasure at its most basic: the smell of burgers and fries, the tingle of

salt and sun on skin, the bracing first seconds of a plunge into the surf. On a hot July day, the scene is a riotous mix of colored beach umbrellas and bare skin, Frisbee-tossers and boogie-boarders. There's nothing new here, and the only "culture" is beach culture at its unrepentant best. (As for parking, bring plenty of quarters and don't forget to feed your meter along Ocean Boulevard, or you will swiftly receive a ticket.)

Even on the most crowded days, beachgoers seeking to escape the throngs will find that the far edges of Hampton Beach tend to remain quiet. On a clear day, if you climb up the bluff and walk the cliffside path at Great Boar's Head, the Isles of Shoals are visible and, far to the south, so is Cape Ann.

John Greenleaf Whittier, the 19th-century poet, wrote many verses inspired by or set in the Hampton area. From his "Hampton Beach" comes this almost Whitmanesque stanza:

> I draw a freer breath—I seem
> Like all I see—
> Waves in the sun—the white-winged gleam
> Of sea-birds in the slanting beam—
> And far-off sails which flit before the south-wind free.

Inland from the beach, east from Route 1 on Park Avenue to Meetinghouse Green, is the original settlement of Hampton. Founded by Puritans, Hampton was not always so fun-loving. Goody Cole landed in jail several times between the 1650s and 1680s for supposedly practicing witchcraft. After her last imprisonment, Hampton residents were ordered to bring her food and firewood, and they weren't happy about it. (The story that she was buried with a stake through her heart—depending on the account, either to exorcise her of her demons or to keep the devil from carrying her soul away—is probably apocryphal.)

To get the flavor of the old town, visit the **Tuck Museum** of the Hampton Historical Society, on the original town green. The complex includes an old schoolhouse, a farmhouse with a collection of early farm implements, and the Seacoast Fire Museum, built by local firemen. *40 Park Avenue, Hampton; 603-929-0781.*

Touring ←🚗→ *Five miles north of Hampton Beach, the road begins its curve along a rocky coast past the elegant mansions of North Hampton's Little Boar's Head. You'll pass rows of seaside cottages punctuated by the occasional restaurant near picture-perfect Rye Harbor, a quiet cove surrounded by a salt marsh. A few more twists in the road bring you to Wallis Sands Beach and Odiorne Point.*

On hot summer days, Hampton Beach is almost always packed.

■ NORTH HAMPTON *map page 53, C-4*

North of Little Boar's Head, North Hampton gives way to Rye Beach, which extends north to the city of Portsmouth. Don't worry that you're missing anything inland; it's mainly residential. The sights along Route 1A are the main attractions.

◆ NORTH HAMPTON STATE PARK AND LITTLE BOAR'S HEAD

About 3 miles north of Great Boar's Head, North Hampton State Park is a great place to park to walk past the mansions of Little Boar's Head, a bluff that projects into the Atlantic. Parking and walking is definitely the best way to see these grand homes, because the road is often busy.

Immediately to the north of the parking lot are 12 shacks, some built as early as 1804 for fishing and lobstering. In the 1930s, the sculptor Malvina Hoffman, a student of Rodin, had a studio here. Up around the bluff on the left, past the fence with jagged vertical stones on the upper course, is a house with an elegant veranda. The home was built in 1874 for Col. George Studebaker, whose company was the

world's largest manufacturer of carriages. Ogden Nash owned the cottage down the little street to the left, at 9 Atlantic Avenue. The whimsical poet began summering on Little Boar's Head in 1930, finally retiring there in 1962.

Beyond Atlantic Avenue on Route 1A is a large yellow house with multiple peaks and dormers called Sea Verger (46 Ocean Boulevard), where both President William Howard Taft and the conductor Arthur Fiedler became engaged to their wives.

Nearby is a vast expanse of lawn, shared by little Union Chapel and four huge houses set back from the road. These were built or bought by the family of Alvan Fuller, the governor of Massachusetts from 1924 to 1930.

A descriptive and highly useful four-color pocket guide lists the historical homes, shops, and hotels of North Hampton. To receive one, send $2 and a self-addressed, stamped envelope to the North Hampton Historical Society, c/o North Hampton Public Library, 237A Atlantic Avenue, North Hampton, NH 03862.

◆ FULLER GARDENS

This fine example of early-20th-century estate gardens was designed by Arthur A. Shurtleff (later Shurcliff) in the late 1920s and reworked by the Olmsted brothers of Boston in the late 1930s. The gardens, including a splendid Japanese one, bloom for nearly half the year, with tulips in May, followed by flowering shrubs and bulbs and more than 2,000 rose bushes, some of which blossom well into October. *10 Willow Avenue; 603-964-5414.*

Lea House, the Colonial Revival–style mansion of Alvan Fuller, visible from Route 1A, is the centerpiece of Fuller Gardens. *23 Willow Avenue.*

■ ISLES OF SHOALS *map page 53, D-4*

Six miles out to sea from Rye are the rocky, windswept Isles of Shoals. Some consider them the birthplace of New Hampshire, as it was here that the state's first regular visitors landed. Five of the islands belong to Maine, four to New Hampshire.

You can visit Star Island, the largest of the nine, with the Isles of Shoals Steamship Company, which drops you off for a three-hour walkabout. On the treeless rock are a hotel, a historic church, and a few gravestones. Seabirds wheel overhead. As your journey progresses, you may see seals or dolphins.

The roses at Fuller Gardens sometimes bloom as late as October.

Cruises leave from Portsmouth Harbor: **Isles of Shoals Steamship Company** (800-441-4620), from mid-May to late September; **Portsmouth Harbor Cruises** (800-776-0915), from May to October.

The Isles of Shoals take their name from the "shoals," or schools of fish once so prevalent here. It is not certain when west-country English fishermen first began to arrive—fishermen are notoriously tight-lipped about their secrets—but they had been fishing off the Shoals for many years before Capt. John Smith first reported this "curious fish pond" in 1614.

Smith, the founder of the settlement at Jamestown, Virginia, in 1608, was forever trying to name parts of the North American coast after ladies he had known during his Turkish campaigns. But he named these lonely islands for himself. Unfortunately for him, "Smith's Isles" never really caught on, and since then their names have tended away from the merely descriptive and toward the fantastic or lyrical—Haley's island became **Smuttynose,** Hog became **Appledore.** The others are **Duck, Malaga, Cedar, Star, Lunging, White,** and **Seavey.**

The Shoals were an ideal spot for fishermen to land because they were safe from mainland tribes and close to the fishing grounds. Here, the "dunfish" so highly prized in Europe could be gutted and dried efficiently, on racks called "fish flakes." Dunfish was the market name for fat winter cod, which was dried and lightly salted.

Cod, which had become a form of currency in Europe, was the most valuable fish caught here, but the seas teemed with rockling, whelk, haddock, hake, ming, lobster, cusk, catfish, sculpin, wolf-fish, sand-dabs, bluefish, sharks, halibut, nursefish, mud-eel, sunfish, swordfish, skipjack, horse-mackerel, herring, shiners, bonito, dogfish, perch, pollock, lumpfish, rudder-fish, alewives, menhaden, and whales.

The fishing trade gave way to the hotel era in the mid-1800s. Resort hotels included the majestic Oceanic, built in 1875. Visitors came to "take the air," enjoy the stark island beauty, and feast at the groaning boards of the hotels. When hoteliers began buying out the islanders, Shoalers wandered the streets of Portsmouth, mourning the loss of their seaward home.

The hotel trade ended in the early 1900s. Today, Star Island is owned by the Unitarian and Congregationalist Star Island Foundation, which hosts religious and educational conferences here.

(following pages) Storm clouds loom over the White Island Light, Isles of Shoals.

FERRY TO THE SHOALS

It was a very bright, warm August day when Mrs. Wishart and her young companion steamed over from Portsmouth to the Isles of Shoals. It was Lois's first sight of the sea, for the journey from New York had been made by land; and the ocean, however still, was nothing but a most wonderful novelty to her. She wanted nothing, she could well nigh attend to nothing, but the movements and developments of this vast and mysterious Presence of nature. Mrs. Wishart was amused and yet half provoked. There was no talk in Lois; nothing to be got out of her; hardly any attention to be had from her. She sat by the vessel's side and gazed, with a brow of grave awe and eyes of submissive admiration; rapt, absorbed, silent, and evidently glad. Mrs. Wishart was provoked at her, and envied her.

"What do you find in the water, Lois?"

"Oh, the wonder of it!" said the girl with a breath of rapture.

"Wonder? What wonder? I suppose everything is wonderful, if you look at it. What do you see there that seems so very wonderful?"

"I don't know, Mrs. Wishart. It is so great! And it is so beautiful! And it is so awful!"

"Beautiful?" said Mrs. Wishart. "I confess I do not see it. I suppose it is your gain, Lois. Yes, it is awful enough in a storm, but not to-day. The sea is quiet."

Quiet! With those low-rolling, majestic soft billows. The quiet of a lion asleep with his head upon his paws. Lois did not say what she thought.

"And you have never seen the sea-shore yet," Mrs. Wishart went on. "Well, you will have enough of the sea at the Isles. And those are they, I fancy, yonder. Are those the Isles of Shoals?" she asked a passing man of the crew; and was answered with a rough voiced, "Yaw, mum; they be th'oisles."

Lois gazed now at those distant brown spots, as the vessel drew nearer and nearer. Brown spots they remained, and to her surprise small brown spots. Nearer and nearer views only forced the conviction deeper. The Isles seemed to be merely some rough rocky projections from old Ocean's bed, too small to have beauty, too rough to have value. Were those the desired Isles of Shoals? Lois felt deep disappointment. Little bits of bare rock in the midst of the sea; nothing more. No trees, she was sure; as the light fell she could even see no green. Why would they not be better relegated to Ocean's domain, from which they were only saved by a few feet of upheaval? Why should anybody live there? And still more, why should anybody make a pleasure visit there?

—Susan Warner, *Nobody*, 1882

■ To Odiorne Point *map page 53, D-3/4*

Jenness Beach, a pocket of white sand on the rocky Rye coast, is the site of a sunken petrified forest, estimated to have originated at the end of the last ice age and still visible at very low tides. The original transatlantic cable, laid in 1874, is also visible at low tide near the historical marker north of the beach.

Odiorne Point, a few miles to the north, is New Hampshire's Plymouth Rock. Here, on a prominent point near the "Piscataquack," David Thomson and crew established the first settlement, a plantation called Pannaway, in 1623. At Pannaway, Thomson and company found fresh water, abundant fishing, and friendly natives.

They built a little fort on the site, along with drying racks on Flake Hill, a smith's shop, and salt works for preserving fish. Their mission was "to cultivate the vine, discover mines, carry on the fisheries, and trade with the natives." Myles Standish came to beg for salted cod to keep his Pilgrims alive for the winter. Thomson obliged him, dividing what little food he had. In 1626, Thomson left Pannaway to settle on an island in Massachusetts Bay off Nahant, Massachusetts, that still bears his name. In the 1660s, two Frenchmen, the Odiorne brothers, settled here. The cemetery of

Sunrise at Odiorne Point State Park, near Rye.

CELIA THAXTER'S GARDEN

As much as anyone, author Celia Thaxter created the Isles of Shoals, at least that comforting vision of a tranquil garden tended lovingly on an idyllic island. The daughter of a failed whaling company investor and defeated politician who retired to White Island Light in disgust, she was the "lighthouse keeper's daughter" and the darling of the Boston literary luminaries who came to her "salon" on the Isles in the late 1800s.

If her less romantic prose holds up better today than her poetry, it is not what the country wanted back then. After the Civil War, Americans, longing for a healing, lyrical vision of their country, could not get enough of her verse. Published in *The Atlantic Monthly* and similar journals, she attracted writers such as Nathaniel Hawthorne (who called her "Miranda" after Shakespeare's island heroine) and painters like the American impressionist Childe Hassam (who illustrated her book *An Island Garden*) to the Shoals. The vision endures: even today "Celia people" plant replicas of her Appledore garden as far away as land-locked Colorado.

Childe Hassam, a frequent guest at the Thaxter family's hotel on Appledore Island, painted In the Garden *(1892), a portrait of Celia Thaxter in her famed garden. (National Museum of American Art, Washington, D.C.)*

the original settlers is on the other side of Route 1A from Odiorne Point State Park, down the road towards Portsmouth from the park entrance a few hundred yards. Walk behind the house and barn to see the cemetery.

At the 330-acre **Seacoast Science Center** at Odiorne Point State Park, naturalists conduct guided walking tours of seven distinct coastal habitats. You can also take a self-guided tour or picnic at a wooded seaside area near the rocky ocean beach and Little Harbor. *570 Ocean Boulevard, off Route 1A; 603-436-8043.*

A few miles offshore of the state park, the first successful rescue by diving bell occurred in 1939, when the *Squalus* went down with all hands. During World War II, massive gun emplacements were built here, camouflaged against an attack that never happened. The only time the huge coastal defense guns were fired, windows cracked in Portsmouth.

Sculpture of herons at the Seacoast Science Center at Odiorne Point State Park.

■ NEW CASTLE *map page 53, D-3*

Touring ←🚗→ *After playing hide-and-seek among the coves and crannies on Route 1A north of Odiorne Point, you'll come to a stop sign at Foye's Corner. Take a right (head north) to continue on Route 1A to Portsmouth. Less than a mile after the turn (before the metal bridge over Sagamore Creek), another right turn onto Route 1B will take you to the town of New Castle, southeast of Portsmouth, home to Fort Constitution and the historic Wentworth-By-The-Sea Hotel. If you ignore Route 1B and continue north, taking a right (past Sagamore Creek) onto Little Harbor Road, after about a mile you'll come to the Wentworth-Coolidge Mansion, the scene of many a swinging colonial party.*

◆ FORT CONSTITUTION (CASTLE WILLIAM AND MARY) *map page 53, D-3*

Tucked away on Great Island, which is part of the town of New Castle, Castle William and Mary was built in 1632 to guard the entrance to Portsmouth Harbor. On a cold December night here in 1774, the real "first shot heard round the world" was fired. Four months before his better-known ride through Lexington and Concord, Paul Revere arrived on horseback in Portsmouth with vital intelligence that sparked raids on Castle William and Mary.

Like most visitors from Massachusetts, Revere stopped to ask for directions. He then met with local patriots at Stoodley's Tavern and told them that her Majesty's ship, *Somerset*, was on its way to fortify or evacuate the weakly defended munitions stores there. The locals stormed the castle twice within the next two days, spiriting away gunpowder, muskets, and cannons that were put to good use in the Battle of Bunker Hill.

Castle William and Mary, later renamed Fort Constitution, was rebuilt numerous times, most recently during the Civil War. Fine views can be had from the castle of shipping lanes, Whaleback Light, and the Portsmouth Naval Prison (the destination of the delinquent sailor played by Randy Quaid in the 1973 film *The Last Detail*).

◆ WENTWORTH-BY-THE-SEA HOTEL *map page 53, D-3*

With her mansard roof and angular frame, the Wentworth-By-The-Sea looks like an aging dowager in high hat and corset, decades out of fashion but still enduring,

BENNING WENTWORTH'S SHOCKING MARRIAGE

Benning Wentworth circa 1760, as painted by Joseph Blackburn.

It was the 64th birthday of New Hampshire's royal governor, Benning Wentworth. A great fire roared, casting long shadows into the spacious dining hall, and servants trundled out heavy trays of roasted meats and poured superb wines. As his guests chatted decorously, Wentworth rose to speak. He was prosperous and powerful, but by 1760 his first wife and their three sons had died. To salve his loneliness he had turned to women far younger than he, and far beneath his station.

Old Benning thanked his guests for attending his celebration, then shocked them to their Anglican roots by announcing his intention to marry Martha Hilton, who had toiled in his kitchen and kept his house since she was a girl. Now 23 (her descendants later claimed she was 35), Martha was beautiful and ambitious. Wentworth turned to Rev. Arthur Browne of Queen's Church and asked him to officiate. Immediately. After some hesitation, wrote Henry Wadsworth Longfellow a century later in his poem "Lady Wentworth":

> The rector read the service loud and clear.
> "Dearly beloved, we are gathered here,"
> And so on to the end. At his command
> On the fourth finger of her fair left hand
> The Governor placed the ring; and that was all:
> Martha was Lady Wentworth of the Hall!"

obstinate if slightly ridiculous. This historic hotel, now closed, still presides proudly over Little Harbor on Great Island.

A Boston distiller built the Wentworth in 1874 during New Hampshire's first tourism boom. The hotel was designed to provide magnificent views from every room, which explains the structure's narrow profile. Bought by the famous Portsmouth brewer Frank Jones in 1902, the Wentworth was a self-contained playground for the wealthy, with a 300-seat theater, a boathouse, and live dinner music.

In her glory days, the Wentworth hosted presidents and potentates. In 1905, President Theodore Roosevelt, eager to boost the standing of the United States and himself, hosted negotiations at the Portsmouth Naval Shipyard to end the Russo-Japanese War. Both delegations stayed at the Wentworth, the six-foot seven-inch Russian diplomat Sergius Witte and the five-foot four-inch Jutaro Komura making an odd couple of guests. At the peace talks (which Roosevelt himself never attended), Witte, unlike his military colleagues, outmaneuvered the Japanese, who had sunk 19 battleships in a major naval battle. Komura went home in disgrace after Witte feigned acquiescence—and then refused to pay restitution or give up any land.

◆ **WENTWORTH-COOLIDGE MANSION** *map page 53, C-3*

"A noble pile, baronial and colonial in its style," rhymed the poet Henry Wadsworth Longfellow about the bright yellow mansion that overlooks Little Harbor. The Wentworth-Coolidge Mansion, built in 1741, was the home of New Hampshire's first royal governor, Benning Wentworth. A man who knew how to party—"high living shows in his corpulent face and figure," accused a contemporary—the governor served sumptuous feasts accompanied by European wines from a cellar so large he hid his horses in it when trouble erupted along the coast. Music, dancing, card-playing, and other after-dinner amusements contributed to his reputation for flouting prevailing moral standards. Wentworth's mansion, which was restored by the artist John Templeman Coolidge in the 1880s and donated by his heirs to the state in the 1950s, is worth a visit for the scenic views and the glimpse the guided tours provide into life in provincial New Hampshire. *Little Harbor Road off Route 1A (just over the bridge, 1 mile north of Foye's Corner); 603-436-6607.*

Touring ←🚗→ *Your coastal driving tour ends in Portsmouth, Kittery, Maine, stares back at you just over the Piscataqua River, on the opposite side of the copper-green Memorial Bridge. To continue exploring, hop a tour boat headed upriver (see page 80),* where the Piscataqua opens into a 24-square-mile tidal basin, or drive inland on Route 4 from Portsmouth to Durham. South along the inner shoreline of this vast estuary and up the Squamscott River lies the old town of Exeter, easily accessed by heading south from Portsmouth on I-93, west on Route 101, and south on Route 108.

■ PORTSMOUTH map page 53, C-3, and below

New Hampshire's only port lies at the mouth of the Piscataqua River, on the southern bank of the wide swift stream that separates New Hampshire from Maine.

The roiling currents of the Piscataqua represent an apt metaphor for Portsmouth's cultural mix. This teeming port threw together fractious patriots and refined royalists, black sailors ("blackjacks") and cotton traders, Abenaki Penacooks and Englishmen, war heroes and widows. In the 1800s, whaling ships, freight-hauling gundalows and merchant vessels would glide past thriving shipyards and brickyards, carrying their varied cargoes to market. The historian Samuel Eliot Morison called

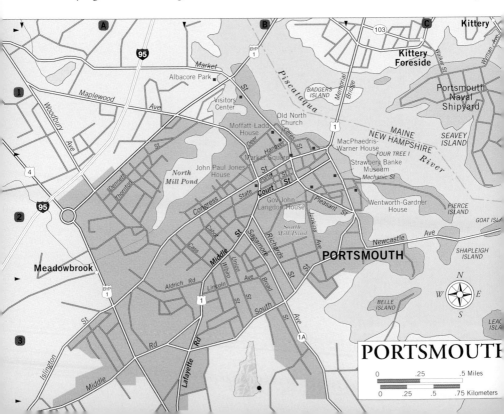

PORTSMOUTH

0   .25   .5 Miles

0   .25   .5   .75 Kilometers

John Paul Jones lived in this former boardinghouse.

the city the "northern counterpart to Annapolis," referring not only to Portsmouth's naval traditions but also to the more worldly, royalist style of its ruling class. In short, it was more Anglican than Puritan.

Walk down Market Street today and you'll see that the melting pot still bubbles, though the Anglicans have all but disappeared. Tourists rub elbows with local youths, and gourmands raise elbows with e-commerce mavens in downtown bars and brew-pubs. Music joints and pubs around town draw all sorts of patrons, from shipyard workers to pierced and tattooed espresso addicts.

Portsmouth continuously reinvents itself, and like any thriving port it has tales to tell about patriots and prostitutes, slaves and abolitionists, heroic acts and bloody murder. Many attractions in this little city with the feel of a big one are within a ten-minute walk of the waterfront. There is much to do—shopping in downtown boutiques for everything from funky fashion to blown glass; hopping a boat to see the harbor, the Isles of Shoals, or Great Bay; touring colonial mansions; walking through the *Albacore*, a submarine; or enjoying a performance at the Seacoast Repertory Theatre. Nearby are bargain outlet malls. And nobody tires of watching the powerful Moran tugboats battle what is said to be the second-trickiest tidal current in the United States.

Scholars of maritime and seacoast history find dusty pleasure in research at the Portsmouth Athenaeum, the Strawbery Banke Museum, and a slew of used book-stores and antique shops. For information about the area, contact the Greater Portsmouth Chamber of Commerce (603-436-3988).

◆ WALKING TOURS OF PORTSMOUTH

Several walking tours explore the old mansions of Portsmouth. The **Portsmouth Harbour Trail** (map and guide available from the chamber of commerce or at the visitors booth on Market Square) is an excellent resource for peripatetic historians and mansion buffs, as is the book *Colonial Portsmouth in Pen and Ink*, by Francis X. Morgan, available at the Strawbery Banke Museum shop.

Along the north side of **Market Square** a fine commercial block dates from the early 19th century—watch for the cast-iron storefronts. Alexander Ladd, a prosperous merchant, once owned the 1763 **Moffatt-Ladd House** (154 Market Street). Opposite the house, which is open to the public in summer, steps descend to **Ceres Street,** a waterfront lane once known as **Merchant's Row.** In the 1800s, the five-story brick buildings to the left contained offices and storerooms for rum and cotton.

◆ STRAWBERY BANKE MUSEUM *map page 68, C-2*

Strawbery Banke Museum is a beautifully restored 10-acre historic neighborhood once known by the less glamorous name of Puddle Dock. Almost 400 years ago, land on this site was granted by the king of England to the former governor of Newfoundland, Capt. John Mason. Because fishermen had noted this as a place where wild berries grew in profusion, the colonists who settled Mason's grant called it Strawbery Banke.

Captain Mason never visited his plantation but you can. There are 40 buildings on the site and a hulking riverboat known as a gundalow, a derivation of gondola. Skilled docents relate the history of Strawbery Banke's many old homes and com-mercial buildings, interpreting local history and illuminating the details of daily life from the 17th through the 20th century.

At the cooper's hut and the dory shop, artisans build barrels and fishing boats using original tools and methods. The craftspeople are happy to share their knowledge of their trades. **Stoodley's Tavern,** which can be viewed only from the outside, was built

Knit one, purl two outside Strawbery Banke's World War II–era grocery store.

by a comrade-in-arms of Robert Rogers, a renowned fighter in the French and Indian Wars. The gambrel-roofed tavern was the site of auctions for goods from the West Indies, including slaves. It was here that Paul Revere brought news that set off the attack on Castle William and Mary.

The **Thomas Bailey Aldrich House** almost exactly matches the description of the Nutter House in Aldrich's *The Story of a Bad Boy*. "Tom Bailey" was the autobiographical invention of Thomas Bailey Aldrich, (a J.K. Rowling of his day), who wrote about his mischievous childhood growing up in his grandparents' house in Portsmouth.

Aldrich's friend Mark Twain admitted that his character Tom Sawyer owed much to Tom Bailey. Twain and Aldrich were inseparable, though Aldrich's wife, Lillian, was never happy to find the inebriated Samuel Clemens at her door in Portsmouth. Twain returned the feeling, referring to Lillian as "A strange and vanity-devoured, detestable woman! I do not believe I could ever learn to like her except on a raft at sea with no other provisions in sight."

William Dean Howells, the editor of *The Atlantic Monthly* in the 1870s, credited Aldrich with creating the modern American novel with his stories of the boy who sneaked out of the house by climbing down a clothesline to set fire to a stagecoach. Like Celia Thaxter's poetry, the tales of "bad boy" Tom Bailey helped Americans relive or reinvent the carefree childhood from which the Civil War had separated them. *Strawbery Banke Museum is across from Prescott Park on Marcy Street; 603-433-1100.*

◆ JOHN PAUL JONES HOUSE MUSEUM *map page 68, B-2*

Sea captain Gregory Purcell built what's now called the John Paul Jones House in 1758 for his bride, Sarah Wentworth, a niece of royal governor Benning Wentworth. After her husband died, the Widow Purcell took in boarders including Jones, a naval hero of the Revolutionary War, who lived here in 1777 during the outfitting of his ship the *Ranger*, and again in 1781 while the *America* was being built. (Jones, who came to love Portsmouth, never took command of the *America*. The U.S. government gave the vessel to the French in thanks for their help during the Revolution.) Rope beds, huge fireplaces, period furnishings, and imposing portraits re-create the time when "the father of the American navy" slept here. Captain Jones—in the form of a life-size and lifelike wax dummy—greets you in his room on the second floor. Since 1922, the bright yellow structure has been the headquarters of the Portsmouth Historical Society. *Open mid-May–mid-Oct. 43 Middle Street; 603-436-8420.*

JOHN PAUL JONES

1747–1792

Born in Scotland and christened John Paul, the future John Paul Jones sailed to Virginia as a cabin boy at the age of 12. As a young man he found work as chief mate on a slave ship out of Jamaica, but he quit after two years and sailed back to Scotland. On that voyage, the captain and the chief mate died of fever and John Paul brought the ship home.

He bought and commanded his own ship in the West Indies in 1772. The crew mutinied and John Paul killed the ringleader. To escape a murder trial, he changed his name to John Paul Jones and fled to Virginia. When the Revolutionary War broke out, he was commissioned as senior lieutenant in the Continental navy and distin-

This lithograph, modeled after a painting by John Collett, depicts a young and pugnacious John Paul Jones. (Library of Congress)

guished himself in battle. Appointed to the *Ranger* in June 1777, Jones captured or sank a number of British ships in the Irish Sea. In 1779, he prowled off the British Isles commanding the *Bonhomme Richard.* Off Flamborough Head he engaged the *Serapis* and the *Countess of Scarborough* in battle. During a three-and-a-half-hour gunfight, Jones famously responded to a request to surrender by calling out, "I have not yet begun to fight." Later, after he had taken the *Serapis,* he watched his own ship sink below the waves.

Jones received a Congressional gold medal in 1787, and later became a rear admiral in the Russian navy. According to legend, late one night in an estuary of the Black Sea, Jones rowed in an open boat into the very middle of a Turkish fleet to scribble in chalk on the hull of the largest ship he could find, "To be burned. Paul Jones." Finding his graffiti in the midst of battle the next day, he proceeded to burn the ship.

A sailor-warrior and lothario, John Paul Jones died in Paris. Later, his remains were returned to the United States by President Theodore Roosevelt, to be buried in Annapolis, Maryland.

◆ MacPhaedris-Warner House *map page 68, B-1*

This is a house with a history. Benjamin Franklin supervised the installation of the lightning rod in 1762, and the Marquis de Lafayette spilled wine on the rug in 1824. There's a Wentworth connection, too. Sarah Wentworth, Benning's sister, married Capt. Archibald MacPhaedris, who built the house between 1718 and 1723 for the sum of 6,000 pounds. Sarah and Archibald's daughter, Mary, married the Hon. Jonathan Warner, a Tory who served on the Governor's Council but looked the other way when patriots broke into the Crown's Commissary, which he was charged to protect. According to Samuel Eliot Morison, the MacPhaedris-Warner House "ranked at the top of the list of the most magnificent homes in the New World." (With 18-inch walls made of brick imported from Holland, the house was built to last, which it has done, admirably.) On the wall by the staircase is one of the first hand-painted murals created in the colonies. A copy of a European mezzotint, it illustrates the European tendency to romanticize Native Americans from a distance. Other frescoes in the home are of biblical and historical scenes. *Open June-Oct. 150 Daniel Street; 603-436-5909.*

The murals at the MacPhaedris-Warner House were painted circa 1719.

First Sail of the *Ranger*

At last, 1 November 1777, when a northwest wind blew down the Piscataqua, the *Ranger* could sail. Her crew hove the anchor cable short, Master Cullam bellowing orders and the boatswains piping shrilly on their new silver calls to annoy Colonel Langdon. Topsail yards were braced sharp, precisely at nine o'clock a gun was fired, the Marines' drums and fifes beat a merry tune while the men heaved on the capstan bars to break out the anchor, and as *Ranger* whipped around under the fresh breeze from the White Mountains, with a strong ebb current under her keel, Captain Jones on the quarterdeck in his best blue uniform and Major Frazer in continentals waved their cocked hats to the ladies ashore. The ship gathered speed as she squared away, nipped around Fort Point "with a bone in her teeth," set lower courses, topgallant sails and studding sails as she passed Jaffrey Point, hauled up short on the port tack to pass the Isles of Shoals, and before night lost sight of the American shore. Bound away at last!

—Samuel Eliot Morison, *John Paul Jones: A Sailor's Biography*, 1959

With John Paul Jones at the helm, the Ranger *captured the British warship the* Drake *on April 24, 1778, just off the British coast. (Mariners' Museum, Newport News, Virginia)*

◆ **GOVERNOR JOHN LANGDON HOUSE AND GARDEN** *map page 68, B-2*
George Washington didn't sleep here, but the home of one of Portsmouth's most prominent citizens was very much to his liking. John Langdon was a merchant, shipbuilder, Revolutionary War leader, a signer of the United States Constitution, and governor of the state. His elaborate home, built in 1784, was updated in the late 19th century by the New York City architectural firm McKim, Mead & White. Don't miss the handsome garden, which contains perennial beds and a pavilion. *Open June–mid-Oct. 143 Pleasant Street; 603-436-3205.*

◆ **BLACK HERITAGE TRAIL**

It comes as a surprise to those who are only aware of New England's role in the abolitionist movement to learn that ships sailing out of the region's ports before 1808 participated in the slave trade. And that some of the leading early citizens owned slaves. The Black Heritage Trail, founded by local historian Valerie Cunningham, who worked three decades on the project, is a self-guided walking and driving tour that relates the history of African Americans in the seacoast area.

Governor John Langdon had slaves whose names we know from their headstones in the Langdon burial ground—Hannah, Pomp, Nanne, Violet, and Scipio. Primus Fowle was owned by the publisher of the *New Hampshire Gazette*. It is possible that Hopestill Cheswell, part African-American, built the house in which John Paul Jones lived. Prince Whipple, who lived at the Moffat-Ladd House, is depicted in the famous Emanuel Gottlieb Leutze painting *George Washington Crossing the Delaware*.

Brochures describing the walking tour are available at the Strawbery Banke Museum, the Chamber of Commerce visitors booth on Market Square, and by mail order from Portsmouth Black Heritage Trail (603-431-2768).

◆ **SUBMARINES OF PORTSMOUTH** *map page 68, B-1*

"Let's go see the submarine races" has been a sly pickup line for as long as there have been submarines, seaports, and the opposite sexes. In Portsmouth, it's been in use since 1915, when the L8 submersible was built at the Portsmouth Naval Shipyard (actually in Kittery, Maine). From Prescott Park, you can look across the water and see where these denizens of the deep are constructed. On a harbor tour you'll usually see a few at berth, being fitted out or repaired. But you'll never see one

(right) Moran tugboats in Portsmouth Harbor. (Robert Holmes)

THE E-COAST

In January 1999, the seacoast woke up to the fact that there were more than 400 technology companies operating in the area. An economic development group was formed, which dubbed the region "the e-coast." And it fit. So many companies are developing Internet infrastructure, managing databases, designing Web sites, or engaging in business-to-business e-commerce that the region has become a mecca for technological high flyers. As a percentage of population, New Hampshire is said to have the second-highest number of high-tech workers in the United States. The seacoast and the Merrimack Valley are the two main areas that account for this ranking.

A dot-com retrenchment as the new millennium dawned caused some shrinkage in Portsmouth, but many important companies survived, including Harbour Lights Productions, a Web design firm; Houston Street Exchange, which provides an online trading platform for commodities; and Newmarket Software.

Which came first, the e-business or the thriving Portsmouth youth culture? All around the seacoast region, corporations are learning to cultivate both. Responding to youthful idealism, area businesses practice community-building philanthropy. Timberland, the footwear and outdoor apparel manufacturer, is but one example. Tucked in a green office park in Stratham, near Exeter, Timberland has funded altruistic efforts such as City Year, a program that hires inner-city youth to work in the community for a year, and Taste of the Nation, a hunger-relief effort. The company, which encourages employees to take sabbaticals to serve the cause of their choice, promotes these charitable endeavors without advertising its involvement. One of its core values, after service and strength, is humility. All these companies depend upon Web designers and developers, who can be seen racing around Portsmouth on their Razor scooters and arguing code at local hangouts.

Nearly everyone here has a Web site. One of the best ways to explore the area's history and attractions is online at **www.seacoastnh.com**. This literate site has one of the most thoroughly cross-referenced explorations of local history anywhere, as well as in-depth guides to businesses, restaurants, and hotels.

U.S. naval police patrol the waters of Portsmouth Harbor during the commissioning of the submarine U.S. Maine.

coming or going—submarines enter and exit Portsmouth Harbor, as their name implies, submerged.

There are too many fantastic Portsmouth submarine stories to relate them all. One that cannot be ignored happened 5 miles south of the Isles of Shoals in 1939. On a shakedown run, the *Squalus* went to the bottom when its main induction valve refused to close. In heavy weather, racing against hypothermia and carbon dioxide poisoning, Lt. Commander Swede Momsen and his team of navy divers attached a huge, pear-shaped diving bell to the *Squalus* and brought up all the men who had survived the first terrifying minutes. Using pontoons, Momsen's crew then raised the *Squalus* itself and towed it into Portsmouth Harbor. It was the first such deep-water rescue, inspired by another Portsmouth sub, the *09*, which went down off the coast in 1929. No one survived that catastrophe. Momsen, who created the rescue chamber and the Momsen Lung—a breathing apparatus for trapped submariners—had been a friend of that sub's skipper. Peter Maas's riveting book *The Terrible Hours* relates this story.

What was life like aboard a submarine before the nuclear navy? Cramped, malodorous, and stressful. The best way to understand the experience is to go below yourself. The ***Albacore,*** a submarine whose construction Momsen supervised, is in permanent drydock north of the waterfront in Portsmouth (Exit 7 off I-95 will take you there). This was the first sub built with a fishlike cylindrical shape and airplane-style controls for diving and climbing (which it performed so rapidly that subway straps were added). What is striking about the vessel is how compact, complete, and, with a mere 12 vertical inches between bunks, claustrophobic it must have been. Fans of 1950s Formica will love the decor. *600 Market Street; 603-436-3680.*

◆ Boat Tours From Portsmouth Harbor

To see the harbor, lighthouse, whales, or fall foliage from the water, take a tour (reservations recommended) with the **Isles of Shoals Steamship Company** (Barker Wharf, 315 Market Street; 800-441-4620 or 603-431-5500), which operates from mid-May through December. Or try **Portsmouth Harbor Cruises** (Ceres Street Dock, 1 Harbour Place; 800-776-0915 or 603-436-8084), from May to October.

■ Exeter *map page 53, B-4*

John Wheelwright, the minister banished from the Bay Colony during one of the Puritan purges, founded Exeter. Wheelwright was a careful man. He settled his congregation far from the seacoast Anglicans and the strict Bay Colony Puritans, gaining title to the land from the Squamscott Indians in 1638. He was also curiously footloose, popping up in Wells, Maine, to escape encroaching Bay Colony zealots, and later in Hampton as a minister in 1647. By then his reputation had diminished greatly. Wheelwright strongly denied being an antinomian yet preached what were considered antinomian beliefs. After being asked to leave one community after another, he sailed to England in 1658, but returned soon after. He died in Salisbury in 1679.

Exeter and the other Piscataqua Basin settlements suffered from "Indian depredations" for many years, and the town's annals abound with tales of early settlers "killed or captured, never returned." Exeter's significance, historically at least, came during the Revolution. In July 1775, Exeter became the revolutionary capital of New Hampshire after colonial governor John Wentworth dissolved the provincial assembly. The Gilmans, the Folsoms, and the Ladds are Exeter natives

(opposite) The Squamscott River flows through the center of Exeter.

who risked everything for the sake of independence.

It is hard to believe today as you drive through seemingly landlocked Exeter, but this was a thriving seaport in the 1800s. The Squamscott River is a saltwater estuary that provides Exeter with access to the ocean via Great Bay. A sawmill was one of the first buildings built by Wheelwright's settlers, and Exeter-sawn lumber (as well as textiles, flour, and meal) was carried to market by the gundalows that plied the Piscataqua Basin. Ships were built here, as many as 22 in a single season and as large as 500 tons. John Phillips, the founder of Phillips Exeter Academy, made his fortune in mercantile trade.

Every Monday night in July, the town's bandstand comes alive with the sounds of America's oldest continuously tootling brass band. The bandstand was designed by Henry Bacon, who also designed the Lincoln Memorial in Washington, D.C. Bacon was a good friend of Exeter native son Daniel Chester French, who sculpted the seated Lincoln in the D.C. memorial and created the Minuteman Memorial in Concord, Massachusetts. Bacon and French worked on another project together, the World War I memorial "Mother Town, Soldier Son," in Exeter's Gale Park.

Phillips Exeter Academy in Exeter.

♦ VISITING EXETER

This quintessential New England town stretches out along the river, with waterfront shops and an established town center, inviting a leisurely stroll. Pick up a walking tour brochure at the Exeter Historical Society, at 47 Front Street, or the American Independence Museum, at Water and Center Streets.

Phillips Exeter Academy

Phillips Exeter is one of the oldest and best known of New Hampshire's many prestigious secondary boarding schools. Daniel Webster, Robert Todd Lincoln (Abe's son), Gore Vidal and other members of America's elite have passed through these halls on the way to Harvard, Princeton, and Yale. Dr. John Phillips, who founded the school in 1781, believed that "goodness without knowledge is weak and feeble, yet knowledge without goodness is dangerous, and that both united form the noblest character, and lay the surest foundation of usefulness to man-kind." An important contribution to secondary school education occurred here, Exeter's Harkness plan, which places students around an oval table (the school maintains a 12-to-1 student-teacher ratio) and emphasizes discourse over note-taking. The modernist architect Louis I. Kahn designed the stunning library, whose contemporary style nods gracefully to the past. *20 Main Street; 603-772-4311.*

American Independence Museum

This museum tells the story of the American Revolution through the lives of three prominent local families, the Ladds, the Gilmans, and the Folsoms. The **Ladd-Gilman House**, a national landmark that contains the museum's artworks and artifacts, dates from the early 18th century. In 1783, 12 of George Washington's officers gathered next door at the **Folsom Tavern** and founded the New Hampshire chapter of the Society of Cincinnati, named for the Roman farmer-general. The society's members included all the army and naval officers of Washington's military. Washington ate breakfast at the tavern, where he made Folsom's sister-in-law immortal by kissing her. *Open May–Oct. 1 Governor's Lane; 603-772-2622.*

Revolutionary War Festival

On the third weekend of July, the Society of the Cincinnati and the American Independence Museum sponsor the Revolutionary War Festival. Participants

LIGHTHOUSES

Who doesn't love a lighthouse? The Portsmouth area has five, though only Portsmouth Harbor Lighthouse can be visited, and only occasionally at that. Boon Island and Cape Neddick are in Maine but are part of the New Hampshire seascape.

Portsmouth Harbor Lighthouse *map page 53, D-3*
The first "lighthouse" was a lantern hung from the flagpole of Castle William and Mary in 1771. Now there is a cast-iron tower on the site, which is maintained by the U.S. Coast Guard. The lighthouse is off Route 1B on Great Island.

Whaleback Light *map page 53, D-3*
On a ledge at the seaward entrance to Portsmouth Harbor, Whaleback can also be seen from Fort Constitution. It has been rebuilt three times, most recently in 1872. Nearby is the defunct Portsmouth Harbor Lifesaving Station, home to the precursor of the U.S. Coast Guard.

White Island Light *map page 53, D-4*
White Island (or Isles of Shoals light), built in 1820, was the childhood home of author Celia Thaxter (see page 63).

Portsmouth Harbor Lighthouse and Fort Constitution.

Boon Island Light *map page 53, D-2*
The island is off York Beach. At 137 feet, the lighthouse here is the tallest in Maine.

Cape Neddick Light *map page 53, D-2*
On Maine's rocky Nubble Point, 80 feet above the waves, Cape Neddick Light, also known as Nubble Light, is one of the most photographed lighthouses in the world.

*(top) Portsmouth Harbor Lighthouse, with Whaleback Light in the distance.
(above) Cape Neddick Light.*

representing British and Revolutionary forces camp along the Squamscott, fight a mock battle, and bring the Revolution back to life. The activities include 18th-century medical-science instruction, lessons in dancing the minuet, hayrides, and junior-militia exercises for kids. *For information, call 603-772-2622 or 603-772-2411.*

Touring ←🚗→ *Head west on Route 101 off I-93, then north on Route 108 to get to the off-the-beaten-track towns of Newfields, Newmarket, Durham, and Dover. To reverse the order, head west from Portsmouth on Route 4 to Exit 2, and then south to Durham.*

■ LIFE ALONG THE PISCATAQUA

The phrase "sleepy backwater towns" could have originated on the Piscataqua. Newfields, Newmarket, Durham, and Dover seem so quiet after the bustle of Hampton, Portsmouth, and Exeter. Along Route 108 north of Exeter are the beautifully restored colonials of Newfields, the blocks of crumbling orange-red brick mercantile buildings of Newmarket's downtown, and the surprising Three Chimneys Inn on the Oyster River in Durham. This is a reassuringly timeless area. Slow? Thank god, yes. But it wasn't always this way. On this rich five-fingered tidal basin began the early-17th-century clashes between colonists and native peoples competing to harvest unbelievable stores of fish, shellfish, maize, berries, furs, salt hay, blue clay, and timber.

◆ SALT MARSH AT SANDY POINT *map page 53, C-3*

The first settlers saw the salt marsh as an abundant resource, not a barren wasteland, as it can appear on a winter afternoon. The vast stretches of salt hay *(Spartina patens)* you see waving delicately around Great Bay provided the settlers with cattle feed, bedding, mattress stuffing, and housing insulation. Salt hay was the all-purpose building material of its day. As late as 1874, towns like Durham on Great Bay shipped more than 1,500 tons of salt hay to the Boston market annually.

A salt marsh is a coastal habitat that acts as a buffer between the ocean and inland areas. By trapping sediment swept down from higher elevations during rainstorms, and mixing it with minerals from the ever-evaporating seawater that washes over it at high tide, the salt marsh creates a rich environment that nonetheless favors only a few salt-tolerant species. The graceful cordgrasses, switchgrasses, and salt hay at Sandy

Point have adapted by absorbing salt and passing it out through their leaves. They preserve moisture by closing their stomata, the minute pores through which plants absorb carbon dioxide and undergo photosynthesis.

The marshy shoreline of Great Bay National Estuarine Research Reserve.

From the boardwalk at the visitors center at Sandy Point, in Stratham, you can see the plants that thrive here as well as the effects of the varying levels of salinity up the slope. Only in this narrow band of low salinity can salt hay and the feathery-tipped switchgrass (*Distichlis spicata*) be found.

The Sandy Point Discovery Center is the conservation and education center for the **Great Bay National Estuarine Research Reserve,** a coastal protection area. *Open May–Sept. and Oct. weekends. 89 Depot Road, off Route 33; 603-778-0015.*

■ NEWFIELDS AND NEWMARKET *map page 53, B-3*

A few miles north of Route 108's turnoff to Sandy Point is another turnoff to Route 85. It's worth the detour (make a left) to see the massive, beautifully restored colonial houses of Newfields, with their centuries-old oaks and maples shading the front lawns.

Up the road on the Lamprey River is Newmarket, which is less upscale than Newfields. A huge restored mill, a symbol of Newmarket's thriving mercantile past, dominates the east side of Main Street. The orange-red brick of the crowded downtown has acquired the soft patina of centuries of service.

■ DURHAM *map page 53, B-2*

If you enter Durham from the south on Route 108, you'll catch sight of a historical marker just as you pass over the Oyster River. The marker commemorates a raid on the settlement here in 1694, when 250 Abenakis, accompanied by a French military attaché and a Jesuit priest, attacked about 300 colonists, killing or kidnapping 94 people, burning 13 houses, and destroying cattle. The victory was a major one for the French, who sought to negate the Treaty of Pemaquid between the English and the Abenakis, signed the year before. Settlers returned to Massachusetts in fear, and Durham took years to recover from the event. A more recent pillaging of town resources was averted in the 1970s, when the citizens thwarted an attempt by Greek shipping magnate Aristotle Onassis to erect an oil refinery at Durham Point.

Beyond the historical marker over the bridge on Route 108, a driveway on the right leads up to the rambling **Three Chimneys Inn** (603-868-7800). The oldest house in Durham, it was owned by a man named Valentine Hill, whose sawmill and gristmill were just upstream. On a rocky promontory overlooking the Oyster River, it survived the great massacre of 1694. On crisp autumn days, the terrace buzzes with the chatter of parents visiting their children at the nearby University of New Hampshire.

North of Three Chimneys about a hundred yards, a left onto Main Street brings you into the downtown of Durham, which is surrounded by a series of one-way streets. The **University of New Hampshire** lies beyond the downtown circle to the west. Founded in 1866 as a school for agriculture and the mechanical arts, today it offers a broad-based curriculum. The campus is replete with green lawns and Georgian Revival "temples of learning." Students hang out at pizza and beer joints downtown like the Tin Palace, Hair of the Dog, and Libby's Bar and Grill.

Two miles east of Durham on the north side of Route 4 is the **Emery Farm,** established in 1655 and still operated by the Emery family. You can pick strawberries, raspberries, and blueberries (the descendants of the fruit that so delighted the first settlers) and purchase maple syrup, honey, and home-baked breads. *Open Apr.–Dec. Route 4; 603-742-8495.*

Beyond Emery Farm on the south side of Route 4 is a huge wagon at the top of a hill. The hill is town land, and visitors are welcome to walk the paths that lead down the far side of the hill to the river. It was along these paths that some survivors of the Indian-French massacre probably ran, escaping by boat across to Little Fox Point.

■ **DOVER** *map page 53, C-2*

Great Bay hangs off the Piscataqua like a great clam belly, but the Cocheco River winds like a goose's neck north to Dover, a major mill center during the 18th and 19th centuries. This is where London fishmongers Edward and William Hilton settled in 1623, which makes Dover the oldest continuously inhabited settlement in New Hampshire, Pannaway having failed in the late 1620s.

◆ WOODMAN INSTITUTE

A 1915 bequest to Dover from resident Annie Woodman made possible this unique campus of museums. *Open Apr.–Nov. and weekends only Dec.–Jan. 182 Central Avenue, at Summer Street; 603-742-1038.*

The **Damm Garrison** dates from the colonial era. William Damm built the garrison to withstand the most determined attack, with thick, iron-studded doors, rifle ports, and a palisade of logs surrounding the property. Arrowheads from Indian attacks are still embedded in the front door.

The **Woodman Institute Museum** is in the redesigned brick home of the town's most famous lawyer, Daniel Christie. Let more modern facilities "interpret" history and the natural world; the Woodman displays its wares randomly, in all their threadbare splendor—polar bears and moths, alligators and a hippo, dolls, birds, Abraham Lincoln's saddle, arrowheads, and rocks. It's a curator's nightmare, but fun, and a fitting homage to area sea captains, who brought many of these curiosities home.

Next door is the **John P. Hale House**. Hale, a U.S. congressman and senator who moved into the 1813 structure in 1840, went from rabidly supporting slavery to courageously advocating its abolition. He ran for the presidency in 1853 on the Free Soil Party ticket against Franklin Pierce and Winfield Scott but received only 5 percent of the vote. In something of a paradox, Hale's daughter, Lucy, was dating John Wilkes Booth at the time the actor assassinated President Abraham Lincoln. The first floor offers more curiosities like those in the Woodman Institute Museum. The bric-a-brac on display here brings to mind these lines from Robert Frost's "New Hampshire":

> Just specimens is all New Hampshire has,
> One each of everything as in a showcase
> Which naturally she doesn't care to sell.

MERRIMACK VALLEY

■ Highlights

■ Area Overview

The Merrimack River and its watershed are the beating heart of New Hampshire. From Franklin in the north to Nashua at the Massachusetts line, Wilton in the west to Derry in the east, the spade-shaped Merrimack Valley is a financial, political, and manufacturing powerhouse that owes its strength, vitality, and identity to the meandering and tumbling, indolent and industrious, but always mighty Merrimack.

With three of the state's largest cities, this is one of its fastest-growing regions. Manchester's huge textile mill has been converted into a museum, and the city's cultural life includes the stellar Currier Gallery of Art. You can poke around the antiques shops in historic Milford, head to the race track (to see Thoroughbreds or autos in action), get your jollies at one of several amusement parks, take the contemplative route along a woodsy path near Robert Frost's home, or see the community created by the Shakers, a religious group, in Canterbury. The best way to explore the Merrimack is on the river itself, by canoe, boat, or kayak.

Weather: Summer temperatures average 69 degrees F, winter 22 degrees, with extremes of 106 and -25. There's some precipitation, on average, every third day, with little seasonal variation in the amount of rain. Fall colors are spectacular, peaking in late September or early October. Winters here are chilly. Heavy, water-laden snow remains until mid-March or a little later.

■ History and the River

The fourth largest watershed in New England, the Merrimack River drops almost 2,000 feet in 115 miles and drains over 5,000 square miles. The first people to encounter this huge river system arrived about 10,000 years ago.

More than 400 archaeological sites along the Merrimack contain evidence of human habitation thousands of years ago. At Amoskeag Falls, these first people would congregate to catch migrating shad, alewives in the small rivulets above the falls, eels wriggling along the pebbly bottom, and fat salmon leaping into the froth at the base of the falls. The Neville site, above the falls in Manchester, is famous for yielding up a 6,000- to 8,000-year-old projectile point, dubbed the Neville point, by which name all similar stone points are now known. The Eddy and Smith sites, also around the falls, have yielded objects that date back 10,000 years.

Indian Hunter with Bow *(date unknown), by Ann Elizabeth Lancaster Hobbs. (Hood Museum of Art, Dartmouth College)*

The Abenakis lived and fished along the river at the time of European contact. Passaconaway, the leader of the confederacy of Abenaki groups across northern New England, presided over the area from several islands on the Merrimack River. He maintained peace with early settlers, but his goodwill didn't prevent more and more of them from moving into the Merrimack region. Wars with other tribes over the fur trade and European diseases like smallpox wiped out more than 75 percent of the population. Settlers, eager for land, pushed those who remained into Canada.

The Pemigewasset River and the Winnipesaukee River, which begin in the White Mountains and Lake Winnipesaukee respectively, meet in Franklin to form the Merrimack. Thanks to the Clean Water Act of 1976 and the closing of logging, paper, and textile mills, the Merrimack, once badly polluted, is now clean enough to swim in.

Near Franklin, the meandering shallow stream flows crystal clear over a sparkling sand bottom, inviting you to plunge in and cool off on a hot July afternoon. Around the next bend, a high bank frames the chopped edge of a verdant cornfield against a high blue sky. Still farther along, bank swallows swoop along a high cliff, each seeking its own private burrow in the pin-cushioned sand cliff.

The shallow upper Merrimack gives way to the broad, deep stretches south of Hooksett where the river gathers steam, then paces majestically to Amoskeag Falls, finally settling down for the long run to Massachusetts and the sea.

Touring ←🚗→ *As you cross the New Hampshire state line in Salem into the wild hills and blasted granite shoulders of I-93, you arrive in Robert Frost country. The poet lived in two of these towns, Salem and Derry, and grew to know the region well on his long "botanizing" walks. Before you get to Manchester on I-93, the highway splits. The left fork—I-293—takes you to the bridge over the Merrimack, then north past the river into Manchester. The redbrick Amoskeag Mills complex hunkers along the riverbank. To the left lies the French West Side.*

■ SALEM *map page 93, D-5/6*

Unless you're a big fan of racetracks and shopping malls, you may want to skip **Salem.** Route 28, which parallels I-93 to the east, is an overdeveloped strip with slow traffic, and there's not much to see. If you do like racing and shopping, though, you'll find plenty of both off Exit 1.

Rockingham Park presents Thoroughbred racing from June to September. You can watch the races from the grandstand, the clubhouse, or a trackside seat in the Picnic Pavilion. Or catch them on big-screen TV in the Sports Club, simulcast from Saratoga, Churchill Downs, and other venues. *I-93, Exit 1; 603-898-2311.*

Salem itself was part of a Massachusetts town, Methuen, before New Hampshire's southern boundary was established in 1741. In the 1880s, it was briefly the boyhood home of Robert Frost. His mother taught fifth grade in Salem, and young Robert did odd jobs around town, working for a cobbler who also raised chickens.

◆ MYSTERY HILL *map page 93, D-5*

Mystery Hill is a stony rise above Salem. The placement and original purpose of its granite stones is considered "mysterious." The fact that people pay to see them may be proof of P. T. Barnum's assertion that a sucker is born every minute. But it's still worth visiting, if for no other reason than to understand something important about New Englanders. For such a famously skeptical lot, we can be downright gullible.

Horse racing at Rockingham Park, named for the Marquis of Rockingham, benefactor of New Hampshire's royal governor John Wentworth.

Collect a bunch of upright rocks and we'll call the assemblage a megalith. Open up an old cellar hole and we proclaim it a "stone chamber." Show us a grooved rock, and we're sure it was used as an altar where people were carved up like Christmas turkeys.

The site has been altered so much over the years there's no certainty about anything at this rocky hill. Who tampered with it the most seems to be the biggest mystery. The Pattee family, which acquired the land in the 1820s? William B. Goodwin, who in the 1930s discarded any evidence contradicting his theory that Irish monks created the place? After two centuries, the question remains: do the stones have ritual significance or is the whole thing a hoax? You decide. *Take Exit 3 off I-93 at Canobie Lake Park, head east on Route 111, go about 5 miles and turn right, following the blue signs to "America's Stonehenge"; 603-893-8300.*

Touring ← 🚗 → *As you head north on I-93, the town of Londonderry lies to the west at Exit 4, and the city of Derry, primarily a bedroom community for Boston and Manchester commuters, lies to the east.*

■ **LONDONDERRY AND DERRY** *map page 93, C/D-5*

In the 1720s, Londonderry was the first of several towns chartered by John Wentworth, the lieutenant governor of Massachusetts (until 1741, the person holding that post ruled New Hampshire). Londonderry and the other new towns were part of his ploy to convince the British Crown that New Hampshire should become an independent colony. Of course, the royal governors of Massachusetts considered this a slap in the face, and rushed to charter their own towns, including Rumford, which later became New Hampshire's state capital, Concord.

Scots-Irish Presbyterians settled Londonderry. The leader of the first 56 families, a Reverend MacGregor, obtained a deed in 1720 for 20 acres. The area had been known informally as Nutfield, for the profusion of chestnut trees on its gentle inclines. Today apple orchards grace the scenic "Appleway" on Pillsbury Road.

The Scots-Irish, known for their energy, independence, and gruff honesty, reintroduced the potato to the New World at Derry (16th-century explorers had taken it to Europe from the Andes), and made a lucrative cottage industry out of weaving flax into delicate linen cloth. Along with flax seed, the Scots-Irish brought sheep, but their fleece hid the seeds of a beautiful but nefarious immigrant: purple loosestrife, a weed that chokes out many native wetland plants.

Mack's Apples grows more than two dozen varieties, including McIntosh, Cortland, Gala, Golden Delicious, Red Delicious, Empire, Jonagold, and Mutsu. The farm's namesake, John Mack, came here in 1732 from Londonderry, Ireland, with his wife Isabella Brown, the Lord Mayor's daughter. John planted a magnificent orchard that still thrives today—a favorite spot to "pick-your-own." In the farm's market you can buy apples (call the hotline to find out what's available), cider, frozen pies made by a local contest winner, maple syrup, honey, jams and jellies, fresh local eggs, pumpkins, squash, and pears. In early May, you can take a blossom tour on a tractor-pulled trailer. *Mammoth Road (Route 128) north of Route 102 (take I-93 Exit 4); 603-434-7619; hotline 603-432-3456.*

■ ROBERT FROST HOMESTEAD *map page 93, D-5*

In 1900, 26-year-old Robert Frost, his wife, Elinor, and their daughter Lesley moved into a small farmhouse in Derry. Frost later claimed that his career as a poet began on this 30-acre plot of land at the base of the long, domed field that still looms behind the farmyard. In this classic New England farmhouse ("big house, little house, back house, barn," as one curator of the site describes the rambling structure), Frost wrote most of the poems that would later appear in his first two poetry collections, *A Boy's Will* and *North of Boston.*

Frost wrote more than 40 poems while he lived here. Some, like "Mending Wall," "Pastures," and "West-Running Brook" are directly connected to the site. The wall being mended in Frost's famous poem still separates his property from the adjoining acreage. You can walk the half-mile path around the field to the footbridges over Hyla Brook, through the shaded woods of large white pines, yellow birch, red oak, hickory, and four rare young American chestnuts. You'll see the wall near marker No. 16, a low pile of lichen-encrusted rock.

After Frost sold the farm, it passed from one owner to the next, finally becoming an automobile graveyard archly named "Frosty Acres." The state bought the property soon after Frost died in the early 1960s, cleared it of car hulks, and restored it under the watchful eye of Lesley Frost Ballantine.

A national historic landmark open from Memorial Day to Columbus Day, the homestead is a worthy cultural shrine, humble yet evocative, with its white house and barn and that quiet path, on which you can experience the contemplative setting that inspired one brilliantly expressive poet's work. *Take Exit 4 off I-93 and head east 2*

"Mending Wall"

...There where it is we do not need the wall:
He is all pine and I am apple orchard.
My apple trees will never get across
And eat the cones under his pines, I tell him.
He only says, "Good fences make good neighbors."
Spring is the mischief in me, and I wonder
If I could put a notion in his head:
"Why do they make good neighbors?" Isn't it
Where there are cows? But here there are no cows.
Before I built a wall I'd ask to know
What I was walling in or walling out,
And to whom I was like to give offense...."

—Robert Frost, excerpted from "Mending Wall," 1914

Wall at Robert Frost Homestead. (Dartmouth College Library)

The moon sets over the Robert Frost Homestead in Derry.

miles through the town of Derry, past the golf course. At the traffic circle, turn south and drive 1.75 miles.

■ **NASHUA** *map page 93, B/C-6*

Nashua, a frontier settlement of Massachusetts called Dunstable in the late 1600s, has the good and ill fortune of being on the southern state line. Boston is only a half-hour drive away, and many out-of-state visitors to the city are Massachusetts residents making purchases here to avoid paying sales tax. Most tourists, though, do not stop in this city so close to the border and so far from the White Mountains.

In Algonquian, *nashua* means "a beautiful river with a pebbly bottom," and portions of the river remain worthy of the name, particularly in **Mine Falls Park,** a 2-mile stretch of easy hiking and biking trails that covertly creeps along the river and the canals that tamed it. *To reach the park, take Exit 6 off the F. E. Everett Turnpike. Take Route 130 west past the Nashua Mall and turn left on Coliseum Avenue. Go behind the Shop and Save to the parking lot.*

Nashua's Main Street exudes charm and quirky small-city character. Look for the gilded eagle perched like a gigantic Christmas ornament atop City Hall, the curious Odd Fellows building, the old library, and the row of upscale restaurants and brewpubs in converted storefronts and bank buildings.

Nashua Pride

The Nashua Pride, an independent professional baseball club (i.e., it's not a minor-league farm team), plays half its 142 Atlantic League games at spiffy Holman Stadium. Taking in a game here is a wonderful trip back to the way baseball used to be played, before gigantic salaries and inflated egos. The team's season runs from early-May to mid-September. *Amherst Street, 1 mile east of F. E. Everett Turnpike Exit 7E; 603-883-2255.*

Nashville Historic District

This neighborhood north of the river is a monument to small-town jealousies. When the town fathers changed the city's name from Dunstable to Nashua, there was disagreement over where City Hall should be. The faction that lost split off in a

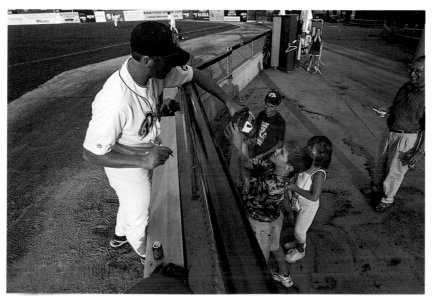

Fans at a Nashua Pride game.

snit, and called themselves Nashville. They came to their senses 11 years later, leaving the name of Nashville to the Athens of the South.

Nashua Symphony

Royston Nash, formerly the conductor of the D'Oyly Carte Opera Company in London, has led the state's oldest professional orchestra since 1985. Past conductors have included the illustrious Willis Traphagen and Walter Eisenberg. The players include a mix of musicians from southern New Hampshire and the Boston area. *603-595-9156.*

Horace Greeley Park

Heading back to the Merrimack via Concord Street to D.W. Highway (Route 3), you cut through an expanse of green park, complete with picnicking families and a bandshell. Why this park is not in Amherst, where the publisher Horace Greeley was born, we'll never know. A genteel promenade at the edge of town, it curves gently all the way down to the Merrimack. This tamed natural setting contrasts with the brushy wilds of Mine Falls Park.

The Big Trike, made by Nashua's Vim Tire company, was a hit at Concord's Bicycle Parade of 1896. (New Hampshire Historical Society)

■ AMHERST *map page 93, B-5*

The towns of the Souhegan Valley west of Nashua stretch along Route 101 toward the Monadnock region. These out-of-the-way places—Amherst, Milford, and Wilton—have for the most part retained the feel of the colonial outposts, mill towns, and farming communities they once were.

In a case of competitive flag-planting, the governor of Massachusetts, Jonathan Belcher, granted the township of Amherst the right to incorporate in 1733, hoping to keep the area out of the grasping hands of New Hampshire, then still under the governance of Massachusetts. Belcher rightly feared that his upstart lieutenant governor, John Wentworth of Portsmouth, would make the case to the king of England that New Hampshire deserved to be a separate colony and that Wentworth would take Amherst, New Hampshire, with him.

Originally called Narragansett Number Three, and later Souhegan West (Souhegan East was the town of Merrimack), Amherst was granted to descendants of the settlers who fought in King Philip's War more than 50 years after that conflict ended. The original settlers moved from towns along Boston's north shore—Salem, Marblehead, Lynn, Gloucester, Andover, Topsfield, and Beverly. Amherst developed into an important governmental center and was the county seat. Incorporated in 1760, it was named for Lord Jeffrey Amherst, a hero of the French and Indian War.

Amherst is one of the prettiest and quietest villages in the state. Its broad thoroughfare lined with big brick colonials could almost be a museum—indeed, the entire town is a historical landmark. Walking down this wide street conjures up images of a world lit only by fire, when a staple like tea was so novel that the first settlers boiled it in an iron pot and promptly declared it unpalatable. Disease was a fact of daily life. Of the 21 Amherst men who died as Revolutionary soldiers, 15 were victims of either dysentery or smallpox.

The **Minot J. Ross Memorial Bird Sanctuary**, near the center of town, is a natural wetland that delights birds with specially constructed birdhouses and bird lovers with a specially constructed viewing platform. *Thornton's Ferry Road.*

■ MILFORD *map page 93, B-5*

Milford, so named because it was a good place to ford the Souhegan River and ideal for sawmills and textile mills, was founded on open land that originally belonged to

Amherst and Dunstable. Amid thriving dairy farms, it became a commercial and manufacturing hub and was incorporated in 1794.

The **Milford oval,** its bandshell surrounded by businesses and a fine old town hall, looks much the same today as it did when it was built in 1869. The town hall's belfry contains a treasure of which even many residents are unaware: one of the last bells (still rung on occasion) that Paul Revere cast. The town's antique shops, most of which lie on Route 101A—Nashua Street and Elm Street on opposite sides of the oval—have excellent collections. The **Milford Diner** (2 Union Square), perched above the rushing Souhegan, serves up coffee and plenty of local color.

Ponemah
A short drive southeast from Milford on Route 101A is Ponemah, the "land of the hereafter"—a name taken from Henry Wadsworth Longfellow's "Hiawatha." Trails in this 75-acre Audubon Society sanctuary lead through an enchanted wetland, woodland, and bog where muskrats, green herons, and pink orchids are only a few of the noble residents. *Rhodora Drive off Sterns Road; 603-224-9909.*

■ WILTON AREA *map page 93, A-5*

From Route 101, across Stony Brook, which spills into the Souhegan River, you can see the town of Wilton perched on a hillside overlooking the river. Wilton is the gateway to the Monadnock region.

Frye's Measure Mill
A measure mill manufactures round wooden boxes that act as units of volume. Tours of the mechanical waterworks at Frye's Measure Mill, with its upright water-powered turbine, take place on Saturdays during spring, summer, and fall. *12 Frye Mill Road; 603-654-6581.*

Wilton Town Hall Theater
Wilton's 1886 theater was first used as a playhouse for traveling minstrels and for vaudeville shows. The original stage remains intact. In 1912, the theater was converted into a silent film house. The creaky floors, ancient seats, musty smell, and freshly popped corn with real butter lend the place old-time charm, but the equipment is strictly state-of-the-art. *40 Main Street; 603-654-3456.*

MERRIMACK VALLEY

Parker's Maple Barn

If you're looking for the perfect pancake—big, fluffy, and very filling—and some perspective on maple sugaring, Parker's, south off Route 13 from Milford, will not disappoint. The occasional long lines are worth the wait if you fancy big breakfasts. In March and April, you can tour the sugar house. Parker's fans claim that because the sap is boiled over a wood fire the syrup has a smoky flavor not to be tasted in commercially made products. For more about maple sugaring, see page 242. *1316 Brookline Road, Mason; 800-832-6564 or 603-878-2308.*

■ **MERRIMACK** *map page 93, B-5/6*

Those looking for the picturesque town square typical of so many New Hampshire towns would be better off up the road in Bedford or farther west in Amherst or Milford. A disgruntled friend from Chicago complains that Merrimack is the "longest, skinniest damn town" he's ever seen. In fact, it is four skinny towns, an amalgamation of Merrimack, Reed's Ferry, Thornton's Ferry, and South Merrimack. Daniel Webster Highway, or Route 3 (often signposted as D.W. Highway and not to be confused with the toll road Route 3, which parallels it less than a mile to the west), is the "back road" that runs up the long stretch from Nashua to Manchester.

During the 1980s, Merrimack played incubator to highly successful electronics concerns, including Digital Equipment Corporation, the state's largest employer, bought by Compaq in 1998. Merrimack is also notable for gourmet restaurants set in historic buildings.

You can learn about the brewing process, from mashing to packaging, on a free tour (days and hours vary by season) of the **Anheuser-Busch** brewery. Tours include tastings and a visit to Clydesdale Hamlet, with its magnificent horses. *221 Daniel Webster Highway, east on Industrial Drive off Everett Turnpike Exit 10; 603-595-1202.*

■ **BEDFORD** *map page 93, B/C-4*

Bedford is a spread-out town, its streets meandering along a hillside. On a crisp autumn day, the town wears a multicolored halo of leaves that frames its picture-perfect town center—the genteel library, the pillared Greek Revival town hall sparkling white against the deep green common, the stunning Congregational Church. In its civic culture, Bedford is old Yankee with new money.

In the 1980s the town's population was oddly transient for such a solid-looking place, full of electronics executives who overspent in real estate, then undersold disastrously after the 1987 stock-market crash. But the town's natural beauty remains transcendent, with a dozen swelling hills to give the landscape contrast and balance.

During primary season, the **Bedford Village Inn** hosts many political correspondents, who broadcast from here or the old buildings in the town center. The inn is built around a farmhouse built in 1810. The original residence contains intimate dining rooms, and there are luxury rooms in the barn. *2 Village Inn Lane, off Route 101; 800-852-1166 or 603-472-2001.*

The inventor Guglielmo Marconi lived in Bedford, England. The **Marconi Museum** celebrates that link with displays of radios and other wireless equipment. *18 North Amherst Road, off Meetinghouse Road (west of Route 101); 603-472-8312.*

Bedford also has its natural wonders, as noted in 1874 by Alonzo Fogg:

In the westerly part of the town is a gulf and precipice, which are worthy of a visit from all lovers of natural curiosities. Over the precipice a small river plunges, falling two hundred feet in a distance of one hundred yards. Excavations in solid stone are found here, sufficiently large to contain several persons.

The formation Fogg describes is **Pulpit Rock,** now part of a conservation area reached by taking New Boston Road left off Route 114. Go about 5 miles, past Wallace, Joppa Hill, and Pulpit Roads. There will be a parking lot (easy to miss amid all the trees) on your left at the trailhead. If you reach the white geodesic dome at the top of the hill, you've gone about a quarter-mile too far.

■ MANCHESTER *map page 93, C-4, and page 105*

The old joke about Manchester is that the city—an hour away from the ocean, an hour from the mountains, and an hour from Boston—is in the middle of nowhere. In truth, it's a central influence in its region and state, a gathering-place for financial, technological, and creative resources. In the Merrimack Valley, all roads lead to Manchester.

◆ SAMUEL BLODGET'S VISION

In 1800, when the little towns along and around the Merrimack were flourishing, what locals called "the 'Skeag"—the area by Amoskeag Falls—remained relatively unpopulated. River traffic couldn't get around the falls, and the falls hadn't been harnessed as a source of energy to power mills. It took the vision of a retired judge, who had once collected mast taxes for the king of England, to build a canal and establish the infrastructure for the future city of Manchester.

Samuel Blodget had seen the great manufactories of Manchester, England, and wondered if it might be possible to build similar ones back home in Derryfield (renamed Manchester to honor him in 1810). But first, he'd need to build a canal, as a place to set the mill wheels that would power the factories, and to provide for transportation past the 'Skeag. In 1793, at the age of 69, Blodget began building the canal. He had already lived a full life: fighting in the Louisburg expedition at Cape Breton Island, acting as provisioner in the Crown Point campaign of 1757, and narrowly avoiding death at the Fort William Henry massacre the same year.

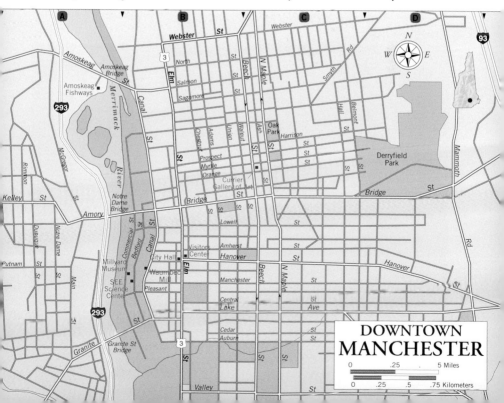

MERRIMACK VALLEY

DOWNTOWN
MANCHESTER

0   .25   .   5 Miles
0   .25   .5   .75 Kilometers

In 1807, after spending $125,000, Blodget finished his canal and died four months later. It was 7,500 feet long, 45 feet wide, and 10 feet deep and walled with stone. Within 75 years, there would be 30,000 people—one-tenth of the state's population—crowded into the area, producing one-sixth of its manufactured goods.

◆ VISITING MANCHESTER

Blodget's canal, built to accommodate boats hauling freight from Concord to Boston, is now a paved thoroughfare, Canal Street, that runs through the heart of the old Amoskeag Manufacturing Company complex. The first mill opened here in 1810, and in its heyday the company had 700,000 spindles and 23,000 looms, which produced 500,000 yards of cloth each week. What Amoskeag didn't have, it made. Its machine shops and forges were a powerful resource, churning out fire engines and muskets for the Union army, to name just a few products.

Amoskeag couldn't provide itself with one thing: longevity. Competition from more modern mills elsewhere and a Boston holding company's eagerness to bail out after several strikes, eventually spelled the end of the Merrimack textile kingdom. The company closed following a 1936 flood.

(above) Conductor J. Bolle of the Manchester Symphony.
(opposite) The equestrian statue of Gen. John Stark.

Where once workers toiled, you can sit outside at trendy restaurants, listen to the river, and enjoy a bruschetta and a glass of chianti. High-tech companies have transformed aging buildings into a thriving center of dining, entertainment, and commerce. More than 80 companies do business in the **Waumbec Mill,** which contains a paintball palace, five gyms, a piano-restoration company, furniture makers, candlestick makers, a square-dancing emporium, and a church. The wonderful Waumbec hosts the most colorful tenants, but other mill buildings contain facilities like indoor driving ranges, the SEE (Science for Early Explorers) Science Center, and the sensational Millyard Museum. The inventor and entrepreneur Dean Kamen, who owns much of the millyard, developed his battery-powered sidewalk cruiser, the Segway Human Transporter, here.

Uphill from the Amoskeag Mill to the east is **Elm Street,** according to *Guinness World Records* the only main thoroughfare to dead-end at both ends. Corporate structures along Elm supply Manchester's modest skyline: the white granite New Hampshire Insurance building; the Fleet Bank at Bridge Street and Elm, with its red Swedish granite polished in Italy; the black, monolithic PSNH (Public Service Company of New Hampshire, the utility system) building; the whimsical AT&T

Veterans Day Parade, Manchester.

tower, across from the heraldic City Hall; and the new Civic Center at Granite Street and Elm. Victorian homes flank the broad north end of Elm. Also here is Notre Dame College (2321 Elm Street), one of six institutions of higher learning in Manchester. There's a magnificently imposing **equestrian statue of Gen. John Stark** on North River Road at Stark Park, and his **boyhood home** is at 2000 Elm Street (for Stark's story, see page 40).

Beyond Elm to the east lies, appropriately enough, the **East Side,** with more magnificent 19th-century homes on "the hill." Much of Manchester's Greek population settled here, and there's a Greek Orthodox Cathedral (St. George's), in the requisite Santorini-blue and white, at the corner of Hanover and Kenney.

Across the river from the mill buildings is the West Side. Many French Canadian millworkers lived here, as do French Canadians to this day. The persistence of French culture is evident in overheard snatches of conversation, in local dishes like *poutine* (french fries with gravy and melted cheese) or roulade, in banks like La Caisse Populaire Ste.-Marie, and in Sainte Marie's Church, which brings to mind the mysterious cathedrals of Montreal.

Germans, Irish, Swedes, and others came to Manchester's mills seeking work, and immigrants from around the world continue to arrive. More than 60 languages and dialects are spoken in Manchester's schools. On Saturday mornings, the **Saigon Market** on Valley Street attracts customers from various Asian lands, shopping for ingredients for everything from Thai *mee krob* (crispy fried noodles) to Indian *gram dal* (lentils) to Chinese pressed duck.

◆ **MANCHESTER SIGHTS**

Millyard Museum *map page 105, B-2/3*
The old redbrick Amoskeag Mill No. 3 houses the new Millyard Museum. Walk through the entrance on Commercial Street, and you'll encounter a fascinating collage of photographs of what was once the world's largest textile mill. Beyond it is a re-creation of a tunnel like the ones that directed water to the mills. In the back of the museum is an iron-lined penstock, 9 feet in diameter that fed water from a canal to a turbine, which provided power to mill machinery.

Mill No. 3 was built in 1844, renovated in 1870, and converted in 2001 into this wonderful museum that exhibits a host of "milliana," including a photograph of the gigantic iron wheel that escaped its mount and broke through the wall of the mills, a perfect stone sphere shaped by the action of the river, and an antique fire pumper made on the premises. Elm Street has been re-created circa the era when electric lights were first installed for Thursday market nights. *Commercial Street and Pleasant Street; 603-622-7531.*

Amoskeag Fishways *map page 105, A-1*

Several eras of history converge at the Amoskeag Fishways, where you can peer through dark glass at salmon swimming up a "fish ladder"—54 pools of water, each a foot higher than the one before it. The ladder permits fish to reach the top of Amoskeag Falls, bypassing a hydroelectric power station. The best views can be had in late May. Walk to the edge of the parking lot, below which the falls flow. Across the river on a bluff to the north was one of Chief Passaconaway's likely encampments. ("Amoskeag" means "place of many fish" in the Abenaki language.) Finds from this site date back 8,000 years. To your left is the dam that pooled water power for the mill-race. Down to the right is the generating plant that provided steam power to the mills. It had been empty for nearly two decades when PSNH began renovating it as its new corporate headquarters in 2000. A section of Samuel Blodget's original canal can be seen where the building meets the river, and a river walk stretches from there down along the east bank. A display in the lobby relates the history of this fascinating building. *Take Exit I-293 at the Amoskeag Bridge (Exit 6), bear right at the Holiday Inn, and take the next right at the light to the Amoskeag Fishways, where the giant salmon sign beckons. 603-626-3474.*

Currier Gallery of Art *map page 105, C-2*

The Currier claims to be "northern New England's finest independent art museum," and it has the pedigree to prove it. Andrew Wyeth held his first solo exhibit here, and his *Spindrift* is on permanent display. The Zimmerman House (1950), the only home designed by Frank Lloyd Wright open to the public in New England, is part of the permanent collection.

The paintings and sculptures on exhibit include works by many of the great ones: Picasso, Monet, O'Keeffe,

Molasses merchant's sign (circa 1850), by an unknown American artist. (Currier Gallery of Art)

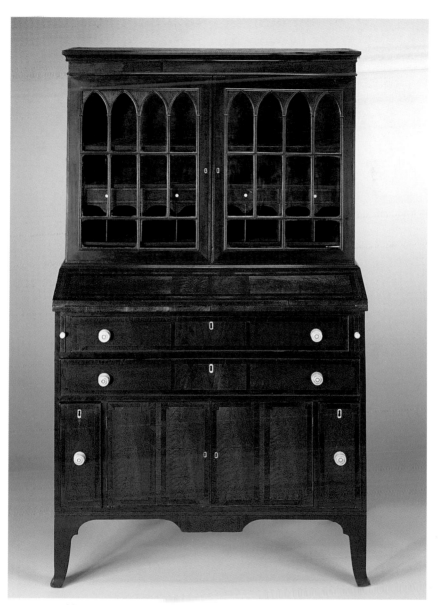

Secretary and bookcase (1813), by Jonathan Judkins and William Senter.
(Currier Gallery of Art)

FROM FARM TO FACTORY: LIFE IN THE MILLS

In the early 19th century, the sprawling Amoskeag Manufacturing Company's mills represented opportunity. Girls from hardscrabble farms would come to work for a few years, earn enough to supply a dowry, get married, and leave. They lived in segregated dormitories, and in the beginning the mill owners provided everything they needed—lodging, church services, schools, and weekend outings to amusement parks like Pine Island. It was a well-regulated life, which reassured parents about the safety of their daughters.

You can walk through restored factories, look at yellowing photographs from the past, and read the letters the mill girls sent home. But if you've never heard the hypnotic clattering of a hundred power looms like a horde of malevolent locusts, and poked your head out on a break to hear a hundred more in the buildings on either side of the one you toil in, you can only guess at what it was like to work here—to breathe cotton dust, hear the noonday whistle, feel a draining exhaustion at the end of a hot, sticky, 12-hour August day. In some ways, these dark buildings are as much monuments to human misery as they are symbols of progress.

Mill buildings at Amoskeag. (Manchester Historic Association)

Gilbert Stuart, John Singer Sargent, Winslow Homer, Andrew Wyeth, Childe Hassam, Alexander Calder, Henri Matisse, Frederic Remington, and Augustus Saint-Gaudens. But the Currier also showcases the arts of New Hampshire, the furniture and works of decorative art reflecting a local tradition of skilled artistry from colonial to contemporary times. *201 Myrtle Way, at Beech Street; 603-669-6144.*

SEE Science Center   *map page 105, B-3*
The center's more than 70 hands-on exhibits are designed to bring science to life. Dean Kamen, inventor of the portable infusion pump, the I-Bot stair-climbing wheelchair, and the Segway human transporter, opened his business here. *200 Bedford Street, between Canal and Commercial Streets; 603-669-0400.*

Pubs and Bistros   *map page 105, B-2*
At or near the intersection of Elm and Lowell Streets are some notable pubs, including the **Wild Rover** (21 Kosciuszko Street) and the **Black Brimmer** (1087 Elm). Also in the neighborhood are **Richard's Bistro** (36 Lowell) and **Baldwin's on Elm** (1105 Elm), which serve contemporary takes on bistro and comfort food. To chat up the locals, head to the **Red Arrow Diner** (61 Lowell), open 24 hours a day since 1903.

Lake Massabesic   *map page 93, C-4*
Lake Massabesic, southeast of Manchester in Auburn, has long been a getaway for locals. A short drive from the city, it has great views and is a terrific resource if you like to canoe, sail, hike, bike, or go snowshoeing. The 2,500-acre lake supplies Manchester's drinking water, so swimming is not allowed, though curiously all types of boating are. The rocky shoreline turns to dense pine forests not a hundred yards inland, with maples, oaks, a few remaining chestnuts, and, along the shoreline, black gums that turn a brilliant red in the autumn.

A resort hotel once occupied Battery Point, and for years 500-pound blocks of ice were cut out of the frozen surface of Lake Massabesic. In the days before refrigeration (and on into the early 1960s), Massabesic ice was used by meatpacking outfits, dairies, restaurants, and hotels. *Exit 1 off Route 101, around the traffic circle toward Derry to Spofford Road.*

Get yourself oriented at the **Massabesic Audubon Center,** where you can check out the exhibits and, in winter, rent snowshoes. *Audubon Way off Spofford Road; 603-668-2045.*

MERRIMACK VALLEY

■ CONCORD *map page 93, B/C-2/3, and page 114*

There's a stark contrast between blue-collar Manchester and the next city north on the Merrimack—Concord, the state capital. The former is all business and big buildings, but the latter has the feel of another time and place, perhaps the Victorian era. Main Street looks right out of *The Music Man*, and quaint homes have rambling verandas and large lawns. This is a town of lawyers and law schools, a proper place where the sidewalks roll up at 9 p.m.

Concord has played a pivotal role in the state's history since Jonathan Belcher, the governor of Massachusetts from 1730 to 1741, granted the city its charter, seeking to solidify his state's hold over New Hampshire.

The capital city became most famous as the town that built "the coach that won the West." In 1813, Lewis Downing set up a wagon shop with $125 in capital, $75

(opposite) Great blue heron.

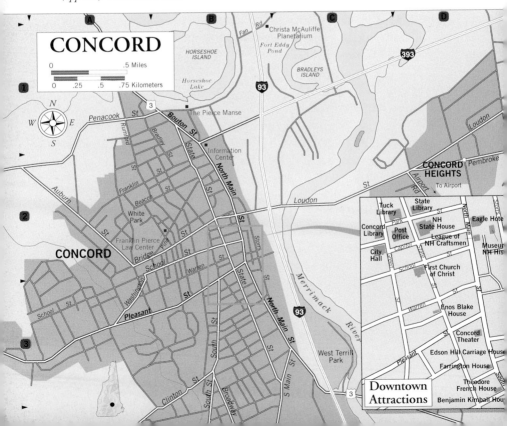

of which he spent on tools. By 1874, the 250 employees of the Abbot-Downing Company, which evolved out of Downing's original enterprise, were producing $600,000 worth of coaches every year.

Concord was also well known for its granite, which was highly prized for its absence of discoloring oxides and minerals. You can see the quarry from I-93 north of town, a long scar in the hills to the west. Though Concord did not have the grand mills of other towns on the Merrimack, it did supply the leather belting that transferred water power to spindles and other machinery.

New Hampshire State House *map page 114, B-2*

Built of Concord granite between 1816 and 1819, this structure cost $85,000, making it the most expensive edifice in the state at the time. The New Hampshire House, with 400 members, and Senate, with a mere 24, meet on the second floor. *Park and North Main Streets.*

Pierce Manse

Franklin Pierce, America's 14th president, lived in this simple home with his wife and two children from 1842 to 1846. Pierce had just resigned as a U.S. senator and had decided to practice law in Concord. In 1846 he left to fight in the Mexican War. (See Pierce's biography on page 45 and a description of his childhood home on page 139.)

The home languished in disrepair until passionate members of the Pierce Brigade held lawn parties and bake sales and scraped together sufficient funds to move it, in 1971, from Montgomery Street to its present location near the river. The state legislature lent the group a paltry sum when it became apparent they wouldn't go away, later forgiving the debt in embarrassment. The house contains a Pierce desk with a glass top, original furniture, plates, and dishes, and a hymnal with doodling in a bored young hand, which might be that of Bennie, Franklin's son. *14 Penacook Street, at the end of North Main Street; 603-224-5954.*

Museum of New Hampshire History *map page 114, B-2*

The fine museum of the New Hampshire Historical Society displays a refurbished Concord coach, one of 3,000 built here in the 19th century. Many were shipped west by rail to St. Louis, Chicago, Omaha, and elsewhere, as depicted in John Burgum's painting *Shipment of Thirty Coaches to Wells Fargo.* The museum's White Mountains Collection showcases paintings, photographs, and souvenirs and other regional

Shipment of Thirty Coaches to Wells Fargo *(1868), by John Burgum.*
(New Hampshire Historical Society)

artifacts. The museum's holdings also include beautiful furniture made in the state from the 18th century to the present. The society's nearby Tuck Library (30 Park Street, across from the State House) exhibits prints, manuscripts, and artworks, among them a sculpture by Daniel Chester French. *6 Eagle Square; 603-228-6688.*

St. Paul's School   *map page 93, B-3*
This might as well be called the Kennedy School of Government North, given how many members of that famous clan have attended it. St. Paul's is the quintessential preparatory boarding school, with rolling lawns and two mobiles by Alexander Calder, one of which is exhibited seasonally.

Christa McAuliffe Planetarium   *map page 114, B-1*
Christa McAuliffe, a social studies teacher from Concord High School, was to have been the first teacher in space, but she perished in the explosion on board the *Challenger* space shuttle during its launch in 1986. The state set aside funds to honor her life and career with this planetarium on the campus of the New

BLOODY HANNAH

After the deaths of Passaconaway and his son Wonalancet, few local Abenakis remained to protect the English from Huron raiders. On the Ides of March in 1697, a raiding party killed or captured 40 people in Haverhill, Massachusetts, and found Hannah Dustin recovering from childbirth at her home. They swung her newborn against a tree, killing the infant, and took Dustin, her nurse, and a boy north along the Merrimack to a sandbar north of what is now Concord. Mad with grief and hatred, Hannah waited until the Hurons fell asleep. She killed and scalped them with their own tomahawks—two men, two women, and six children—and in a single day made her way south to what is now Nashua.

That's the story in a nutshell, but more than a little ambiguity surrounds Hannah's tale. In his history of Massachusetts, Cotton Mather, whose writings inspired the witchraft trials in Salem, memorialized Hannah as a symbol of female fortitude. To Nathaniel Hawthorne, she was that "bloody old hag."

The fateful sandbar still exists, on Route 4 (off I-93 at Exit 17), but today it's a gathering place for lazy paddlers and sun- and water-worshippers. A granite statue of Hannah, clutching her scalps in one hand and a tomahawk in the other, stands 30 feet tall downstream of the Route 4 bridge over the Merrimack.

To see the statue, pull into the Park and Ride lot and take the little path to the island where the Contoocook River meets the Merrimack. Vandals have shot off Hannah's nose and her hatchet has been spray-painted red, but she still stares balefully upriver, a dubious tribute to a dubious past.

Hampshire Community Technical College. At what is the "ultimate field trip" for thousands of New Hampshire students, the programs blend computer-generated effects, video, slides, and music. Walk-ins are welcome, but reservations are highly recommended. *3 Institute Drive (take Exit 15 off I-93); 603-271-7831.*

Silk Farm Audubon Center *map page 93, B-3*
A hiking trail at the New Hampshire Audubon Society's headquarters leads into the woods, through an old orchard, and down to Great Turkey Pond, where a moose might happen by. Owls, eagles, and hawks are often part of the educational activities at the visitor center. *Silk Farm Road off Route 89 Exit 2 (turn right); 603-224-9909.*

Canoeing on the River

The Merrimack's wildlife alone makes the river worth a look, best taken from a canoe or kayak. In late August when it's hot, quiet paddlers on the upper Merrimack sometimes spot snowy egrets. Bank swallows nest in June, and bald eagles, red-tail hawks, osprey, cormorants, kingfishers, and blue herons inhabit the area.

On Route 4 (Exit 17 off I-93), before the bridge over the Merrimack, is the little road to **Hannah's Paddles.** Joyce and Ann, a 10th-generation descendant of Hannah Dustin, will transport you north to one of three put-ins upstream. *Open Memorial Day–Columbus Day. 15 Hannah Dustin Road; 603-753-6695.*

◆ CANTERBURY SHAKER VILLAGE *map page 93, C-1/2*

In the bucolic town of Canterbury lived a religious community that probably came as close to achieving a utopian society as did any group. The first Shakers in America settled in Albany, New York, in 1776, as the American Revolution kicked into full gear. The Shakers, who emigrated from Manchester, England, initiated another sort of revolution, based on celibacy, the confession of sins, and labor. Though they called themselves the United Society of Believers in Christ's Second Appearing, outsiders dubbed them "shaking Quakers" for their dramatic gyrations during worship. (The services subsequently became less kinetic.) The group, which arrived in Canterbury in 1792, eventually adopted the name Shakers.

At its height just before the Civil War, the entire Shaker sect had nearly 6,000 members in 18 communities as far south as Florida and as far west as Kentucky and Indiana. More than 300 men and women lived in Canterbury Shaker Village at that point. The last of the Canterbury Shakers, Sister Ethel Hudson, died in 1992.

The narrow tree-lined common and more than 20 buildings of the Canterbury Shakers remain intact. The highly informative tour of them takes about 90 minutes. Parts of the schoolhouse look as if they had been painted yesterday. A national paint company analyzed samples to figure out the secret of the paint's durability but couldn't. Furniture on display throughout the site demonstrates the genius of Shaker design, a perfect balance of form and function. Artisans at the site create Shaker-style objects, including baskets, boxes, and brooms. *Open Apr.–Dec. (days and hours vary); Route 132 north from Concord or Exit 18 off I-93; 603-783-9511.*

The **Creamery Restaurant** serves lunches and four-course prix-fixe dinners in the 1905 Creamery building, where Canterbury Shakers once prepared dairy products from their prized herd of Guernsey cattle. Diners sit at handcrafted, communal

Sisters Cora Helena Sarle and Jessie Evans, Canterbury, circa 1900.
(Canterbury Shaker Village)

tables and feast on simple, traditional Shaker fare prepared with local ingredients. Candlelight dinners are followed by live entertainment or a tour of the village. *Open Apr.–Dec. (days and hours vary); 288 Shaker Road; 603-783-9511.*

◆ NEW HAMPSHIRE INTERNATIONAL SPEEDWAY *map page 93, C-1*

As you drive north on flat, straight Route 106 north of Concord, a huge viewing stand emerges from the trees. It's the New Hampshire International Speedway, New England's largest sports complex, capable of seating more than 91,000 fans. If you arrive with a ticket for one of two Winston Cup NASCAR events held here (in July and September), you'll find yourself in what is temporarily the second-largest city of New Hampshire. To racing fans, this is the "miracle mile," a 1.058-mile oval track that can be configured to a 1.6-mile course for sports car races. Every Father's Day weekend, the Loudon Motorcycle Classic is run here, the oldest motorcycle race in the United States and the culminating event in Motorcycle Week. In addition to professional and amateur motor sports, the speedway hosts bicycle racing, driving,

After the Shakers come the movers, at the Loudon Motorcycle Classic.

racing schools, and soapbox derby trials. If a major event is not being run, you can wander in and take a look, visit the souvenir shop, or buy a pit-pass for lunch at the infield restaurant. *Route 106, Loudon; 603-783-4931.*

■ **NORTHFIELD** *map page 93, B-1*

No, you're not in Rome, and that's not the forum. The splendid arch you see poking up out of the woods as you drive north from Concord on I-93 is patterned after the Arch of Titus at the southern end of the Forum in Rome—the arch that commemorates Titus's triumph over Israel in A.D. 70. The **Tilton arch,** on the other hand, immortalizes a defeat. Charles E. Tilton, who had made a fortune supplying miners during California's mid-19th-century gold rush, came back East to bestow his name on a town. He offered to build his arch and be buried in the sarcophagus below if the town of Northfield would change its name to South Tilton. The results speak for themselves: the arch, made of New Hampshire granite, is in Northfield and the sarcophagus is empty. Charles Tilton is buried in the neighboring town that bears his name. *Take Exit*

(following pages) Autumn at Canterbury Shaker Village. (Peter Guttman)

19 off I-93 and turn left onto Route 132. Turn left at the far side of the bridge on Main Street. A dirt road next to Northfield Town Hall heads up a hill to the arch.

In downtown **Tilton,** look for other statues: an Indian princess standing over an alligator (symbolizing America), a robed woman holding a bird and standing over a lion (symbolizing Asia), and a crowned and robed woman leaning on a horse head (symbolizing Europe). There is also a zinc statue of Chief Squamtum, or Squanto, of Plymouth Rock fame. The statue symbolizing Europe is affectionately known as Timetable Mabel, alluding to the days when the artwork graced a fountain at the Tilton train station.

A walker's map of the statues and other points of interest is available at the library (a mile from Exit 19) and in many local stores. The library, a resplendent specimen of Victorian excess, was Tilton's mansion.

■ **FRANKLIN** *map page 93, B-1*

Franklin, built where the Winnipesaukee River and the Pemigewasset River join to form the Merrimack, was created out of land taken from five towns: Andover, Sanborton, Northfield, Canterbury, and Salisbury.

Franklin's claim to fame is its association with **Daniel Webster,** a famous lawyer and politician who was born on a little farm southwest of town in 1782 (see page 43 for his biography). Nearby are Webster Lake, Webster Place, Webster Bridge, Webster Avenue, Daniel Webster Highway, and farther south, Daniel Webster College. Though Webster was born in New Hampshire, graduated from Dartmouth, and practiced law in Boscawen and Portsmouth for a time, the association is a tad forced; he was far more at home in Massachusetts.

Once a year, Webster would visit, "with his invited friends," to reflect at the altar of his home, his parents' graves, his boyhood haunts, and then rush back to Boston's Union Oyster House and civilization. **Webster's childhood home** is open on weekends between Memorial Day and Labor Day. *North Road off Route 127 southwest of town; 603-934-5057.*

Parts of a covered bridge, called the Sulphite Bridge, are still visible over the Winnipesaukee River. It's a shame that vandals damaged this bridge a few years back, because it was an important piece of the town's history. Not only was it the world's only "upside-down" bridge (trusses under the roadbed rather than over it), but it served the industries that made Franklin prosperous—paper and woolens.

Practically from the time the river was dammed in 1818, there was a paper mill in Franklin. Albert Garneau, the town historian, born in 1919, claims that three of the original founders of International Paper, a conglomeration of 17 pulp and paper mills founded in 1898, were from Franklin. And he remembers the prodigious output of the woolen mills, which operated in Franklin for more than a century. The mills were heavy polluters that eventually closed, leaving the town with high unemployment and a mess to clean up.

In 1999, Franklin was awarded a small grant to help redevelop the J.P. Stevens textile mill under the Brownfields redevelopment program. "Brownfields" are abandoned or underutilized industrial facilities whose transformation into new uses is being hindered by fear of contamination.

◆ FRANKLIN SIGHTS

The Abenaki Mortar
On the corner of Central (Route 3/11) and Dearborn Streets is a large stone mortar. It was common for the Abenakis to find such a hollowed surface in which to grind maize. It is unknown how far back this use dates. Settlers used the same stone for the same purpose when they moved here.

Nearby is another boulder, on which is carved the outline of a shad—one of the anadromous fish that swam up this far in the Merrimack to reproduce. It is said that at this point in the river the shad continued up the Winnipesaukee and the salmon continued north to the Pemigewasset. The blossoming of a plant called the shadbush was a sign that the fish were running.

Franklin Falls Dam Project
Franklin is the town that saved the Merrimack Valley. North of here on the Pemigewasset is the Franklin Falls Dam. In 1936, a flood destroyed homes and livelihoods downriver. "Almost immediately afterward, an army of surveyors showed up," says Garneau. "That dam project put 1,500 people to work, but it buried Hill." The Franklin dam backs up water all the way to Bristol, 8 miles upstream. Hill was a town about 6 miles upstream that was flooded by the dam. With odd echoes of the Tennessee Valley Authority, Hill and all its people were relocated across the river, north from Franklin on Route 3A.

MONADNOCK REGION

Map page 129

Keene
Peterborough

■ Area Overview

The Monadnock region takes its name from bald-capped Grand Monadnock, the shouldered 3,165-foot peak that dominates the surrounding hills. Grand Monadnock is the most-hiked mountain in the world, and the villages that surround it, with their white church spires and dignified town halls, look like dreamscapes from Currier & Ives. Nestled in wooded hills, busy little Peterborough, Jaffrey, Keene, and the sleepy hamlets of Dublin, Fitzwilliam, and Hancock are what many people see when they close their eyes and think of New England.

Huge mills dominated the economic life of cities along the Merrimack River, but the economies of cities and towns in the Monadnock region remained more balanced. Unlike Manchester's monolithic mills, Monadnock's working mills, such as Frye's Measure Mill in Lyndeborough, and the old brick mill in Harrisville, are smaller, friendlier, and, frankly, more fun to visit.

Weather: Winter days average near freezing and can drop into the teens. Ample snow brings cross-country and alpine skiers. Spring is beautiful, with river-running on the Contoocook and maple sugaring. (Mud season is from mid-March to early May.) Summer temperatures average 68 degrees F, with highs in the 80s and occasional rain. Autumn is hustle-bustle time, with leaf-peepers traversing scenic byways and crowding cafés and bookstores.

MONADNOCK REGION

■ History

As early as 1605—18 years before New Hampshire's first settlement at Odiorne Point and 15 years before the Pilgrims landed at Plymouth Rock—the French explorer Samuel de Champlain passed through this region, portaging between Chemong Lake and Little Lake to the site of the present town of Peterborough on the Contoocook River. By the mid-1600s, nearly all the native people had succumbed to epidemics of smallpox and measles. The few who survived moved north to Quebec.

It was not until 1739 that the Monadnock area was settled, when a roughly six-square-mile tract was granted to a group of prominent citizens of Concord, Massachusetts. The grantees never visited their land, and the right to settle it was quickly sold to some of the same industrious Scots-Irish who established Londonderry on the east bank of the Merrimack. Making a life here was not easy. Wrote gazetteer Alonzo Fogg of the settlers, "Unaccustomed to clearing and cultivating wild lands, they endured great privations."

Plowing the Fields *(1917), by William Zorach. (Currier Gallery of Art)*

Frye's Measure Mill.

After harvesting grains from rock-strewn fields, they hauled their harvest by oxcart 25 miles to the nearest gristmill, in Townsend, Massachusetts, along a rough path. They learned to harvest the wild foods of their upcountry surroundings, including berries, elephant ferns, and the sap of local maples. By dint of Calvinist severity and sheer Scottish stubbornness, the farming community of Peterborough was incorporated as a town in 1760.

By the first decade of the 1800s, the Peterborough Cotton Mfg. Co. was spinning cotton thread, which it distributed to local women to weave into cloth on hand looms. This cottage industry gave way to waterpowered looms in 1817. By 1831, the Noone Mill (still standing south of town on Route 202) was creating satinettes, cashmeres, and roller cloth, all of which required sophisticated finishing operations. The mill owners brought in French and Irish laborers, who established Catholic churches and working-class enclaves in towns like Jaffrey, Troy, and Harrisville.

Between Keene and Peterborough lie the Monadnock townships granted between 1749 and 1752. Keene and Peterborough were accessible by the Contoocook River or over open country, but these townships and their settlers remained isolated in swampy regions or on out-of-the-way inclines.

The Monadnock's inaccessibility fostered a sense of separation from the evolving centers of commercial and political power: Portsmouth, Exeter, and Concord. This manifested itself in ways peculiar to the region—in artist-recluses, solitary cabins on remote hillsides, and alternative spiritual communities and communes. The Monadnock still cherishes its distance from the bustling Merrimack Valley, Boston, New York, and the worldly world "out there," even while it generously accepts their refugees.

Touring ←🚗→ *Route 101 west from Wilton takes you into the heart of the Monadnock region. Curving along the tumbling Souhegan River at Wilton, the road meanders, then climbs increasingly rough terrain. Roadside hotdog stands and nurseries soon give way to wooded slopes. The climb is gradual—almost imperceptible. Eventually you'll see Pack Monadnock Mountain, at Miller State Park. Grand Monadnock is 10 miles down the road on the far side of Dublin. Route 101 descends*

MONADNOCK
REGION

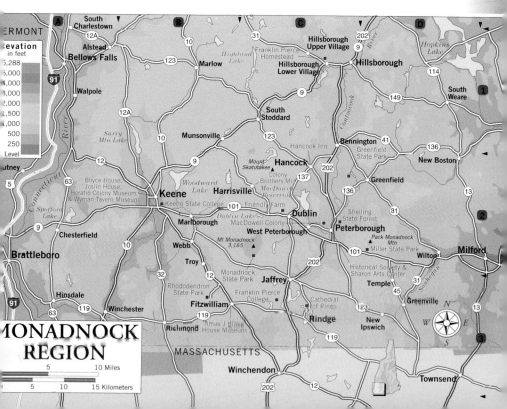

MONADNOCK
REGION

from this elevation of 1,480 feet into a perfect bowl of a valley, the spiritual seat of the Monadnock region—the town of Peterborough.

■ **PETERBOROUGH** *map page 129, C-2*

On a raw mid-March day in 2001, after two nor'easters had dumped close to three feet of snow on New England in three days, a lunch patron at Harlow's Pub in Peterborough looked up from his steaming barley soup and *The New York Times* to watch five Tibetan acolytes pick their way carefully in single file through the slush, their burgundy robes silhouetted against the stark white of shoulder-high snow mounds and the softer white of fog and freezing rain. In town to chant their triple-throated prayer at the Peterborough Town House, the monks had been invited to perform by student members of the Free Tibet Society at local Conval High School—an example of the blend of idealism and cultural sophistication that defines this town.

Peterborough (population 5,600) is a center of culture that would be the envy

(above) Main Street, Peterborough, as photographed by Gregorio Prestopino in 1901. (New Hampshire Historical Society) (opposite) Weathervane atop town office building.

of towns five times its size. The first free public library in the world was established in Peterborough in 1833, and the town's Summer Lyceum lecture series is more than 170 years old. Peterborough also hosts artistic, religious, and academic retreats, as well as arts groups and musical ensembles.

As you descend into Peterborough on the last bend around a stand of white pines on Route 101, it's hard to shake the feeling that the curtain has just gone up on Act I of *Our Town*, the Pulitzer Prize–winning play written by Thornton Wilder during his stay at the nearby MacDowell Colony, an artist's retreat, in the early 1930s. Visitors make the connection so often that locals just roll their eyes, waiting for the inevitable sample declamation. But they do speak reverently of the time James Whitmore, who got his start with the Peterborough Players, performed the role of the narrator in Wilder's play.

Downtown Peterborough is filled with upscale shops within easy walking distance of newly renovated Depot Park, by the Contoocook River. At the single traffic light at the bottom of the hill on Route 101 (just past the A&P), turn right onto Grove Street. Drive a hundred yards or so and make a right turn onto School Street. Park anywhere you can and wander around the revitalized riverfront area. Drop by the famous **Peterborough Diner,** at 10 Depot Street, or grab a sandwich at **Twelve Pine** and sit on the granite steps overlooking the swirling Contoocook. Twelve Pine, in Depot Square, is like a Horn & Hardart's for the Monadnock, with a glass case of daily gourmet specials and specialties.

Peterborough Historical Society

Unlike most such local historical repositories, Peterborough's was funded, designed, and built in 1917 specifically for its exalted purpose. It's an excellent example of the Colonial Revival style in public architecture, with its U-shape, understated formality, and utilitarian, no-larger-than-life scale. Designed by Little & Russell of Boston, the preeminent firm doing such work in their day, the building houses an outstanding collection of early-American furnishings, including tall-case (grandfather) clocks and pewter pieces from Europe and America.

There's also a colonial kitchen and exhibits on mill life. "People who come for the arts don't realize that Peterborough was a working mill town fairly early in the industrial revolution," says Michelle Stahl of the Peterborough Historical Society. "And it stayed that way right up to the First World War." According to Stahl, there's some controversy about whether the town was named after Peter

The MacDowell Colony's mission is to provide artists with privacy and seclusion. (Library of Congress)

Prescott, one of the most active early merchants of the town, or the English Earl of Peterborough. She doubts the latter explanation because the earl was no friend of the Scots-Irish. *19 Grove Street; 603-924-3235.*

Arts and Culture

Professional summer theater thrives in the presentations of the **Peterborough Players.** *Stearn Farm, Hadley Road; 603-924-7585.*

Monadnock Music presents chamber music year round and a summer festival; *603-924-7610.* The 100-voice **Monadnock Chorus** sings at well-attended recitals; *603-924-8899.*

In 1896, composer Edward MacDowell and his wife Marian bought a farm for summer residence, envisioning it as a haven for artists. Since the establishment of a fund in 1906, the **MacDowell Colony** has fed and housed prominent and not-so-prominent composers, visual artists, and writers, at no cost. Every summer on the third Sunday in August, luminaries gather at the colony for Medal Day. Under a canvas tent one stifling day in the late 1980s, John Updike rose to introduce George Plimpton, who then presented William Styron with the MacDowell Medal. *100 High Street, northwest of town; 603-924-3886.*

◆ SHEILING STATE FOREST *map page 129, C-2*

Follow the Contoocook River north from Peterborough on Route 202, and you'll soon come to Sand Hill Road on your right. This will take you to Old Street Road and Sheiling State Forest, a pine forest with 45 acres of wooded ridges, gentle walking trails through wildflower preserves, and gigantic boulders left behind by the glaciers. Here, on the site of an old gristmill, are almost a hundred varieties of flowering plants, from trailing arbutus (*Epigaea repens*) to gall of the earth (*Prenanthus trifolata*), all identified by low markers and maintained by the

Peterborough Garden Club. Sheiling (Scottish for "shelter") was left to the state by the children's author Elizabeth Yates McGreal. In the summer, it's a beautiful spot for a picnic in the woods or a leisurely walk. In winter, cross-country skiing and snowshoeing are popular.

◆ Contoocook River

The Contoocook River—named for the Kon-wa-teg-ok, an old Abenaki trail—is one of the unique features of the Monadnock region. Unlike most rivers in New Hampshire, it flows northeast, for 71 miles from Poole Pond in Rindge to the Merrimack River in Concord. This northeasterly flow made the Contoocook an invaluable pathway for travelers and settlers looking to come upcountry from Massachusetts. Its dramatic rapids, which drop 700 feet, powered the water wheels of early mills. Today, paddlers and floaters run the whitewater rapids. One of the most popular runs in the region is between Hillsborough and West Henniker and includes the famous Freight Train Rapids.

Touring ←🚗→ *From Peterborough, you can head north on Route 202 to Hillsborough, with a detour to historic Hancock, or you can travel south on Route 202 to Jaffrey and Rindge (and continue northwest on Route 12 to Fitzwilliam). Another option is to head west from Peterborough on Route 101 to Dublin and Keene. The tours below list the towns along Route 202 north, followed by the ones along Route 202 south (see page 141) and finally those along Route 101 (see page 149). Route 202 winds north from Peterborough through a pine forest to Bennington and the rural countryside near Hillsborough. Before you get to Bennington, a detour west on Route 123 takes you to Hancock, a postcard-perfect town curled around Norway Pond.*

North on Route 202 out of Peterborough, you will pass on your right the headquarters and retail store of **Eastern Mountain Sports** (EMS), which sells outdoor recreational gear. Founded in 1967 in Boston, EMS has become a major employer in the Monadnock; its outdoor workshops and climbing school are renowned resources for wilderness lovers.

About 6 miles north of Peterborough, turn left on Route 123, which has a fine view of Mount Skatutakee ("Sku-TOO-tu-kee") over the fields to the west. On a clear day you can see Grand Monadnock to the south, peeking through the distant hills. After a few miles you'll come to the quintessential New England hamlet of Hancock.

■ HANCOCK *map page 129, C-2*

As you stroll through Hancock, you may think you've happened upon a living painting of an impossibly perfect world. Two rows of well-kept brick-and-clapboard colonial buildings face each other across a quiet street. Well-dressed residents can be found at the general store, swapping stories over coffee. The town is close enough to Peterborough to feel connected to culture, yet far enough away to afford peace and quiet.

Hancock has just one of everything it needs. A faux-primitive painting of the town, available at the local inn, captures this succinctly: one general store, one café (Fiddleheads), one serene pond, one curved carriage shed (that once sheltered 19 buggies on town-meeting day), one Revolutionary War Memorial, one Paul Revere Bell (#236) in the Town Hall, and one historic New England inn.

It's all very pretty, but be careful—a deep-seated grudge smolders in the hearts of true Hancockians. The Revolutionary firebrand and wealthy Boston merchant John Hancock was an early landowner. Hancock (the town) was originally known as "Societyland"—the area drew farm families to its meeting hall and the ballroom

(above) Hancock's village green.
(following pages) Village of Hancock *(1995), by Barbara Appleyard. (Courtesy of the artist)*

Rufus Porter and His Murals

To Victorian America, heaven was an exotic, faraway place—a paradise. What better analogy on earth to native New Englanders, then, than Hawaii? When Rufus Porter saw those distant islands in 1818, they changed him forever. This "Yankee da Vinci"—itinerant muralist, silhouette artist, inventor, and entrepreneur, the publisher and founder of *Scientific American*—was so enamored of the Pacific islands that he painted palm trees everywhere, even in the murals of the bucolic New England hillsides he created all over the region.

One of the more notable features of the Hancock Inn is the Rufus Porter mural in the coveted guest bedroom that bears his name. If you are lucky enough to book the room, you will wake to gaze upon an interior hillside dotted with the houses of Hancock, its stately elms, and the fronds of a palm tree poking through.

But the palm trees are a story all their own. Early Americans fashioned a rich and exotic visual symbolism from an amalgam of Bible stories, personal experience of nature, and tales of faraway lands—sea captains returning from the China trade and whaling expeditions in the Pacific spun fabulous tales. In colonial days, pineapples connoted "hospitality" throughout New England. Willows, found often on gravestones, were symbols of mourning. Palm fronds signified divine benevolence, and Porter fit them in wherever he could, as much for his audience as for himself.

Detail of Porter mural in the Samuel Benjamin House in Winthrop, Maine. (Maine State Museum, Augusta)

at the inn—and early settlers thought it would be a nice touch to change the name to Hancock, perhaps as much to acquire a benefactor as to compliment Hancock the man. Visiting him at the governor's office in Massachusetts, they sat in the waiting room and waited. And waited. Hancock never saw them (or the town they named for him, for that matter). They returned to New Hampshire and vowed to change the name of their town again, to York. It didn't take, but to this day no portrait of the inhospitable Mr. Hancock hangs anywhere in town.

The **Hancock Inn** is well known, as is the inn's signature dish. A bartender at the Ritz-Carlton in Boston likes to tell this story: "Where to next?" he asked a British couple sitting at his bar. "Why, to the Hancock Inn," they replied. "Where's that?" "In Hancock, New Hampshire." "Why would you want to go there?" "For the Shaker Cranberry Pot Roast, of course!"

The recipe for the inn's famous dish isn't complicated, though you may not want to try it at home. Simply reduce 20 pounds of oven-braised veal bones to a rich velvety stock over the course of three days. Then cook three scalped beef shoulders in it, ladling the result carefully over a fourth shoulder on a bed of garlic mashed potatoes. Serve with a soupçon of fresh cranberry sauce and two crunchy gaufrette potato chips as a rabbit-eared garnish. But first serve an appetizer, as chefs Ben Cass and Julie Cordatos do, with crostini topped with a perfectly balanced mélange of red and yellow peppers, eggplant, and pignoli.

The Hancock Inn is one of only six Original Historic Inns, a self-invented category of New England establishments built as inns and of sufficient age. The Hancock was built in 1789 to feed and house drovers who brought their cattle north to the lush local pastures. Today you're more likely to find executives from Eastern Mountain Sports. *33 Main Street; 603-525-3318.*

■ **HILLSBOROUGH AND THE FRANKLIN PIERCE HOMESTEAD**
map page 129, C-1

Pastoral Hillsborough is best known as the birthplace and childhood home of Franklin Pierce, the 14th president of the United States. After serving as a general in the American Revolution, Franklin's impoverished father, Benjamin Pierce, found 50 acres of affordable, forested land in the area known as Lower Village. Continuing a life in public service, he prospered, and in the year of his son Franklin's birth, 1804, he was able to build the elegant homestead.

MONADNOCK
REGION

The 1804 home of Franklin Pierce in Hillsborough.

Great care has been taken to restore the Pierce Homestead to the appearance it had during the 1830s, when Benjamin Pierce was governor of New Hampshire. The house holds some surprises, one being the intense colors used throughout the beautifully appointed rooms. These vivid hues have been restored to match spectrometer readings of the underlying layers of paint. The striking Dufour wallpaper is in excellent condition. *Open late-May–Columbus Day. Route 31 at Route 9; 603-478-3165.*

For more about Franklin Pierce, see his biography on page 45, and a description of his home in Concord on page 116.

Touring ←🚗→ *Head south from Peterborough on Route 202 and you'll come to Jaffrey, within whose borders sits Monadnock State Park (the peak itself and park headquarters are in Jaffrey, but Dublin shares the 6-mile ridge). South of Jaffrey is a chain of lakes, reservoirs, and wetlands, the perfect setting for Franklin Pierce College, perched high on a hill overlooking Rindge, where the rambunctious Contoocook River originates. To the west of Route 202 on Route 119 lies Fitzwilliam, another town steeped in history.*

■ JAFFREY   *map page 129, C-2/3*

South of Peterborough, Route 202 heads upstream along the Contoocook River. A few miles up this well-traveled road you will encounter on your left Noone's Mill, home today to a few boutiques and an auctioneer's facility. A few miles farther lies the modern version of those early mills, the New Hampshire Ball Bearings factory. Then there is D. D. Bean, which still makes almost every safety match used in the world. (It is said that the market for matches shrank by 70 percent when the Bic lighter was introduced.) Luckily, and somewhat paradoxically, D. D. Bean also sells fire-protection equipment through Jaffrey Fire Protection.

Jaffrey is a mill town that drew Irish and French-Canadian immigrants to weave its textiles, build its boxes and barrels, and produce its clothespins and metal tacks. The immigrants built a no-nonsense culture that is upriver yet down-market from Peterborough, that magnet for the shopping class. Relations have been strained between the towns through the years, as they have been between local working families and the pocket of gentility up in Jaffrey Center, a few miles up Route 124.

MONADNOCK REGION

A colorful sunset reflected on a pond near Jaffrey.

Willa Cather is buried in Jaffrey. The famous writer from Nebraska *(My Antonia, Death Comes for the Archbishop)* fell in love with Jaffrey after a visit to the Monadnock Inn (now the Inn at Jaffrey Center). Her gravestone reads, "The truth and charity of her great spirit will live on in her work which is her enduring gift to her country and all its people." Sarah Orne Jewett, another famous regional writer of undetermined sexuality, introduced Cather to Jaffrey. In that Victorian era, a "Boston marriage" was a euphemism for two women who took up housekeeping and companionship. Cather and Jewett were both in such an arrangement, though not with each other. Boston marriages were commonplace and even accepted in New England, whose male population had been decimated during the Civil War.

Jaffrey was the adopted home of Amos Fortune, one of the most remarkable African-Americans to live in the Granite State. Fortune was free almost 100 years before the Emancipation Proclamation of 1863, having purchased his own freedom and that of his wife, Violate. He owned a successful business in Jaffrey and is listed as the first town benefactor in the Jaffrey Town Report. He is also

The landscape surrounding the Cathedral House Bed and Breakfast.

the subject of the children's book *Amos Fortune, Free Man* (1949), for which Elizabeth Yates McGreal won the Newbery Award. In a 1999 article in the *Concord Monitor,* McGreal explained how a trip to the Jaffrey cemetery led to her interest in Fortune's life. "I followed the grassy center path almost to the far stone wall, and then I saw the Fortune stones. They were of slate, equal in height, slender, weathered, and finely carved. Standing beside them, I read the inscription on each one."

Amos's stone reads, "Sacred to the memory of Amos Fortune who was born free in Africa, a slave in America, he purchased his liberty, professed Christianity, lived reputably and died hopefully Nov. 17, 1801 Aet 91." On Violate's: "To the memory of Violate by sale the slave of Amos Fortune, by Marriage his wife, by her fidelity his friend and solace, she died his widow Sept. 13, 1802 Aet 73."

South of Jaffrey is **Rindge,** home of **Franklin Pierce College** and **Cathedral of the Pines,** a memorial to those lost in this country's military service. This natural setting is far more conducive to spiritual thought than the most elaborate steel-and-glass tabernacle. The simple bell tower was the first memorial dedicated to women veterans. A museum and gardens are also on the site. *Cathedral of the Pines is open May–Oct. Cathedral Road, 1 mile off Route 119; 603-899-3300.*

■ **GRAND MONADNOCK** *map page 129, C-2*

At 3,165 feet, Mount Monadnock (known as Grand Monadnock to distinguish it from Pack Monadnock, in Temple) is the tallest peak for 70 miles in any direction. Its summit provides views of mountains in all six New England states—Washington in New Hampshire, Mansfield in Vermont, Wachusett (and the Boston skyline) in Massachusetts, Agamenticus in Maine, Woonsocket Hill in Rhode Island, and Bald Hill in Connecticut.

How wonderful that Monadnock did not begin as a mountain, but as a valley. The grain of the rock at its shoulders juts upward, not downward, suggesting that mighty Monadnock was once the dainty dip between two giant sisters. Its cap of durable schist, formed deep in the earth's bowels 400 million years ago, was thrust upward along with much taller mountains around it. Only Monadnock resisted the scouring of the glaciers, which took all else away, leaving us with this magnificent climb.

MONADNOCK REGION

Monadnock rises behind Perkins Pond, near the villages of Jaffrey and Troy.

◆ WHAT "MONADNOCK" MEANS

Most linguists agree that *monadnock* is an Algonquian word meaning "he who stands alone," but they arrive at the definition by different routes. The dominant theory puts together *man*, meaning "wonderful" (as in *manitou*, the Algonquian word for "Great Spirit"), *adn*, meaning "mountain," and *auke*, for "place." A few linguists, betraying a Scots-Irish bias, claim the word is a Gaelic compound of *monadh*, meaning "mountain," and *cnoc*, meaning "round hill."

Whatever the origin of the word, it has taken on scientific import. For geologists, monadnocks are any "isolated remnants of hard rock which remain distinctly above their surroundings in the late stages of an erosion cycle," as the *Encyclopaedia Britannica* stated in 1911. After all the theories of why Monadnock survived—it was a volcano, diluvial floods eroded everything else, higher surrounding peaks protected it—what it comes down to is that Monadnock has always been just plain too tough to disappear. In New Hampshire, and geology, the ornery endure.

◆ Transcendentalists Come to Monadnock Mountain

The distant northern mountain mesmerized the transcendentalists from Massachusetts. In 1847, Ralph Waldo Emerson wrote the poem "Monadnoc." In another, he compared its curious shape to the Sphinx. Henry David Thoreau slept at the peak three times and wrote of the experience in his Walden journal. Rudyard Kipling, James Russell Lowell, Willa Cather, John Greenleaf Whittier, and Mark Twain climbed it. Some of the most haunting images of Monadnock were painted by Abbott Handerson Thayer (1849-1921). Like others who came later, Thayer was a New Yorker who left the city at the age of 52 and settled in Dublin, New Hampshire, joining an ad hoc colony of artists, writers, scientists, and cultural figures living at the foot of the mountain.

Monadnock has its legends of dubious origin. Farmers supposedly burned the top of the mountain to kill wolves living there. The view from the peak is so commanding that spies supposedly hid out in its caves during World War II to send signals to German submarines in outer Boston Harbor. FBI reports at the time cited the blinking lights on the mountain and burned lighting-fixture screens in New Ipswich as evidence of searchlights.

◆ Monadnock Mountain Trails

The White Mountains possess a plethora of peaks, but Monadnock has just two: the main bald peak and Monte Rosa, a smaller point with a weather vane. Monadnock trails, though, vary so greatly they might as well be on separate mountains.

The casual hiker today might take the advice of Thoreau, whose list of what to take (in 1852) included: an umbrella, a rubber coat, three false white shirtfronts (known as "bosoms"), and a nightcap. Perhaps the bosoms were proper attire aboard the train—Thoreau would take it as far as Troy, and then hike overland to the mountain. For six days' provisions, he suggested hikers take two-and-a-half pounds of salt beef and tongue, 18 hard-boiled eggs, two-and-a-half pounds of sugar, a little salt, a quarter-pound of tea, two pounds of hard bread, half a loaf of homemade bread, and a piece of cake.

One can only imagine what gastronomic misadventures caused him to add in the margins that on the next trip it would be better to leave out the tongue and the eggs and that he "might have taken more home-made bread and more solid

MONADNOCK REGION

sweet cake." On June 28, 1852, Thoreau wrote in his journal:

> I have camped out all night on the tops of four mountains,—
> Wachusett, Saddleback, Ktaadn and Monadnock,—and I usually took a
> ramble over the summit at midnight by moonlight. I remember the
> moaning of the wind on the rocks, and that you seemed much nearer
> to the moon than on the plains. The light is then in harmony with the
> scenery. Of what use the sunlight to the mountain-summits? From the
> cliffs you looked off into vast depths of illumined air.

White Dot and White Cross Trails

Those new to Monadnock usually climb the "White Dot Trail," as I did on a
sophomore class field trip one crisp September day in 1968. The White Dot, full
of excited beginners eager for the summit, presents numerous switchbacks through
the woods. It begins with a wide path that comfortably accommodates four or five
people walking side by side. But don't be fooled—the trails become narrower and
steeper almost a mile in. The climb is challenging, with many opportunities for
twisted ankles, but the splendor of the summit makes the effort worth the risk.
Allow between four and six hours, round-trip, for a leisurely climb.

The parking lot at Monadnock State Park provides access to the White Dot Trail
and, its near parallel, the White Cross Trail. The White Dot itself provides access
the more challenging trails (the Red Dot and Spellman) near the summit. The state
park is in Jaffrey, off a little road lined with trees. If you are on Route 101 in
Dublin, turn left on Upper Jaffrey Road and go about 5 miles. If you are coming
from Jaffrey, take Route 124 and turn right on Dublin Road. No pets are allowed
in the park, which is strictly carry-in, carry-out.

Pumpelly Trail

For those who prefer less-traveled trails, Monadnock has a number of options. The
meandering Pumpelly Trail, named for white-bearded Professor Pumpelly of
Dublin, follows the ridgeline south from Dublin for 4.5 miles (the trailhead is in
Dublin, on Marlborough Road off Route 101 on the west side of town). Watch for
the large coffin-shaped glacial erratic called the Sarcophagus. The shorter (a little
more than 2 miles) but steeper Marlboro Trail, on the west side of the mountain,

provides great views of Vermont's Green Mountains. Turn onto Shaker Farm Road from Route 124 and drive almost a mile. The trailhead is behind the small parking lot on your right. You will see the stone foundations of the deserted Shaker community. Farther up the trail is a huge overhanging slab called Rock House.

As with any climb in New England, water is an absolute requirement—bring a quart per person at least. So is warmth. Monadnock is notoriously windy, and the peak will be 10 to 15 degrees cooler than the parking lot. Bring a sweater and a windbreaker. Leave by 9 or 10 in the morning and you won't feel rushed. Topographical maps and compasses (valuable on any climb) can be purchased at Eastern Mountain Sports on Route 202, about a mile north of Peterborough.

■ FITZWILLIAM *map page 129, B-3*

The gleaming white Greek Revival buildings of Fitzwilliam huddle together around the swath of lush grass that is the town common, and though the place never exactly bustles, it hums with the comings and goings of town business. Citizens are proud of their historic common, where a marker commemorates early settler Brigadier Gen. James Reed, who fought with John Stark at Bunker Hill. Also on the common, the 12-room **Amos J. Blake House Museum** presents a picture of local life in the early 19th-century.

◆ RHODODENDRON STATE PARK *map page 129, B-3*

Down the road is Rhododendron State Park, named for the profusion of heath shrubs with their clusters of showy flowers and waxy oblong leaves. The park is known for its stand of Rhododendron Maximum, one of the largest on the East Coast, with bushes 20 feet high. This National Nature Landmark has walking paths, picnic grounds, and fine views of Monadnock. Blossoms are best seen in mid-July. *Rhododendron Road off Route 119.*

Touring ←🚗→ *West of Peterborough on Route 101, up a steep slope, lies Dublin, the "highest town in New Hampshire." One of several roads that lead to Mount Monadnock State Park is just past Dublin town center. From Dublin you can head north to untouristy Harrisville or west on Route 101 to Keene. If you're in Fitzwilliam, drive north on Route 12 to reach Keene.*

■ DUBLIN *map page 129, C-2*

On the roller-coaster road between Peterborough (elevation 743) and Keene (elevation 508), the town of Dublin (elevation 1,439) is at the very top of the ride. If you're not careful, you'll go through it before you know it. So slow down. Pull into Yankee Publishing's parking lot, past the big rock in the middle of Route 101, and look around. Everything you see has a story attached to it. Even the rock.

Dublin Town Hall is a delightfully Gothic public building. Built in 1882, it once had a spire and entrance that resembled a ski slope. But John Lawrence Mauran, a successful architect and one of a number of "summer people" from St. Louis, didn't like it. He offered to redesign the edifice in 1916 and got his way.

Mauran was not the only powerful person to leave his stamp on Dublin. A great influx of summer rich folk took over the town in the late 1800s. "Summer people came in here like the English into India," says Thomas Hyman, a native son who returned after a career as a New York editor and novelist to write the definitive local history. "The poor local dirt farmers didn't know what hit them, but they liked the money." The interlopers renovated the town hall, built Emmanuel Episcopal for themselves, and, at an appropriate distance down the hill, Our Lady of the Snows Catholic church for the Irish maids who cared for their children and households.

Dublin Community Church, the white building next door to Yankee Publishing, has a unique claim to fame, though not all locals buy into it. During a rainstorm, water hitting one side of the roof will supposedly find its way to the Atlantic Ocean via the Merrimack River, while a drop hitting the roof just two inches away on the western slope, will drain to the Connecticut and down to Long Island Sound.

If you follow the first raindrop west, it will take you to **Dublin Lake,** really just a pond, whose shoreline Route 101 hugs for about a mile. It's as nice a spot as any to pull over and view Monadnock. A few miles past the pond on the left is **Friendly Farm** (603-563-8444), a petting zoo for children that is open from late spring to early fall.

Every September, Dublin holds a **Gas Engine and Tractor Show**—part swap meet, part show. There's no limit to what's shown: a Fairbanks Morse Diesel might be found huffing away next to an Alpha DeLaval milking vacuum pump.

The Congregational Meetinghouse in Fitzwilliam.

ARTISTS WHO CAME TO DUBLIN

Painters like **Abbott Thayer,** a leader in the New York art scene from a prominent Boston family, came to live in Dublin on the north end of the ridge that climbs to Monadnock, as did other artists, writers, scientists, and cultural figures. This group was less a formal colony like the MacDowell than a loose circle of friends centered around Thayer, who moved to Dublin in 1901 and painted some of the most evocative images of Monadnock.

Abbott Thayer	painter
Joseph Lindon Smith	painter
Barry Faulkner	muralist
Alexander James	painter
Richard Meryman	painter
George deForest Brush	painter
Rockwell Kent	painter
Amy Lowell	poet

Many of his works are in the collections of the Smithsonian Institution.

Thayer and his wife were true eccentrics who believed fervently in the healing powers of fresh air. They slept in little lean-tos hidden in the bushes and kept the windows of their cottage open almost all the time. Washed vegetables would freeze on the kitchen table. Muralist **Barry Faulkner's** works in the State House in Concord and in the Keene National Bank (now the Fleet Bank) on the Keene common depict the ascetic-looking Thayer holding court.

In houses and cottages around the pond and the hills, the artists who moved here in the early 1900s would gather in the evening to talk. Tomb-painter **Joseph Lindon Smith,** who re-created what he saw on sarcophagi from Egypt to Sumatra, would stage elaborate theatricals and *tableaux vivants* on the shores of Dublin Pond.

The painter and printmaker **Rockwell Kent** apprenticed himself to Thayer and later married his niece. Relations between the artists became strained after the couple divorced. Painters **Alexander James** and **Richard Meryman** also came to Dublin. **George deForest Brush**, a painter of Native Americans, lived for a time in Cornish. During social visits between the two art "colonies," violent arguments about who had the better mountain view would ensue.

Amy Lowell, the cigar-smoking Imagist poet, had a house on Beech Hill in Dublin, but she retreated to Boston. Lowell found Dublin and Monadnock inspiring, but she couldn't stand the locals, an attitude for which Robert Frost took her to task in his poem "New Hampshire." She was not the first, nor the last, smug Bostonian to feel that the beauty of the state is wasted on the woodchucks.

The Old Farmer's Almanac AND *Yankee* MAGAZINE

The Farmer's Almanac was founded in 1792 by Robert B. Thomas to provide advice and entertainment for farmers, gardeners, and the merely curious. In 1832 it became *The Old Farmer's Almanac* to distinguish it from 1,500 other contemporary publications. The only one that survived, it is said to be the oldest continuously published periodical in North America.

The Old Farmer's Almanac, published by Yankee Publishing Inc. since 1941, has never laid claim to infallibility. It has always predicted the weather based on sunspot cycles (not woolly worms, wasp nests, and other signs of nature, as rumored by some), and today is aided in that effort by the former chief scientist on NASA's Mercury program, Dr. Richard Head.

First and foremost, *The Old Farmer's Almanac* is an almanac, which is Arabic for "calendar of the heavens." Those who feel compelled to know to the minute when high tide will occur on September 4, or when the moon and sun will rise and set, will absolutely require a copy. What fascinates other readers is the host of temporal trivia and practical advice dispensed along with its eternal astronomical truths. Take, for example, these "Rules for a long life" from 1793: "Never look out the window after getting out of bed," and "What to do if someone moves next door: Leave them alone."

Yankee Magazine is a well-read (circulation 500,000) magazine about New England. Full of stories about New England and its people, it also contains tips about travel, the home, gardening, and cooking, along with the "Yankee Emporium," a catalog of intriguing ads for everything from custom-cast bronze bells to chemical toilets.

Early and recent Yankee *issues.*

■ HARRISVILLE *map page 129, C-2*

Head north of Dublin on Dublin Road about 4 miles and you'll be in Harrisville, a textile town where woolen yarn has been spun since 1790. You'll still find quality yarns and home looms at **Harrisville Designs** in the middle of town.

Harrisville is almost impossible to negotiate in the dead of winter, but in other seasons it's a beautiful town that shows off its best features from the walkway around Harrisville Pond. With its granite and brick buildings, some of them perched over the waterfalls of Goose Brook, Harrisville claims to be New Hampshire's most photographed village. If true, it must be because Harrisville's consistent architecture provides such a refreshing break from suburban sprawl. The

Harrisville. (Robert Holmes)

Colony Brothers Mill and the entire town were designated National Historical Landmarks in 1984 (see the Horatio Colony Museum, in Keene, for more on this important family).

As expressed in the literature of Historic Harrisville, the entity formed to preserve the character of the town, the goal here is not to encourage tourism but to "maintain the essential character of Harrisville as a small, quiet, relatively isolated village where people work and live." So don't go looking for public restrooms, gas stations, tours of the historic mill, or a visitors center. That isn't what this well-preserved burg is about. And you won't find big tour buses, either—there's no place for them to park.

■ KEENE *map page 129, B-2*

Settled after 1736, this little city with a wide Main Street was named for Sir Benjamin Keene, a British diplomat and friend of colonial governor Benning Wentworth. Then at the edge of the frontier, Keene became a pawn in the struggles between France and England as their imperial ambitions were played out in North America. Keene was burned to the ground in 1748 by French and Indian attackers, but the local settlers had deserted the town, convinced that it could not be protected without a military presence. As it turned out, they were right.

Since then, Keene has been built and rebuilt in splendid style, financed by riches earned from its position as a railhead and manufacturing center. Everything being so formal, it's a surprise to learn that as recently as 1921 cattle were driven down Main Street on their way from Vermont to a livestock center in Brighton, Massachusetts. One old photo captures a herd in front of the gazebo on the square, surrounded by determined-looking gentlemen in bowler hats and greatcoats.

When the railroads came in the mid-19th century, the busy depot off Main Street began exporting Keene furniture, flannels, pottery, glass, and toys to international customers. Today Keene is a city of 23,000, a number that bulges every workday with another 9,000 nonresidents, many of them working in its

(above) Keene's wide Main Street.
(following pages) Jack-o'-lanterns aplenty near Keene's gazebo. (Peter Guttman)

Darby, the Fictional Keene

"I grew up in Keene, New Hampshire," writes novelist Ernest Hebert, the fictional Tuckerman in the five-book series of novels revolving around Darby. "North of Keene in Sullivan, I built a cabin; south in Dublin, my parents met on a blind date; east in Westmoreland, I own three remote acres of woods where I camp, cut wood, and just sit and think. Fictional Darby is a mix of these three towns, all of which I love dearly."

Immense wealth lies hidden in the hills of the Monadnock region, and it's not the fool's gold one Jaffrey farmer mistook for the real thing. Family fortunes were made in timber and textiles, yet many less fortunate families still live in tatterdemalion pockets of rural poverty in the hills around Keene. This split reality and the battles it engenders for the soul of the Monadnock are the setting and subject of Ernest Hebert's Darby novels. These five novels, set in Cheshire County (*The Dogs of March, A Little More Than Kin, Live Free or Die, Whisper My Name,* and *The Passion of Estelle Johnson*) were inspired by the people of reduced circumstances Hebert met as a young newspaper reporter. He is at his best when capturing the folkways and speech of these marginalized citizens of the hills. They rise from the page simply as they are, without condescension or glorification. His characters are real, true, and surprisingly eloquent.

The Old American is a departure from the Darby series. Hebert had often passed the stone marker at Main and Winchester Streets that marked the spot where six generations of the Blake family had lived. Hebert's novel is based on the 1746 abduction of Nathan Blake, who built the first log house in Keene. He was captured by the Algonquins during one of the many wars over who would control the Ohio Valley: France, England, the Iroquois, or other native groups. Blake's wife ransomed him in 1749, and he lived to be 100.

insurance, aerospace, precision instruments, machine tools, and industrial-marking equipment businesses.

◆ Visiting Keene

Four well-marked exits along Route 101 lead into Keene. Detour north off Route 101 onto Route 12, or Main Street, and you'll find yourself driving down a grand boulevard lined with Federal-style and Italianate homes, glass and furniture manufacturers, and the Catholic church complex. As you drive up Main Street, you can thank the town fathers, who voted in 1736 to double the street's width to

164 feet. Even in olden times traffic was an issue—as many as 70 wagons a day would rumble down Main Street hauling goods to market.

Keene State College

The permanent collection at **Thorne-Sagendorph Art Gallery** on the Keene State College campus includes an impressive selection of works by artists who flocked to areas near Mount Monadnock a century or so ago. They included Alexander James, Richard Meryman, Joseph Lindon Smith, and Barry Faulkner. *Off Main Street at Wyman Way; 603-358-2720.*

Historical Society of Cheshire County

Keene was once a center for glass and pottery manufacturing. Many fine pieces of antique glass and Hampshire pottery can be seen at the Historical Society, in an old brick building with a black iron fence in front on Main Street. The Italianate house was built by the clothing merchant and brickyard partner George Ball. This is the place to pick up the truly superior brochure "Shire Town by Foot," which contains a **walking tour of the town** with fine examples of every style of architecture from Georgian through Art Moderne. *246 Main Street; 603-352-1895.*

United Church of Christ

The huge white-spired edifice that overlooks Main Street and the town is the United Church of Christ, built in 1787. On the National Register of Historic Places, it gracefully integrates three architectural styles: Greek Revival, Italianate, and Colonial Revival. Pull into a parking space near the church and stroll the shopping district. The lobby of the Fleet Bank contains Barry Faulkner's mural *Men of Monadnock*, depicting Emerson, Thoreau, and Thayer. *23 Central Square.*

Jumanji

Parts of the movie *Jumanji,* starring Robin Williams and inspired by Chris Van Allsburg's children's book, were shot in Keene. The gazebo on Central Square may look familiar to fans of the film.

The Ingersoll Collection

Maj. George Ingersoll fought under Gen. Arthur St. Clair during the French and Indian War, then against Gage, Burgoyne, and Cornwallis during the Revolution.

He was in command at West Point from 1796 to 1800 and later at Philadelphia and Governor's Island in New York. His papers are typical of a military man of his day, but along with mundane letters are papers signed by Washington, Jefferson, Hamilton, Hancock, Thomas Pickering, St. Clair, and other distinguished Americans. These papers are on display on the first floor of City Hall. *3 Washington Street.*

Painted Ladies

North of Central Square on Court Street are grand Queen Anne–style homes. At 122 Court Street is the **Boyce House,** a "painted lady" with a cross-gable roof, a round tower, and a neoclassical wraparound porch. On the same side one block down is another Queen Anne, the **Joslin House,** built by the owner of the Cheshire Chair Company.

Colony Mill Marketplace

To combine history and shopping, go around the circle at Central Square and head west past a store called Sotto Voce to the **Colony Mill** marketplace, a renovated mill with antiques, bookstores, and other shops. Colony was the name of a famous mill-owning family—the Colony Mill in Harrisville still stands.

Horatio Colony Museum

Horatio Colony, a descendant of Keene's notable Colony family, built his Federal-style house in 1806. The museum within contains the family's outstanding furniture, art, books, and silver. *Open May–mid-Oct. 199 Main Street; 603-352-0460.*

Wyman Tavern Museum

Built in 1762, the Wyman Tavern hosted the first meeting of the Dartmouth College trustees, and in April 1775 its lawn served as a gathering place for local men heading to Lexington and Concord. Open from Thursday to Saturday, it is furnished as a tavern and residence. *Open June–Labor Day. 339 Main Street; 603-352-1895.*

MONADNOCK
REGION

LAKES REGION

■ **Area Overview**

The railroads made the Lakes region a desirable vacation spot in the 19th century, and as the state's fastest growing area it has become hot again. Roads here wind past lakes and islands, around little coves, and under rocky cliffs, serving up vistas of great variety. The towns that encircle these shores are refreshingly informal. One of them, Wolfeboro, lays claim to being America's oldest summer resort, dating back to pre–Revolutionary War times as a place where royal governors and grandees would come to doff their silks, dip their feet in blue waters, and bob for the local fish known as the horned pout.

The carnival strip at Weirs Beach, across from charming Wolfeboro, is a zany adventure, but you can also sail or boat big blue Lake Winnipesaukee. A baronial mansion on a burned-out volcano, the nearby jewel called Newfound Lake, the perfect peak of Mount Chocorua—who wouldn't want to experience this casual paradise?

Weather: Summer temperatures average 68 degrees F, winter 18 degrees, with extremes of 102 and -38. Winter is wet, heavy snows swell the Winnipesaukee come spring (late March), yet precipitation of 38 inches is distributed fairly evenly throughout the year. In late September, striking foliage decorates the lakeshores.

■ History

The Wisconsin Glacier, which had been creeping southwest over the Sandwich Range, came to a halt when the earth's climate began to warm about 13,000 years ago. For a time, the mile-thick mass of ice sat there like a dense dollop of light blue paint scraped off on the rim of a bucket, until it slowly melted into the deep rock hollows it had scoured. Left behind was the landscape now known as the Lakes region, which holds 273 sparkling lakes and ponds and hundreds of islands, hidden bays, and magical, undulating shorelines.

A compelling print from the 1890s of the largest of the lakes, Winnipesaukee, shows the vast, beautiful bowl in which it sits. One of the first "tourist pictures" created of the region, by the Boston & Maine Railroad, reminds us that even the "oldest resort in America" had to be marketed. But how brilliantly the railroad and steamboat companies did it.

The first boat to ply Lake Winnipesaukee was the *Belknap,* launched in 1833. Powered by the steam plant from an old sawmill, it was wrecked off present-day

LAKES
REGION

Hand-colored engraving of Lake Winnipesaukee by William Bartlett.
(Old Print Barn, Meredith)

Steamboat Island in 1841. In 1849, the Winnipesaukee Steamboat Company launched the grand *Lady of the Lake,* for years the fastest boat on the lake. Railroad officials saw the potential for integrated service, and the Boston & Maine launched the *Mount Washington* in 1872—the most graceful-looking steamship in the United States. The era of steam competition was born, with boats like *James Bell, Maid of the Isles, Mineola, Belle of the Waves, Lamprey, Eagle, Cyclone, Roxmount,* and *Meredith* vying for passengers.

The railroads brought the tourists, the steamboats distributed them around the lake, and the resort hotels and camp meetings prospered. Weirs Beach became a summer getaway for Methodists, who stayed and built gingerbread cottages. The deluxe Hotel Weirs catered to refined tastes. The lakes brought together people yearning to escape the gritty industrialized cities. The Boston & Maine Railroad, dangling a bucolic retreat before their eyes, offered the means to get there.

But before the awe-inspiring power and luxury of the steam era, before the steamship *Mount Washington's* shrill whistle-blasts and 42-inch single piston with 10-foot throw, there were stranger and more wondrous conveyances on the lake.

Lake Winnipesaukee was a destination for weekend vacationers from New England and New York. (New Hampshire Historical Society)

LAKES
REGION

Poster for the Mount Washington *steamer. (Boston Athenaeum)*

Gundalows, shallow-drafted sailboats developed on the Piscataqua River, also plied Winnipesaukee, hauling heavy loads between towns. Between 1830 and 1890, a bizarre contraption sailed the lake—the horseboat. This barge had an angled treadmill in the back. Horses trudging up the treadmill ramps powered paddlewheels on the sides of the boat.

Touring ←🚗→ *Route 3 heading east from I-93 Exit 20 passes through a commercial area, then skirts the shores of Silver Lake. Soon you'll cross the bridge over the southern tip of Lake Winnisquam (great views of Chocorua to the right and Red Hill to the left) and come to the tiny town of Winnisquam. Continue northeast on Route 3/11, and in less than two miles you'll enter Laconia.*

■ LACONIA *map page 165, C-3/4*

After easy Winnisquam, the traffic in Laconia can be jarring. Suddenly you're in the center of town, faced with a choice of turning left on East Beacon Street in the direction of the "business district"; south toward Gilmanton on Route 107; or continuing north toward Weirs Beach, with traffic coming every which way. It's even worse in June, when Motorcycle Week brings up to 350,000 metal locusts to the region. Resist the impulse to floor it—make the turn onto East Beacon Street, and you'll see the redbrick Belknap Mill next to the white gazebo by the river. Find a spot to park and relax.

Horseboat on Lake Winnipesaukee. (Wolfeboro Historical Society)

LAKES REGION

Ice-cutting, Newfound Lake, 1968. (New Hampshire Historical Society)

"Constructed in 1823," reads the historical marker, "the **Belknap Mill** is the oldest unaltered brick textile mill in the U.S. Once a hosiery mill, it houses an intact hydraulic power plant and a bell cast by George Holbrook, apprentice to Paul Revere."

Roger Gibbs, Curator of Mechanical Systems at the mill, is careful to point out the difference between this little operation and the sprawling Amoskeag complex. "Down there, it's all about weaving—interlacing parallel threads with cross-threads—on a massive power loom." Knitting machines, by contrast, are compact, almost cute, with a circular ring of needles that pop up in sequence, clicking along like a typewriter—or an automated grandmother. A knitting machine produces a continuous tube of stretchy fabric, which eventually becomes a sock. Here is how it was done: first the tube was cut to length, and then a turner boy (the lowest-paid worker in the plant) turned the sock inside out so the looper could seam the toes. Then the turner boys reversed them, right side out, so they could be boarded (put on a pattern) and steamed, which shrank them to the right size. *East Beacon Street; 603-524-8813.*

Laconia's **train station** is an amusing example of Richardson Romanesque architecture, named for the late-19th-century architect Hobson Richardson and a

Ice sailing on Lake Winnipesaukee.

popular style for public buildings. It's now occupied by the Chamber of Commerce and, incongruously, a pizza joint. *Main Street north of Beacon Street.*

■ LAKE WINNIPESAUKEE   *map page 165, D-2/3*

The clear blue waters of Lake Winnipesaukee are surrounded by a forest of oaks, maples, birches, and white pines, the latter often framing white sand beaches tucked into coves along the shoreline. Mountains rim the lake to the north and east. Along the shore are boat launches and camping sites, cottages, motels, and hotels. The western shore is completely developed, but conservation areas, state parks, and mountain trails make it easy for you to escape the crowds.

◆ THE WEIRS

The famous weirs, named for the fencing placed in waterways to catch fish, are on the shore side of Route 3, north of the bridge over Paugus Bay, but in the channel that runs under the bridge.

(following pages) Boats docked at Mountain View Yacht Club, Gilford.

As far back as 9,500 years ago, Paleo-Indians encamped on the then-barren landscape around the lakes, sheltering themselves from the wind and hunting for bison and caribou. Perhaps 8,000 years ago, in the Late Archaic Period, the population increased all along the channel that begins at Weirs Beach and extends west to Franklin. Stone fences were built to gather migrating shad, which native peoples speared or scooped out in baskets and smoked. Archaeological digs along the weirs have yielded rich finds, including pottery shards.

In the same channel lies **Endicott Rock,** left in 1652 by a surveying party from Massachusetts that ventured north to establish that colony's northern boundary. The party chiseled a rock with Gov. John Endicott's name (misspelled) on it to mark the spot. The rock was lost until 1833, when a work crew found it in the channel in the town of Weirs Beach.

◆ WEIRS BEACH   *map page 165, C-3*

Weirs Beach is one of New Hampshire's busiest beach towns, a summer carnival surrounded by nature's more sedate charms. "Where the Boats meet the Train," says the sign on the wharf, and it's true—a scenic train departs every hour. But "Where old-time religion met Coney Island" might be more accurate. A hundred years ago, places like Weirs Beach and Oak Bluffs on Martha's Vineyard became popular as tent-revival retreats. All that remains of that era of religious fervor are the gaudy, whimsical Victorian cottages on the hillside facing the lake. Not long after they were built, vacationers began taking their carnival delights undiluted by religion.

North of the ornate New Hampshire Veterans Association building on Lakeside Avenue, a strip of stores sells timelessly trashy delights. A couple of generations of Americana are packed into the store signs alone: Pizza, Penny Arcade, Bumper Cars, Hart's Homemade Slush, Cook's Candy Kitchen, Weirs Jewelry Outlet, Family Fun Center, Laser Tag Fog-Filled Arena.

Across the street is the Weirs Beach stop of the **Winnipesaukee Scenic Railroad,** which departs from Meredith and travels along the lakeshore daily from late June through Labor Day and on weekends in September and October. *603-745-2135.*

Weirs Beach becomes downright frenetic during June's **Motorcycle Week,** which spreads out from Laconia, with locals selling beer, burgers, tattoos, and trinkets. Motorcycle Week typically coincides with the Loudon Motorcycle Classic, at the New Hampshire International Speedway, northeast of Concord (see page 120).

SALMON RUN ON THE RIVER

In the excerpt below from The Old American, *a historical novel by Ernest Hebert set in mid-1700s, the wise old native of the title anticipates the yearly salmon run.*

The salmon run is always an exciting event. Winter is over. If we've been lucky (and this has been a lucky winter), we have avoided death by starvation, freezing, and diseases, and can now look forward to months of plenty before the next hard winter, so all the people are in a playful mood upon arrival at the salmon stream. This year adds poignancy to joy because this is the last great task that this réfugié tribe embarks on in common before it will divide into two bands. The sight of cold water thrashing rocks, spray like busy fog, colorful fish slippery in the hands, sharp cuts of sunlight, stir the blood.

Does Nathan Provider-of-Services understand that the nomadic life, though more prone to disasters than the farm life, is also more ecstatic, and the salmon run is one of those ecstatic moments? This life that you are throwing away, will you miss it, Black Dirt?...

This kind of fishing is for the nimble and the strong. It takes strength to set up the weirs in the fast water to slow the fish so they can be stabbed. It takes good balance to perch on a ledge of slippery granite while at the same time stabbing at jumping fish in frothing water. It takes agility to climb to the best spearing stations, and it takes timing and dexterity to actually spear the fish.

—Ernest Hebert, *The Old American,* 2000
University Press of New England

■ MEREDITH–WINONA AREA *map page 165, C-2*

Meredith is the upscale version of Weirs Beach. Everything is newly minted, then carefully distressed to look old. Giant handmade wooden fish, fishing photos from Vermont—it's a Ralph Lauren fantasy, replete with fly rods, fowling pieces, and fancy duds (minus the messy fish guts).

Café Lafayette Dinner Train

From late May until Labor Day you can enjoy a five-course dinner on restored

CRUISING LAKE WINNIPESAUKEE

To truly experience 72-square-mile Lake Winnipesaukee, you must get out on it. Try a cruise of the lake aboard the historic *Mount Washington,* or the *Sophie C.* or the *Doris E.* between Weirs Beach and Meredith. If you've brought your own sailboat or motorboat, you'll find yourself zipping past wooded islands, with the wind in your hair and the spray in your face. Watch in the distance for Red Hill to the north, Mount Major to the southwest, and Mount Ossipee to the east. Take a chart; it's easy to become disoriented in the maze of islands.

Cruise Boats

Mount Washington
This boat departs several times a day from Weirs Beach, Wolfeboro, Alton Bay, and Meredith between mid-May and mid-October. There are dinner-dance cruises and brunch cruises on Saturday and Sunday, depending upon the town and the boat. For information on all other boats except the *Winnipesaukee Belle* (see below), contact *888-843-6686; www. msmountwashington.com*

Winnipesaukee Belle
From June to October, this Mississippi-style paddlewheel boat cruises out of Wolfeboro for an hour and a half along the shoreline; *800-451-2389; www.wolfeboroinn.com*

Sophie C.
Sophie delivers the U.S. mail and carries passengers along for the ride.

Doris E.
The *Doris E.* runs between Weirs Beach and Meredith and offers scenic and sunset cruises. The boat operates between mid-May and mid-October; *888-843-6686 or 603-366-5531.*

Motorboats

You can rent a motorboat for waterskiing or cruising at marinas around the lake. A few include:

Meredith
Meredith Marina; *603-279-7921.*
Brown's Boat Basin; *603-279-4573.*

Weirs Beach
Anchor Marine; *603-366-4311.*
Thurston's; *603-366-4811.*

Sailboats

Fay's Boatyard rents sailboats. *Follow Route 11B south from Weirs Beach, turn left on Route 11, then make another left onto Varney Point Road; 603-293-0700.*

Pullman cars as they tour the shore. The dinner train departs from South Main Street in North Woodstock. *Route 112 off I-93 Exit 32; 800-699-3501 or 603-745-3500.*

Old Print Barn

Winona's Old Print Barn, a Civil War–era structure, houses a sublime collection of images by master printmakers. Steel engravings, lithographs, wood engravings, chromolithographs, Korean oils, etchings with aquatint, mezzotints, and subtractive woodblocks are all on display. The works exhibited along one corridor provide a wonderful overview of printmaking, from the red chalk drawing of a Florentine boy (circa 1550) to contemporary mezzotints of breathtaking subtlety. There are also prints by Currier and Ives, Audubon, Gould, Homer, and Whistler, to name just a few.

One section is devoted to views of New Hampshire, including a famous series by William H. Bartlett (1830s), as well as *White Mountain Scenery* (1848), a series by William Oakes. Upstairs in the loft are wood engravings by Herbert Waters. His stark *January Thaw* (1985) depicts a covered bridge over a half-frozen stream beneath lacy bare branches silhouetted against the sky. Sophia and Charles Lane, the publishers of *The Journal of the Print World*, live next door in a 1790 farmhouse. Sophia is an excellent guide, with unique perspectives on the art of printmaking. *Winona Road west of Meredith; 603-279-6479.*

Lakes Region Summer Theater

The Lakes Region Summer Theater is not the area's oldest summer theater (that would be Barnstormers in Tamworth), but it is the oldest professional theater on the lake. Watch a boffo Broadway hit in this casual lakeside setting after a sunset cruise on the lake. *Route 25, a half-mile north of Meredith; 603-279-9933.*

Annalee Doll Museum

Every doll collector knows the name Annalee. Barbara Annalee Davis first created her elfin-faced collectibles in the 1930s. Selling the dolls through craft outlets in New Hampshire and Massachusetts, she parlayed her hobby into an international enterprise. The museum displays 900 Annalee dolls, the earliest from 1934, along with a few antique autos. *Gift shop open year-round, museum May–Oct. Hemlock Drive south of Route 104; 603-279-6542 or 603-279-3333.*

■ HOLDERNESS: SQUAM LAKE *map page 165, C-2*

To the northwest of Lake Winnipesaukee lie Squam and Little Squam Lakes. Some wealthy "summer people" who own homes on Squam Lake have been reluctant to open it up to boat traffic, which irks many year-round residents. An official boat ramp was finally installed on the little neck of land between Squam and Little Squam, in Holderness, on Route 3 (Exit 24), near Walter's Basin restaurant.

There's no denying that Squam is a beautiful lake. For generations, important landowners with names like Coolidge, Armstrong, and Preston have favored understated development—low camplike buildings stained dark brown—to the more ostentatious displays, particularly some recently built condos, around Winnipesaukee.

Squam Lakes Natural Science Center operates naturalist-led summer cruises on 28-foot-long pontoon boats. Excursions include sunset cruises and a daytime search for loons. Summer evening cruises sometimes include a snack by campfire on Moon Island. *Open May–Oct. Route 3 at Route 113, Holderness; 603-968-7194.*

■ MOULTONBOROUGH AREA *map page 165, D-2*

Moultonborough straddles the road with a few nondescript buildings and a unique general store ("rabbit pelts, $2.50"). Beyond, where Route 25 meets Route 109, you can go up in an airplane to tour the lakes.

◆ CENTER SANDWICH *map page 165, C/D-1*

Come to this small town north of Moultonborough to see what a country store looked like circa 1848. Follow Route 109 up to Center Sandwich, then go right about 50 yards on Route 113. The headquarters of the **Sandwich Historical Society** (4 Maple Street; 603-284-6269) is a house restored to look as it did in the mid-1800s; the attached barn contains the country store. On your way into town you'll see a crumbling orange brick building, formerly **Blanchard's Store,** a famous stagecoach stop. Continue down Route 113, over a beautiful hill with a view of the Sandwich Range to the north, and you'll come to a little dirt road, easy to miss except that Route 113 takes a sharp turn to the left.

Turn right and you're on **Top of the World.** As you drive along this dirt road (passable in most seasons, but be careful if it's muddy or icy), you'll see the sharp tooth

(opposite) Squam Lake.

of Chocorua behind you, the bowl of Ossipee ahead and to your left, and a bit farther along and to the right, Red Hill, at the shoulder of Moultonborough Neck. You'll pass by a hilltop farm and a portion of the Bearcamp Trail, before this bumpy wagon path comes out at Little Pond Road about two miles later.

◆ **Moultonborough Neck** *map page 165, D-2*

About two miles east of Center Harbor on Route 25 at Murphy's Mobil Station, Moultonborough Neck Road extends south to the end of a long peninsula, connected to an island in the big lake. The drive down the Neck will take you past a marshy area and then into a dense pine forest. On your right, down Kona Farm Road, is **Kona Mansion Inn** and golf club, originally built to be a "gentlemen's farm" by one of the founders of Jordan Marsh department stores. Travelers and cartographers take note: The Winnipesaukee Post Office, which has inspired at least five mapmakers to put a black dot denoting a "town center" at the south end of the Neck, has been closed since 1964. There is no town of Winnipesaukee.

About seven miles from Route 25, you'll come to a bridge over Braun Bay onto **Long Island**, a magical spot with a handy boat launch. White-sand beaches curve along a shallow wading cove, framed by a stand of white pines. It's the best spot on the Neck.

◆ **Marcus Wildlife Sanctuary** *map page 165, D-2*

At the Marcus Wildlife Sanctuary's **Loon Preservation Center,** go through the trees in the back to find the trail that hugs Halfway Brook. If you follow it to the lake in June and July, you might see loons nesting on an artificial island. There's plenty to learn at the center, from the exhibits and the Thursday night natural history lectures. The sanctuary itself encompasses 200 acres of forests, marshes, ponds, and streams. *Off Route 25 between Center Harbor and Moultonborough; turn south on Blake Road and follow the signs ("Loon viewing") one mile; 603-476-5666.*

Wild Meadow Canoes rents canoes and kayaks. *Route 25; 603-253-7536.*

◆ **Castle in the Clouds** *map page 165, D-2*

The area's main attraction is **Castle in the Clouds**, the baronial manse of Thomas Gustave Plant, which sits atop Ossipee Mountain. Friendly docents will show you the spectacular view high above Winnipesaukee as well as the mansion's conveniences, revolutionary for their day, like a central vacuum system, surround shower-jets, and an early refrigeration system.

What the docents don't divulge is how the mansion got here. Plant, who made his fortune designing shoe machinery, bought the land from B. F. Shaw in 1911. Shaw, a rich and quirky inventor, had bought a great deal of land from the Lee family to establish Ossipee Mountain Park. Plant blasted the top off Ossipee Mountain and built his fantasy. When the Lees, who had lived on the slopes of Ossipee since the late 1700s refused to sell the rest of their land, he built a huge spite fence, with spiky protrusions to obscure their view of the lake, and splashed outlying buildings with black paint. After the family sold out to the relentless Plant, he set out to destroy their cemetery.

But time has a way of righting wrongs. The diminutive Plant, who practically worshiped Napoleon, died penniless, having invested in Russian rubles—on the advice of Theodore Roosevelt—just before Vladimir Ilyich Lenin and the Bolsheviks came to power.

Castle in the Clouds is run as an attraction by the Castle Springs bottling company, which sits down the slope. An informative display explains that Ossipee is an ancient volcano, formed about 120 million years ago. As glaciers moved south, they filled the crevices of the Ossipee range with deposits, forming a vast bowl of sandy soil called a ring dike—the only one north of Mexico. This natural bowl is a highly effective filtration system for the pure water that is bottled at the Castle Springs plant.

You can take a horseback ride around the grounds or follow hiking paths to two waterfalls and a feeding pond, where you can make already obese trout gargantuan by tossing them food pellets. You can't angle for these fish, but a local who caught one "by accident" said it tasted more like cat food than fish. *Open late May–mid-Oct. (days and hours vary). Route 171 northeast of Lake Winnipesaukee; 800-729-2468.*

Touring ←🚗→ *As it heads north, then east, Route 25 takes you downstream through the open fields and wetlands of the Bearcamp River Valley. A left turn on Route 113 takes you through more open fields separated by wooded areas, lightly settled, north to the village of Tamworth.*

■ TAMWORTH AREA *map page 165, E-1*

As you turn off Route 16 into quiet little Tamworth on Route 113, you'll encounter the Lakes region's version of Hancock (the little town with one of everything it needs). Small and perfect, Tamworth is like a model-railroad town come to life.

Barnstormers Playhouse

The oldest summer playhouse in New Hampshire, founded in 1931 by presidential son Francis Grover Cleveland, hosts one play a week in July and August. The company (all Equity performers) converted the beautiful old Kimball's Store as their theatrical home. *Intersection of Cleveland Hill and Great Hill Roads and Main Street, Tamworth; 603-323-8500.*

Remick Country Doctor Museum and Farm

The last two of six generations of Remicks to live in Tamworth were country doctors (from 1894 to 1993) on the grand farm founded by their forebears in the late 1700s. When Edwin Remick died in 1993, he provided in his estate for this unique and wonderful place, both working farm and museum, devoted to remembering the life and work of the country doctor who also farmed.

The day I visited, schoolchildren were learning how to bake muffins in the huge beehive fireplace in the great room of Edwin's home, where the museum proper is situated. Over their heads hung a sampler admonishing, "Patience is bitter, but the fruit is sweet."

Programs at the Remick explain cooking and preserving, flax processing, candle making, butter and cheese making, wool carding and spinning, and soap making. The museum commemorates the farm year with seasonal events like maple sugaring in spring, stone wall building in summer, a pumpkin festival and Victorian Thanksgiving in fall, and ice harvesting in winter.

The doctors' antique medical instruments are on display, as well as an old examination room, a waiting room, and living rooms above the medical offices—just the way they might have looked in the early 1900s. The stories keep it interesting (reaching influenza patients in the hills around Tamworth meant donning snowshoes, or a ride in a jury-rigged snowbuggy), and the photos of the doctors' lives and loves (harness racing and animal husbandry) keep it personal and immediate.

Across the road from the museum, a walking trail (15 minutes) straddles the banks of the Swift River. Grab a trail guide at the parking lot or at the Remick Museum. It contains thoughtful clues for reading the natural environment for signs of humans, animals, and weather-related events such as the Hurricane of 1938. *58 Cleveland Hill Road; 800-686-6117.*

(previous pages) Pitch pines frame White Lake and the White Mountains, White Lake State Park, near Tamworth.

The Common Loon

One night long ago, as I lay in my Cowboy Eddie sleeping bag near Lake of the Woods, I heard a quavering, disquieting laugh that raised the hairs on the back of my neck. I learned later from loon experts that this "tremolo" is the sound the loon uses to signal danger. The bird has three other cries: wails, yodels, and hoots. A wail sounds like a howling clarinet and is the loon's "how do you do." Yodels are produced only by males, to defend territory. And hoots are intimate calls between paired loons, or between parents and chicks.

A beautiful bird with a unique black and white pattern on its feathers, the loon lives on and near lakes, except in winter when it moves to the seacoast and molts to a drab color.

Loons can live 20 years or more, but that life span has been at risk in New Hampshire, for a number of reasons. Loss of nesting habitats due to shoreline development, powerboats, loss of food (fish) due to pollution, fluctuating water levels that obliterate their nests, and acid rain are a few. But the most common cause of loon mortality — from 50 percent to 80 percent according to the Loon Preservation Center—are the lead sinkers used by fishers. The center's field biologists surveyed 267 lakes statewide in 2000 and found only 216 mating pairs.

There is cause for optimism, however. Lead sinkers were banned on the lakes, and loon lovers are optimistic that the birds' numbers may increase because of it.

■ CHOCORUA *map page 165, E-1*

Standing like a jagged tooth above the Sandwich Range, Mount Chocorua was noted in the first records of the region. Darby Field, that impetuous Irishman, on his way to becoming the first European to climb Mount Washington, called it a "striking sentinel," while others referred to it as the most perfectly shaped of the White Mountains. Its legend is fascinating.

Supposedly, many Native Americans feared retribution after their devastating raid on Dover in 1686, and they retreated to Canada. But Chocorua, a Pequawket chieftain, stayed in his beloved White Mountains. The family of Cornelius and Caroline Campbell cared for his son when Chocorua went to visit his kinsmen, but the boy died. Blaming his son's death on the Campbells, Chocorua killed Caroline and her children. Cornelius chased Chocorua up the slopes of the jagged mountain, where, rather than surrender, he jumped off the peak. As recorded in the book *The White Mountains: Names, Places & Legends,* he screamed this curse before he leapt:

"May the Great Spirit curse when he speaks in the clouds and his words are fire! Lightning blast your crops! Wind and fire destroy your homes! The Evil One breathe death on your cattle! Panthers howl and wolves fatten on your bones!"

At 3,475 feet, Mount Chocorua is one of the most climbed mountains in the Whites. Three popular routes are the Piper Trail from the east, Liberty Trail from the west, and Champney Falls Trail from the north. The Hammond Trail, off Route 16 north of Lake Chocorua, is a less-traveled path to the summit and its sweeping views of the Presidential Range to the north.

Touring ← 🚗 → *To return to Lake Winnipesaukee and Wolfeboro, head back from Castle in the Clouds on Route 171 to the left turn onto Route 109. Follow Route 109 south through Melvin Village (where a granite marker in the graveyard behind the Melvin Village Church commemorates John Greenleaf Whittier's poem "The Grave by the Lake"), past Union Wharf, around Nineteenmile Bay, and finally to Mirror Lake.*

■ WOLFEBORO AREA *map page 165, E-3*

The town on the southeast shore of Lake Winnipesaukee is named for James Wolfe, a frail British general who was despised by his subordinates and whose last-ditch attempt to storm the faraway city of Quebec in 1759 resulted in his death. But his last deed earned him immortality, at least in these parts. Wolfe defeated the French army, ending raids on New Hampshire and opening up this frontier to settlers.

The modern history of the Lakes region begins in 1769 with the road that the royal governor, John Wentworth, built from the Piscataqua River to Wolfeborough, now Wolfeboro (it took an act of Congress to drop the "ugh"), linking the seacoast with these beautiful environs. Governor Wentworth believed the road would open up a region vitally important to the future development of the state. Enamored of the area, he built a summer home on 4,000 acres of land along the shores of Lake Wentworth. Wentworth's "humble habitation" was a fine mansion with four drawing rooms, white and black marble fireplaces, and an elaborate deer park fenced in by trees.

Today Wolfeboro bills itself as the oldest summer resort in America, based on the fact that Wentworth built his summer home near Wolfeboro in 1771. Wentworth brought his patrician friends with him, and one wonders if the sedate quality of the west shore owes something to their legacy. But as if to tweak their British hauteur, another of Paul Revere's ubiquitous bells peals forth here.

LAKES
REGION

(above) The dock at Wolfeboro.

Watercraft entering Wolfeboro Bay on Lake Winnipesaukee.

Wolfeboro is among the classiest towns on the lake, with expansive green lawns that slope down to Wolfeboro Bay. Smart homes along Route 28 South flank the brick halls of the local institution of learning, Brewster Academy. People are friendly and polite, and they clearly enjoy their picturesque town.

Brewster Academy

Brewster is both a preparatory school and a model educational facility, with a fully networked campus and state-of-the-art video and multimedia laboratories. Educators from around the world study the Brewster Model, which is based on a flexible curriculum that allows students to develop at their own pace. A cordial relationship exists between town and gown, but it's not without humor.

"You can always tell a Brewster kid," says one local. "They never say 'I'm good,' as in 'I'm good 'n' you?' It's always, 'I'm well, thank you.'" But his tone is wry, not angry. Locals know that Brewster is better for Wolfeboro than anything you'd find across the lake. "And you always know when it's parents' weekend—all the limos line up at the ice-cream joint."

Clark House

Down the street from Brewster's main gate, across from Huggins Hospital, is the Clark House, the headquarters of the Wolfeboro Historical Society. This 1778 farmhouse is typical of the era, with one large "keeping room," which served as kitchen, living room, dining room, and bedroom, and a "borning room" for bringing babies into the world. The house has two notable attractions: scale models of Gov. John Wentworth's estate and of an ungainly horseboat that "trod" the lakes in the late 19th century. *Open in summer only. 233 South Main Street; 603-569-4997.*

Farm at Frost Corner

Virginia Taylor runs the Farm at Frost Corner, a restored early-19th-century working farm with historic buildings and animals of the era: a short-horn milking cow, dairy goats, sheep, chickens, geese, and rabbits. Aaron Frost, one of Wolfeboro's original settlers, started the farm in the 1760s. You can learn how folks cooked in the fireplace, made candles and soap, and spun sheep's wool. *Call ahead for directions and an appointment. 44 Stoddard Road; 603-569-1773.*

Canoeing and Kayaking

Whether by canoe, kayak, or horseboat, traveling on the water is the fastest way to get around these parts. One couple I know regularly boats across "the Broads" to **Love's Quay,** in Wolfeboro, in just 20 minutes, tying up at one of the two slips the restaurant makes available to diners.

If you drive past Love's Quay on Mill Street, then turn right on Bay Street, you'll come to the **Winnipesaukee Kayak Co.**, which from April to November rents boats and offers boating lessons and conducts tours of the region's lakes and rivers. *17 Bay Street; 603-569-9926.*

Fishing on the Lake

Another way onto the lake is with a reputable fishing guide. Curt Golder of Gadabout Golder Guide Service is all that and a box of bait. He's been fishing all over the United States for more than four decades and has been a New Hampshire certified guide since 1989. "The whole thing about being a guide on the lakes is that it's not about the fish," says this former service manager from Connecticut. "It's about memories. So many clients say it takes them back to what it was like to fish with their dads years ago. Some want to catch the big one, others want to drift, cast a little,

remember, and talk. Most of the time, though, we just shut up and fish."
79 Middleton Road; 603-569-6426.

Wright Museum of American Enterprise

If you take a turn north off Main Street onto Center Street (Route 109 departs from Route 28 here), you're on your way to Wolfeboro Falls. After you pass the post office, on your right you'll see something a little odd—a tank charging through the side of a brick building. The building houses the collections of David Wright, a veteran of the Korean War who restored World War II military vehicles. The museum also commemorates the social changes and sacrifices that occurred on the home front during World War II. The building closest to the street contains period rooms from that era: a living room, a kitchen, dentist's offices, and a soda fountain. The building in the rear houses Wright's remarkable military vehicles, including one of the few remaining Pershing heavy tanks. A third structure at this memorial to the "greatest generation" will contain rooms devoted to events of the years 1939 to 1945. *Open Feb.–Oct. 77 Center Street; 603-569-1212.*

New Hampshire Antique and Classic Boat Museum

The antique pleasure boats on display here include mahogany runabouts from the 1920s and '30s, such as a 1930 Garwood (only nine were made of this model), a Dee-Wite Lumber that cost $1,185 at the height of the Depression, and any number of Chris-Crafts. *Open Memorial Day–Columbus Day. 397 Center Street (Route 28, 2 miles north of intersection of Route 109 and Route 28); 603-569-4554.*

Libby Museum   *map page 165, E-3*

Dr. Henry Forrest Libby, a local dentist who was something of a Renaissance man, established this museum in 1912. Natural history exhibits include many local plant and animal species. Two other areas of emphasis are Abenaki artifacts and items from the estate of Gov. John Wentworth. *Open June–Sept. Route 109, three miles north of downtown Wolfeboro; 603-569-1035.*

Lake Wentworth   *map page 165, E-3*

East of Wolfeboro is a pretty little lake named for Governor Wentworth. From **Lake Wentworth State Beach** on the northeast shore, there's a stunning view across the lake through the tall pine trees. No wonder John Wentworth built his estate here. The

WORDS OF THE ABENAKIS

The early people of New Hampshire spoke a dialect of the Algonquian language, itself spoken by peoples as far south as the Carolinas and as far north as Canada. A few words can provide the key to the meanings of many New Hampshire place names.

ROOT WORDS

Algonquian	English
amos	fish
apee	lake
asquam	broad sheet of water, large lake
aukee	high place, hill, mountain
cook	quiet stretch of water
coos	pine tree
keag	place
kunnaway	bear
mag, mass	large, big, high
nashua	lovely river with pebbly floor
nipi	lake or pond
papoeis	child
penna	crooked
saco	flowing out, outlet
segu	river
sippee	river
suna	goose

PLACE NAMES

Algonquian	English
Amoskeag = Amos + Keag	Place of Many Fish
Ossippee = Coos + Sippee	River with Many Pines
Pennacook = Penna + Cook	Riverbend
Papisseconewa = Papoeis + Kunnaway	Child of the Bear

—Compiled from *New Hampshire: Crosscurrents in Its Development*, by Heffernan and Stecker, and *The History of Manchester*, by C. E. Potter

house is gone, but the location is a national historic site. *Take Route 28 east out of Wolfeboro, then Route 109 south; 603-569-3699.*

■ **ALTON BAY**   *map page 165, E-4*

At the south end of Lake Winnipesaukee is Alton Bay. In 1851, the Cocheco railroad turned this town into a transportation center with the completion of the line from Dover. Ice harvested on Winnipesaukee was shipped south from Alton Bay, and tourists were shipped north. The first *Mount Washington* was built here in 1872, and until the railroad was extended to Lakeport in 1890 it was a far more comfortable alternative to the stagecoach.

Many consider Alton Bay the most "New Hampshire" of the lake towns, an authentic alternative to Meredith's ersatz nostalgia, perhaps less classy than Wolfeboro yet full of local color. The best place to experience that is at the **Olde Bay Diner**, a little breakfast joint on Route 11, a few yards up the west shore from the center of town. Each of the booths has a navigation chart of the lake under its glass top, and the famous Boston & Maine tourist print of the lakes framed on the wall. For a great start to your day, sit over pancakes and sausage and ponder your next step on the map.

Touring ←🚗→ *To take in the scenery along Route 11, drive north from Alton Bay, not south from Weirs Beach, because the view is better in the lane closest to the lake. A turnout along Route 11 puts you at the top of it all, looking down on Little Mark Island, with its lone house and, off to the east, the majestic volcanic molar of the Ossipee range.*

For a fine hike in this area, take the **Mount Major** (1,130 feet) trail, a two-mile path climbing to the peak's spectacular views of the lake. You'll find the trailhead a few hundred yards down Route 11 from the turnout described above.

Ellacoya State Beach is a bit of a letdown if you've read the legend of Ellacoya before you get there. Ellacoya was the Juliet of the native world, who fell in love with her Romeo, a young brave named Kona, against her father Ahanton's wishes, then protected Kona from Ahanton's wrath. Sixty-five-acre Ellacoya is an RV park that offers row upon regimented row of hook-ups. There is a beach with a bathhouse and changing area; the park is open from mid-May to mid-October; *603-293-7821.*

A few miles north of Mount Major on Route 11 north from Alton Bay, Route 11A splits away from the shore, toward **Gunstock Mountain,** one of the finest family ski areas anywhere. Gunstock may not be as popular as areas farther north, like Waterville

Valley or Loon, but it's a friendly place in scale with its environment. The 50 or so trails range from easy to double diamond. Skiing fanatics may find Gunstock not sufficiently challenging, but for hassle-free skiing it's a good choice. *Route 11A, Gilford; 800-486-7862.*

■ **GILFORD** *map page 165, D-3*

Gilford is a hamlet south of Route 11A on Belknap Mountain Road. Past the tiny town center, with its 1800 homestead and historic store (in the Thompson-Ames building) are some fine old homes with well-kept flower gardens. The mountain you see at the end of the road is not Belknap but the "back" side of Gunstock (the ski area is on the "front" side). Gilford is the only New Hampshire town named after a Revolutionary War battle—Guilford Court House, 1781, in which the town's founder fought.

Gilford is best known for the **New Hampshire Music Festival** in July and August. *Performances are on Friday nights at the Gilford Middle School; reservations recommended; 603-524-1000.*

■ **NEWFOUND LAKE** *map page 165, A/B-2*

Newfound Lake is crowded with islands, peninsulas, and a wandering shoreline backed by thick woods. Two of the best views of this sparkling lake, the cleanest in the state, some say, can be found on the south shore at Cummings Beach, opposite the Bungalo Village and on the west shore at Wellington State Park.

The smell of spruce pitch and the sight of flowering columbine make **Wellington State Park** a fine setting for picnics and walks. The beautifully maintained park has a pavilion and a boat launch. *Route 3A off I-93 Exit 23 (left onto Route 104W, then north on 3A), Bristol.*

Opposite Route 3A from the entrance to Wellington is the trail to **Mount Cardigan,** a 3,121-footer 12 miles to the west. To see another fascinating geological feature, follow Route 3A north along the mountainous west shore. South of the town of Nutting, a huge granite bluff comes up to the water's edge, with the merest lip of a ledge for the road at its base, built over fallen boulders.

S U N A P E E
& THE UPPER VALLEY

■ **Highlights**   *page*

The Fells and Hay National Wildlife Refuge 193
Sunapee Crafts Fair   196
Ruggles Mine   199
Dartmouth College   201
Saint-Gaudens National Historic Site   208
The Fort at # 4   215

Map page 195

Hanover
Lebanon

■ **Area Overview**

The Connecticut, New England's longest river, begins at the Connecticut Lakes, at the very tip of New Hampshire. Nearly two-thirds of its 410 miles are in the state, and its watershed takes in 33 percent of New Hampshire's area. The river was once the northwestern frontier from which military expeditions were launched during the French and Indian and Revolutionary Wars. Under threatening skies, scenes along its low flood plain bring to mind Rembrandt riverscapes like *The Mill.*

The upper Connecticut River Valley has always harbored rebelliously creative types, from seditious pamphleteers operating out of Dartmouth College to the mischievous painter Maxfield Parrish to the reclusive author J.D. Salinger. A pocket of undervisited tranquillity, the area is rich with diversions. You'll find a restored colonial fort, creaking covered bridges, kayak and canoe runs, stellar inns, a national wildlife refuge, Dartmouth College, and New Hampshire's only national park. In the region's center is big, blue Lake Sunapee, with skiing, lake cruises, the stunning gardens of an old estate, and nearby, the college town of New London.

Weather: Summer temperatures average 68 degrees F and can go as high as 101. Winters are snowy with average temperatures of 18 degrees and extremes to -37. Autumn colors peak in mid to late September.

■ CONNECTICUT RIVER VALLEY

The Connecticut River Valley was the site of New Hampshire's second great border rebellion, the first being with Massachusetts over the southern border. More than half of what is now Vermont had been granted to favorites of Benning Wentworth. Between 1760 and 1764 alone, his New Hampshire Grants encompassed 3 million acres, including most of the west valley and the flat fertile land east of Lake Champlain.

Most people who lived in the area had moved up from Massachusetts and Connecticut, buying land from the grantees. The local governments they established were more democratic than those on the royalist coast. Out on their remote western frontier, the locals felt greater solidarity with the people of the Green Mountains (with whom they shared defense and agricultural concerns) and with folks downstream in Connecticut (with whom they traded) than with the aristocratic lace-ruffle set on the seacoast.

The Connecticut River forms a natural border between Vermont and New Hampshire.

A View Along the Connecticut River *(1850), by Nicolino Calyo, shows the river from the New Hampshire side. (Shelburne Museum, Shelburne Falls, Vermont)*

By 1779, the north country's fiery patriot Ethan Allen was maneuvering to carve a "Green Mountain State" out of the disputed lands between New York and New Hampshire. Emboldened by pamphlets from Dartmouth College, which declared the area to be in a "state of nature," the residents of 16 towns declared themselves part of the as yet hypothetical state of Vermont, which was not established until 1791.

The secession was quashed by a strongly worded but discreet letter from George Washington in 1781. "There is no calamity within my foresight, which is more to be dreaded than a necessity of coercion," he wrote. His threat worked. Both the Green Mountain Boys and the New Hampshire state government hastily agreed that perhaps nature's boundary—the Connecticut River—was good enough for man. The 16 towns on the eastern bank rejoined the Granite State.

Steamboats once plied this boundary river, though most of them did so south of the massive falls in northern Massachusetts. In 1793, Samuel Morey of Orford launched a prototype for the steamboat on the upper Connecticut. The *Aunt Sally* was a log dugout with a steam-powered paddlewheel at the prow. According to Morey, Robert Fulton, who is credited with inventing the steamboat, swiped his plans. Fulton's *Clermont* sailed the Hudson 14 years later.

Touring ←🚗→ *Almost halfway to Lebanon (and Vermont) up Route 89 is Lake Sunapee, a miniature Lake Winnipesaukee, with the same meandering shoreline, ski mountain, and chuffing tour boats. But Sunapee has fewer people, less development, and a scenic circuit you can easily traverse in a day or less. Take Exit 12 to Route 11, then Route 103A south. You'll pass through little towns like Lakeside (Sunapee's Merrick Cove lies to your right) and Hastings. Farther south is the Fells State Historic Site, where the estate of statesman John Hay (open to the public) overlooks the lake. A trail in the National Wildlife Refuge winds through the forest. At the southern tip of Sunapee is the cottage-resort town of Newbury.*

■ THE FELLS AND HAY NATIONAL WILDLIFE REFUGE
map page 195, C-5

In 1883, the author and statesman John Milton Hay built a large country cottage on the eastern shore of Lake Sunapee in Newbury. Over the next three generations, the family transformed this 1,000-acre rocky upland overlooking the lake into a beautiful natural showcase, **The Fells,** the British term for a rocky upland pasture. Today, it's a historic estate and neighbor to a wildlife refuge.

Sunapee and the upper valley contain several such refuges, originally created by the wealthy and influential as country getaways. Hay, who had been secretary of state, ambassador to Great Britain, and Abraham Lincoln's personal secretary, intended to colonize the Fells with "the Five of Hearts," a charmed circle of influential friends that included Clarence King, a geologist and the founder of the U.S. Geological Survey; the writer and historian Henry Adams; and Adams's artist-photographer wife, Clover. Unlike Aspet, the artists colony of Augustus Saint-Gaudens, this one did not take. King could not afford to move to Sunapee. Clover Adams committed suicide (Saint-Gaudens created the haunting Adams Memorial figure for her tomb). John Hay died at the Fells in 1905.

In 1987, after the last of the Hays died, the Fells became a public-private conservation partnership, serving as a model for similar arrangements. The Garden Conservancy, the U.S. Fish and Wildlife Service, the State of New Hampshire, the

Lake Sunapee Protective Association, the Society for the Protection of New Hampshire Forests, and local volunteers work together to ensure the preservation of the house and its surrounding landscape. The 1890 Victorian is open for viewing.

The Fells is a horticulturist's dream. Beyond the 1930s gatehouse (now the visitors center) are gardens full of perennials—the rock garden alone has more than 600 species of rock-garden and alpine plants, including rhododendrons, azaleas, and a magnificent Chinese dogwood. The maple at the end of the stone wall was planted by Theodore Roosevelt in 1902. You can even buy a perennial or shrub for your garden at home.

Across the street is the **Hay National Wildlife Refuge,** full of plants and animals native to these fields, wetlands, and woods. Red and gray porcupines live here, as do coyote, deer, weasels, and, occasionally, otter and mink. Moose and bear make infrequent showings. Seventy-six species of birds nest in the refuge: thrushes, tanagers, vireos, as well as broadwing hawks, barred owls, and goshawks.

The wonderful hikes include a mile-long trail through the forest along the shore of Lake Sunapee that returns through Beech Brook to the Grassy Road. Paths cross beneath striped maples, shadbush, hobblebush, and tupelo, and past native ferns, mosses, and wildflowers. The popular Sunset Hill and Beech Brook Trails lead to the top of Sunset Hill, which overlooks Lake Sunapee and has views of Mount Sunapee to the west. *The Fells and Hay National Wildlife Refuge are off Route 103A, about 2.5 miles north of Newbury. No pets; 603-763-4789.*

Touring ←🚗→ *Turn right on Route 103 and head up the lake's western shore. Gingerbread cottages abound. Wind your way on this pleasant drive, through the town of Edgemont to a little traffic circle. Three roads diverge here: south to the ski hill and state park, west (Route 103) to Newport, and north (Route 103B) to the town of Sunapee.*

■ **MOUNT SUNAPEE** *map page 195, C-5*

A popular fall attraction in the Sunapee region is the **Skyride at the Mount Sunapee Ski Area.** Ride the ski lift for a breathtaking view of the autumn colors. With southern New Hampshire's longest vertical drop (1,510 feet), Mount Sunapee has nearly 60 trails. The emphasis here is on fun, not fashion.

Summer can be as much fun as winter. The **Summit Trail,** located at the base of the Ridge Trail, is a pleasant 2-mile hike through the woods. The trail follows the Ridge

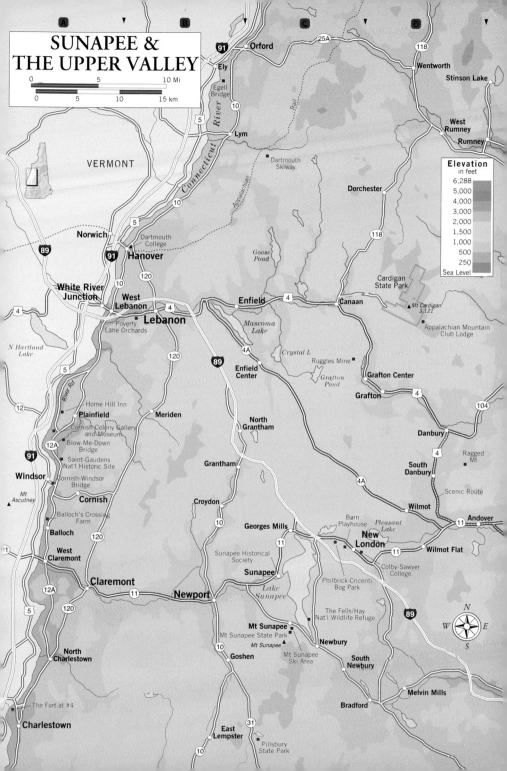

SUNAPEE &
THE UPPER VALLEY

Elevation
in feet

6,288	
5,000	
4,000	
3,000	
2,000	
1,500	
1,000	
500	
250	
Sea Level	

A · B · C · D

Orford
Ely
Egell Bridge
Lym
25A
Wentworth
Stinson Lake
West Rumney
Rumney

VERMONT

Dartmouth Skiway
Dorchester

Norwich
Dartmouth College
Hanover
Goose Pond
118
Cardigan State Park

White River Junction
West Lebanon
Lebanon
Poverty Lane Orchards
Enfield
Canaan
Mt Cardigan 3,121
Appalachian Mountain Club Lodge

Mascoma Lake
N Hartland Lake
Crystal L
Ruggles Mine
Grafton Center

Enfield Center
Grafton Pond
Grafton

River Rd
Home Hill Inn
Plainfield
Meriden
North Grantham
Danbury
Ragged Mt

Cornish Colony Gallery and Museum
Blow-Me-Down Bridge
Saint-Gaudens Nat'l Historic Site
Grantham
South Danbury
Scenic Route

Windsor
Cornish-Windsor Bridge
Mt Ascutney
Cornish
Croydon
Wilmot
Andover

Balloch's Crossing Farm
Georges Mills
Barn Playhouse
Pleasant Lake
New London
Wilmot Flat

Balloch
Sunapee Historical Society
Sunapee
Colby-Sawyer College

West Claremont
Claremont
Newport
Lake Sunapee
Philbrick-Cricenti Bog Park

North Charlestown
Mt Sunapee
Mt Sunapee State Park
Mt Sunapee
Mt Sunapee Ski Area
The Fells/Hay Nat'l Wildlife Refuge
Newbury
South Newbury

The Fort at #4
Goshen
Melvin Mills

Charlestown
East Lempster
Pillsbury State Park
Bradford

N
W · E
S

Trail to the summit and brings you to the back side of the Summit Lodge. From the summit, either hike down the mountain or follow the Andrew Brook Trail (off Mountain Road) to Lake Solitude, on the back side of Mount Sunapee. *Route 103, Newbury; 603-763-2356 or 603-763-4020.*

Sunapee Crafts Fair, the oldest such fair in the United States, was first held in Crawford Notch in 1934. The Mount Sunapee Ski Area now hosts the event. All the participants are members of the peer-reviewed League of New Hampshire Craftsmen. Wandering in and out of the tents, you can watch the highly skilled blacksmiths, painters, jewelers, and other artists and artisans practice their craft. Fine jewelry, wood accessories, decorative glass, pottery, fiber arts, metalwork, and furniture are on display.

All the while, musicians, storytellers, and actors from all over New England will keep you entertained. The fair begins on the first Saturday in August and lasts for nine days. *Mount Sunapee Ski Area, Route 103, Newbury; 603-763-2356.*

A blanket of fog obscures the sunrise in the hills surrounding Mount Sunapee.

SUNAPEE &
THE UPPER VALLEY

THE LEAGUE OF NEW HAMPSHIRE CRAFTSMEN

The League of New Hampshire Craftsmen was founded during the Depression thanks to the efforts of Mrs. J. Randolph Coolidge of Center Sandwich and A. Cooper Balentine of Wolfeboro, who sought "to encourage, nurture and promote the creation, use and preservation of fine craft through the inspiration and education of artists and the broader community." But it took the visionary Gov. John Winant to fund the League of Arts and Crafts in 1931, making New Hampshire the first state to recognize the value and, indeed, existence of the crafts industry. Today, six league galleries display the works of craftspeople recognized by their peers for their accomplishments.

GALLERY LOCATIONS:

Concord   *map page 114, B-2*
36 North Main Street; 603-228-8171

Hanover   *map page 195, B-2*
13 Lebanon Street; 603-643-5050

Meredith   *map page 165, C-3*
279 D.W. Highway; 603-279-7920

North Conway   *map page 231, F-2*
2526 White Mountain Highway;
603-356-2441

Center Sandwich   *map page 165, D-4*
Main Street; 603-284-6831

Wolfeboro   *map page 165, E-3*
64 Center Street; 603-224-3375

■ **LAKE SUNAPEE** *map page 195, C-5*

The most convenient way to get out on the lake is from the little harbor of Sunapee on the western shore. Sunapee is a charming town whose economy is based on tourism. Turn east off Route 11 to find the harbor. Stop in at the **Anchorage** for lunch at a table overlooking the harbor, where cruise boats come and go.

You can set sail with Captain Bob Henry on the MV *Mount Sunapee* (a two-decker that holds about 120) or enjoy dinner on the MV *Mount Kearsarge*. The same outfit, Sunapee Cruises, also rents canoes and kayaks; *603-763-4043*.

To learn more about the region, visit the **Sunapee Historical Society,** whose artifacts include a restored pilot house, a horseless carriage, and a fire pumper. *74 Main Street, on Sunapee Harbor.*

Touring ←🚐→ *Directly across Route 89 from Lake Sunapee to the east is the New London area. Take Exit 12 east to Newport Road. You'll pass Little Sunapee Lake on your left, the spooky Philbrick-Cricenti Bog Park on your right, the Barn Playhouse, and the little college town of New London.*

■ NEW LONDON AREA *map page 195, C/D-5*

Bogs are peculiar places. They're formed when a pool of water grows a thick layer of vegetation. If the water is deep enough, and the mat of tundra plants (so called because like the tundra, a bog is nutrient-poor) is thick enough, you get a "quaking bog"—one that wobbles when you walk on it. **Philbrick-Cricenti Bog Park** has a fine quaking bog, and a lot of mosquitoes—it is stagnant water, after all. It's also a wonderfully spooky place, with its little boardwalk through the murky lowland. Don't expect Atlantic City: this walk consists of two boards that sometimes get a little submerged. Traffic noise from Newport Road mars the effect somewhat. *East a half-mile off Route 89, Exit 12. No sign, just a wider shoulder on the right.*

Boats on Sunapee waterfront.

The sun sets behind Burkehaven Lighthouse on Lake Sunapee.

The **New London Barn Playhouse,** like Barnstormers in Tamworth, claims to be the oldest summer theater in America, with talented hopefuls and seasoned veterans putting on a mix of Broadway favorites. If you're not looking for Eugene O'Neill or Tom Stoppard, you won't be disappointed by show-stopping musicals like *South Pacific, Ain't Misbehavin',* and *The Man of La Mancha.* The performers shake the rafters of this circa-1820 converted barn. *Mid-June–early-Sept. 209 Main Street, at Newport Road; 603-526-4631 or 603-526-6710.*

■ RUGGLES MINE *map page 195, C-3*

What kind of book has no pages? You'll find out at the Ruggles Mine in **Grafton.** Commercial mining of huge "books" of mica, a fire-resistant, transparent mineral, began here in 1803. This was the first producer of isinglass (the transparent sheets used in stove windows) in the United States. Pit A is a canyon with white quartz and feldspar. Ruggles is an open-pit mine, but there are many interior caves and caverns to add visual interest. It's also on Isinglass Mountain, hence the tag "the mine in the sky." Rock hounds will be pleased to know that mineral collecting is permitted. More than 150 minerals can be found here, including beryl, amethyst, gummite, autunite, rose quartz, and garnet. Sam Ruggles owned the land and at first hauled his valuable minerals to Portsmouth by ox team, shipping them to relatives in England to keep the secret of his mine. Finally, Ruggles hired a mine boss, "a ferocious driving man who directed the operations with abundant profanity." *Open mid-May–mid-Oct. Grafton village green off Route 4; 603-523-4275.*

■ ENFIELD SHAKER VILLAGE   *map page 195, B-3*

In 1793, a year after the Canterbury Shaker Village was formed, Shakers came to the shore of Lake Mascoma in Enfield. In keeping with the sect's belief in the equality of the sexes, two elders and two eldresses governed each of the communities. Residents of Canterbury and Enfield often visited each other, and the boys of the two communities would meet for picnics in Andover, halfway between the two towns. Between 1837 and 1841, the **Great Stone Dwelling** was built. A hundred feet long, 58 feet wide, and 100 feet tall, the white granite structure was the largest the Shakers ever constructed.

At Enfield's peak, its farms covered more than 3,000 acres. The community disbanded in the early 1920s for lack of new members, but the **Enfield Shaker Museum** preserves this vital piece of state history. The Great Stone Dwelling is now an inn. On the grounds are 12 other buildings, some with exhibits of furniture, tools, clothing, and historical photographs. Also here are the Shaker Gardens, and nearby is the Shaker Sacred Feast Ground, part of a state-owned 2,500-acre nature preserve. *Open Memorial Day–Oct. and winter weekends. 24 Caleb Dyer Lane; 603-632-4346.*

The 24 airy rooms of the **Shaker Inn at the Great Stone Dwelling** have been updated with private baths and exquisite reproduction Shaker furniture, but some original detailing remains. The restaurant serves Shaker-inspired fare including pan-seared Atlantic salmon and roasted duckling. *447 Route 4A; 888-707-4257 or 603-632-7810.*

If you are in the area come apple-harvest time, from Labor Day weekend into early October, you can pick your own at **Poverty Lane Orchards,** in Lebanon. Traditional varieties include McIntosh, Cortland, and Macoun, and there are some mouth-puckering varieties grown especially for the company's Farnum Hill Ciders. *98 Poverty Lane (Exit 19 off I-89); 603-448-1511.*

■ HANOVER AND DARTMOUTH COLLEGE *map page 195, B-2*

The best way into Hanover is to take Route 120 (Exit 18 off Route 89) north. This town has drawn the high-minded and erudite since Eleazar Wheelock first established Dartmouth College as the "voice in the wilderness." It was the ninth college created in the United States and the last to be supported by a grant from the king of England. Hanover is no longer a wilderness. Everyone seems to have business around the historic green, even hikers (the Appalachian Trail passes by it). The buildings of the Baker and Berry Libraries face south, directly across from the Hanover Inn.

The inscription on the gravestone of Dartmouth's founder, Eleazar Wheelock reads:

By the Gospel he subdued the ferocity of the savage,

And to the civilized he opened new paths of Science.

Traveler, go if you can and deserve the sublime reward of such merit.

Dartmouth's campus at the dawn of the 21st century. (Robert Holmes)

If the founder of the college was high-minded, its students have enjoyed singing a less than reverent ditty about him written in the 1890s by the poet Richard Hovey.

> Eleazar Wheelock was a very pious man.
> He went into the wilderness to teach the Indian,
> With a gradus ad parnassum, a bible and a drum,
> And five hundred gallons of New England rum.

A gradus ad parnassum (literally a step to Parnassus) was a guide to Latin poetry, and it was only a barrel of rum (about 31 gallons) that Wheeler's wife brought north by wagon. But in 1769 Gov. John Wentworth granted a charter to Eleazar Wheelock for Dartmouth College, as a religious school "for the education and instruction of Youth of the Indian Tribes in this Land...and also of English Youth and any others."

Eleazar Wheelock may indeed have cared about the souls of savages; he had founded a "charity school" in Connecticut to educate native clergymen. But his holy mission to the Native Americans served mostly as a convenient justification for founding Dartmouth. When his English benefactors stipulated that their money

be used solely for educating the local natives, Wheelock craftily established his charity school as a separate institution, leaving his beloved Dartmouth College free to pursue its own potential.

In years to come, the college educated

Dartmouth alumnus Joseph Steward received a commission in 1793 to paint this portrait of the college's founder, Eleazar Wheelock. (Hood Museum of Art, Dartmouth College, Hanover)

famous alumnae such as Daniel Webster, Theodor "Dr. Seuss" Geisel, Vice-President Nelson Rockefeller, former U.S. Surgeon General C. Everett Koop, and the writer Louise Erdrich. Robert Frost dropped out after one term but returned to teach.

Dartmouth became caught in a political struggle between Federalists and Republicans in 1815, when Gov. William Plumer attempted to turn the college into a state-run university. Orford shopkeeper John Wheeler put up the first thousand dollars to cover legal fees to defend Dartmouth against the State of New Hampshire in 1816. Daniel Webster and two other attorneys took the case to the Supreme Court, where Webster's grandiloquence won the day.

An ice sculpture, The Starshooter, *at Dartmouth Winter Carnival, circa 1940. (Dartmouth College Library)*

Dartmouth Winter Carnival

In early February, Dartmouth College holds its Winter Carnival. The oldest collegiate winter festival, it's a way for north-country spirits to overcome the February blahs. This celebration of the great white outdoors includes ski races, a children's carnival, and snow- and ice-sculpting contests. *603-646-3399.*

Hopkins Center for the Performing Arts

On the south side of the green is the performing arts center, designed by Wallace K. Harrison, who also designed the United Nations headquarters and Lincoln Center in New York City. The term "center" truly applies here, as "the Hop" houses art studios, three stages, the Paddock Music Library, recital halls and practice rooms, workshop facilities, and the Hop café. More than 500 music, drama, dance, and speaking events take place each year, as well as fine-arts exhibits. *On the green; 603-646-2422.*

Hood Museum of Art

This generously endowed art museum has Ancient, African, American, European, and Indian collections notable for their scope and depth. The specialties include Assyrian reliefs, Roman mosaics, Hudson River School paintings, and primitive art from Papua New Guinea. An entire suite is devoted to Picasso's Vollard etchings. *On the green, next to the Hopkins Center; 603-646-2808.*

Touring ←🚗→ *A short drive west on Route 89 to Exit 20 points you south on Route 12A along the Connecticut River (if you go a little farther on Route 89 you will end up at the spectacular Quechee Gorge, in Vermont). North on Route 10 out of Hanover to Orford is another scenic drive along the river.*

■ ORFORD   *map page 195, B/C-1*

Washington Irving described Orford as the most attractive little town he'd ever seen. The row of close-set Federal houses on Ridge Street was not designed by the great Charles Bulfinch, as legend has it, but by skilled local artisans who were inspired by plans from a design book published by Bulfinch's student, Archer Benjamin. The itinerant painter Rufus Porter (see also the Hancock Inn in the Monadnock, page 139) created murals in one of the Ridge Houses in 1824.

Touring ←🚗→ *The magical drive south on Route 12A from West Lebanon to Walpole winds through a charmed landscape, past Cornish, where many artists lived and worked. Farther south are the vestiges of a settlement along the Connecticut River from the mid-1700s.*

■ PLAINFIELD   *map page 195, A-4*

As you pass through the little town of Plainfield, about 8 miles south of Route 89, watch for the **town hall** on your left. If it's open, you'll enjoy the rare treat of viewing an entire stage set by painter Maxfield Parrish—a backdrop, six wings, and three overhead drapes—depicting Mount Ascutney and environs. Parrish used casein on linen that was woven at Nashua's Indian Head Mill. The original lighting, which mimics daybreak, sunset, and any gradation in between, still operates. Every Columbus Day weekend there's a sale of vintage Parrish prints at town hall, which is on the

SUNAPEE & THE UPPER VALLEY

THE APPALACHIAN TRAIL: TAKING A REST IN HANOVER

Refer to map page 195, A2-C1

The Appalachian Trail—the AT for short—runs along the Appalachian Range from Springer Mountain in Georgia to Mount Katahdin in Maine. New Hampshire's stretch of this 2,100-mile trail offers some of the most exposed and difficult terrain of the entire journey. It's a mighty endeavor to hike the whole thing (Earl Shaffer was the first to do it, in 1948) and requires planning, stamina, and the will to keep pushing—through brambles, bad weather, and exhaustion. Since the AT became a federally protected footpath in 1968, more than 2000 hikers have completed the trip on the knife-edge of Katahdin.

In New Hampshire, the AT begins at the Ledyard Bridge, passing through downtown Hanover. For many hikers this is a golden opportunity to shake off the trail dust for a bit of fun, which is why so many of them call the town "Hangover." The Dartmouth Outing Club maintains the trail for 50 miles in New Hampshire. Just past the area of Mount Moosilauke, the Appalachian Mountain Club takes up the task. From there, the AT passes through the three notches of the White Mountains, climbing Franconia Ridge, both the southern and northern Presidentials, and the Wildcat Ridge. After crossing the Androscoggin River east of Gorham, the trail passes through the Leadmine State Forest, curves to the east, and leaves New Hampshire just past Mount Success.

National Register of Historic Places and the National List of Historic Theater Buildings. *Route 12; 603-675-6866.*

At the Plainfield Grange Hall is the restored mural **Women of Plymouth,** painted by Lucia Fairchild Fuller, a member of the Cornish art community, and commissioned for the Women's Building in the 1893 Columbian Exposition at the Chicago World's Fair.

◆ HOME HILL INN

The Home Hill Inn is more than just another inn. It's a stellar restaurant, a boutique of scents and soaps, a horse farm, a collection of exceptional paintings in a beautifully restored 1818 home, and a bit of Provence in Plainfield. Dinners are inspired by Stephane du Roure's French origins and reinterpreted by his wife Victoria, who

Hunt Farm *(circa 1948), by Maxfield Parrish. The artist joined the Cornish Colony in 1898 and lived and painted in the area until his death in 1966. (Hood Museum of Art, Dartmouth College, Hanover)*

trained at the Ecole Ritz-Escoffier in Paris, to take advantage of New England produce. Still, many ingredients are flown in daily from France. Staying in one of the
inn's four rooms (there are two more each in the carriage house and the pool house)
is sheer luxury. They're decorated with French fabrics, the bedding is sprinkled with
lavender water, and guests experience it all without television or telephone. They pay
a great sum, but it's worth it.

Paintings by Stephen Parrish, Maxfield's father, enliven the walls of one of three
elegant dining rooms. The brushwork of Parrish the elder manifests the full visual
vocabulary of a master. The surface of one painting, a winter scene, bulges with
thick gobs of white paint, as though applied by knife, or nature. A harvest scene's delicately scraped verticals mimic hay left behind by the scythe. *River Road, 3.5 miles
south on Route 12A from I-89, Exit 20, Plainfield; 603-675-6165.*

◆ MAXFIELD PARRISH AND THE OAKS

During the golden age of American illustration, when giants like N.C. Wyeth and
Maxfield Parrish created astonishing images of fairy-tale worlds for magazines, cal-
endars, and department stores, crowds would gather to see the unveiling of a new work.
Mothers would frame Parrish's calendar prints for the parlor. His *Daybreak*, depicting two lolling women on a mock-classical veranda with a fantastic mountainscape
in the background, is perhaps the best-selling print of all time. In many of his
intensely luminous paintings, crafted by applying multiple monochromatic layers of
thin oils over stretched paper, you can see mighty, gnarled trees. They were inspired
by the oaks that surrounded his estate, the Oaks, in Plainfield. He lived at the Oaks
most of his life with his wife and a mistress/model. (How this unconventional house-
hold got on is not a matter of public record.) Parrish built most of the buildings at
the Oaks by himself, aided by a local carpenter. The estate, whose original buildings
were destroyed by fire long ago, is not open to the public.

◆ CORNISH COLONY GALLERY AND MUSEUM *map page 195, A-4*

Inside a large yellow building on a beautiful property called Mastlands, the museum
is said to have the largest exhibit of Parrish's works in the country. Depending on the
day or time you can have tea or brunch in the garden, *Open Memorial Day–Oct. Route
12A; 603-675-6000.*

◆ **BLOW-ME-DOWN COVERED BRIDGE** *map page 195, A-4*

If you're fond of covered bridges, Blow-Me-Down is worth a peek. You cannot drive over it, but walk you can, and must. The instant you open your car door at the end of this dirt road, you're greeted by the unmistakable roaring sound of an invisible cataract. You must peer around the edges of the bridge or, better yet, peep through a gap in the boards to see the rushing torrent of Blow-Me-Down Brook. James F. Tasker, an imposing man of few words, built this bridge and many others in the area.

Locals refer to "Blow-Me-Down" so often you'd think they would know where the term came from. The only explanation I've heard is that it came from the Nova Scotia loggers who once worked these forests. They hailed from Mount Blomidon, and Yankee tongues twisted the word. But that's a stretch that even James Tasker would not have been able to bridge. *South of Plainfield on Route 12A, left on Lang Road (watch for the bridge marker).*

Less than a half-mile south of Blow-Me-Down Bridge Road is a right turn onto Ferry Hill Road (if you get to the Winston Churchill historical marker you've gone too far). This road, which becomes a dirt road after a bit, will take you back in time and across the Atlantic to that little bit of Provence in Plainfield, New Hampshire, the Home Hill Inn (see page 205).

Touring ←🚗→ *On Route 12A, a few miles south of Plainfield, watch for the little gristmill, probably the only one the architect Stanford White ever designed. It was paid for by Charles Beaman (of Blow-Me-Down Farm), who convinced Augustus Saint-Gaudens to move to Cornish. Opposite the mill, below road grade, is a stone arch built by Jabez Hammond, who also built the mill. Just past the mill to the left, Saint-Gaudens Road climbs through a shaded pine grove to the Saint-Gaudens National Historic Site.*

■ **SAINT-GAUDENS NATIONAL HISTORIC SITE**
map page 195, A-4

A celebration of the life and work of one of America's finest sculptors, Augustus Saint-Gaudens (1848–1907), the 150-acre Saint-Gaudens National Historic Site includes his home, gardens, and studios.

The best-known Saint-Gaudens piece may be the Shaw Memorial on Boston Common, which commemorates the courage of Col. Robert Gould Shaw, a young white Bostonian lieutenant, and his black troops, who died fighting for the Union during the Civil War. The ranks of the 54th regiment are depicted in bas-relief, marching determinedly, their thrusting legs and angled rifles forming a resolute vector into the future. The regiment's stoic features are in calm contrast to those of Shaw's frightened steed. The men seem to know exactly where they are going, and to be resigned to the fact that they will not be coming back.

After placing the sculpture in Boston, Saint-Gaudens continued to work on details that displeased him. The final version, which the artist considered superior to the Boston installation, can be found in a quiet setting on the way to the New Gallery. The revised memorial is one of many examples at the site of the visual genius of Saint-Gaudens, who lived in Cornish from 1885 until his death.

Born in Ireland and brought to the United States in 1848 during the potato famine, he was apprenticed to a cameo cutter at the age of 14. This training gave him an eye for detail and the skill to realize it. He created works of remarkable natural grace, sculpting the likenesses of major political and cultural figures of the late 19th century, many of whom he counted among his closest friends. He had four major works on exhibit at the Exposition Universelle in Paris, was awarded the Grand Prix, and made an officer of the Legion of Honor, a remarkable achievement for a foreigner. President Theodore Roosevelt asked him to design a $20 gold piece that many collectors consider the most beautiful coin ever minted in this country. Other works include major public commissions such as the "Standing Lincoln" in Chicago and the memorials to the Civil War heroes Admiral David G. Farragut and General William Tecumseh Sherman in New York City. Augustus married Augusta Homer, a distant relative of the painter Winslow Homer, and for the rest of their lives they were "Gus" and "Gussie" to each other.

Aspet, the artist's Cornish estate, is the embodiment of the man and a living testament to his life. Sitting on the lawn in the shade of the double row of white birches on a Sunday afternoon, with a picnic lunch and a bottle of wine, listening to the music of a string quartet or

The $20 gold piece designed by Augustus Saint-Gaudens.

Augustus Saint-Gaudens standing in front of a draft for a version of the Amor Caritas, *1898, Paris, France. (U.S. Department of the Interior, National Park Service)*

piano soloist waft across the lawn, you'll half expect the gregarious sculptor to bound around the hedge of his studio, greet you, and humorously apologize for his long absence. Two hiking trails explore the park's natural areas, and full-scale copies of Saint-Gaudens's work are on display in two studios and in gardens on the grounds.

The Saint-Gaudens National Historic Site does an excellent job of re-creating the artist's life. In the **New Gallery**, you enter a room to see *The Puritan* bearing down on you, his square-booted toes crushing a tiny pine tree, thick fingers clutching a bible and a cane, powerfully evoking both good and evil. Also on exhibit are copies of the Farragut statue and seated and standing Lincolns, many bas-reliefs, and caricatures Saint-Gaudens did of himself and friends like Mark Twain and Robert Louis Stevenson. So many in-progress models accompany the finished pieces that, again, you may feel as though the famous man is still at work.

Inside the **Little Studio** is a scale model of his famous and scandalous *Diana* bending her bow (mothers used to hide their children's faces from this nude) as well as a superb bust of General Sherman that captures every line and wrinkle in his haunted face. The Little Studio is where Saint-Gaudens, ill with cancer and carried there every morning by his assistant, sculpted his last standing relief. He hid a few affectionate private jokes in the piece. Gussie is wearing a "heart on her sleeve" and the park rangers say the sculptor's face is hidden in the shaggy mane of their sheep dog. I couldn't find it, but I found his spirit everywhere. *Buildings and exhibits open Memorial Day–Oct.; grounds year-round. Off Route 12A, Cornish; 603-675-2175.*

◆ **CORNISH-WINDSOR COVERED BRIDGE** *map page 195, A-4*

Your car wheels will make a feathery sound on the thick wooden floorboards of the Cornish-Windsor Bridge as you pass under its canopy. There has been a bridge here since 1796. The original one and two more (built in 1824 and 1849) washed away. James Tasker built the present span in 1866. At 450.5 feet it is the longest covered wooden bridge in the United States.

Tasker, a big man with a bushy beard and a strongman's build, was an intuitive bridge engineer who substituted 6-by-8-foot timbers for planks in the lattice truss, which he framed up in a nearby Windsor meadow. The bridge remains essentially as he built it in 1866, still carries traffic, and in 1970 was designated a National Historic Civil Engineering Landmark by the American Society of Civil Engineers.

The Windsor-Cornish covered bridge is the longest covered wooden bridge in the nation.

◆ BALLOCH'S CROSSING *map page 195, A-4*

Mount Ascutney looms across the wide Connecticut River from the spot that Scotsman William Balloch picked, circa 1770, for his farm, where he distilled Scotch whiskey and daydreamed about his home across the sea. His heirs allowed the Boston & Maine Railroad to cross the river at Balloch's Crossing and, later, to install a little depot in which farmers stashed their cows' output for the daily milk run. Today, the farm's owners, the Hammond family, breed that most rare of draft horses, the Suffolk Punch. The family also runs a canoe livery. They'll put you in the water north of the covered Windsor-Cornish Bridge, which John Hammond's great-grandfather helped build. You can paddle leisurely back downstream, stopping on Chase Island for a picnic lunch. *Three miles south of Windsor-Cornish Bridge; 603-542-5802.*

Horse-pulling competition at the Cornish Fair.

■ **CLAREMONT** *map page 195, A-5*

Claremont is a poor little town that started a revolution in the state of New Hampshire. The north end is full of boarded-up or underutilized buildings, but on the south side of town along Route 12/11 are beautiful old Victorian mansions set well away from the road at the top of a long sloping lawn.

Claremont is the only town in New Hampshire with commuter rail service (Amtrak stops once a day), but that's not what makes this place unique, and uniquely powerful. Claremont brought a lawsuit against the state concerning the way it funds education, by property tax. A number of New Hampshire's poorer towns, Claremont foremost among them, claimed that this condemned children from property-poor towns to substandard education. To everyone's surprise, the Supreme Court of the State of New Hampshire upheld the decision in favor of the plaintiffs. In a state where "the pledge" not to institute an income tax is all but sacrosanct, the Claremont lawsuit has caused all sorts of legislative gymnastics. Taxes on gambling, electricity, liquor, and (albeit with great trepidation) income, have all been proposed and discarded.

The Fort at #4 is a replica of a 1744 stockaded settlement.

SUNAPEE &
THE UPPER VALLEY

Touring ←🚗→ *Continue south on Route12A past Claremont and make a right onto Route 11 to get to the Fort at #4, which figured in the French and Indian and Revolutionary Wars. Farther south on Route 12 is Walpole, notable for its beautiful green surrounded by white houses and for its famous son, the documentarian Ken Burns.*

■ THE FORT AT #4 *map page 195, A-6*

At one time this stockaded village was among the most strategically important spots in colonial America. The Fort at #4, named after Massachusetts Grant Township #4, was the supply link to Fort Ticonderoga and Fort Crown Point, at the southern tip of Lake Champlain. Lord Jeffrey Amherst's campaigns to defeat the French depended upon this crude but well-fortified village, attacked in 1747 by an enemy force that was sent away limping.

The first thing you notice outside the timber palisade is the three-dimensional relief map. Six feet tall and three feet wide, it provides a wonderfully tactile way to get to know the topography of New Hampshire and surrounding areas. It was funded by Emma A. Hunt, who taught science at Framingham State College, from which she earned an honorary doctorate at the age of 99 (she was 101 when she died, in 1992). When you run your hands over New Hampshire's old volcanoes, river valleys, and north-south ridges, you'll understand how topography affected the way people moved into the state, why there aren't more east-west roads, and why the rivers became so important.

The herb garden inside the palisade contains some savories you know, like dill and oregano, and some you might not: cheese mallow, feverfew, dianthus. The fort is several hundred yards from the river. Beyond the herb garden are log buildings interconnected to prevent entrance by the unwelcome. *Open Memorial Day–Oct. Route 11 (Springfield Road), 10 miles south of Claremont; 603-826-5700.*

In **Charlestown** proper, on Main Street, look for a marker and a boulder. That's where the original fort was built in 1743—the reconstruction is closer to the river. Thirty-four years later, Gen. John Stark stopped here on his way to fight in Bennington, Vermont. His force of 1,500 men used the Fort at #4 as a muster point, where they were given food, medical supplies, and military provisions. On August 3, 1777, they marched west and on August 16 defeated British and German forces at Bennington.

WHITE MOUNTAINS

■ Highlights

■ Area Overview

"The White Mountains in the northern part of New Hampshire have, from the earliest settlement of the country, attracted the attention of all sorts of persons," wrote Jeremy Belknap in 1792. What an understatement! Adventurers and artists, scientists and alchemists, day-trippers and through-hikers, timber butchers and tree-huggers have all found their way to these magnificent peaks.

Driving the Whites, through passes (called "notches" in the local parlance) under craggy outcroppings thousands of feet above, is spectacular. Odd natural attractions constantly reveal themselves: flumes, basins, giant faces in the rock you can see from the car or within a short walk. The best way to enjoy these mountains is to hike uphill and look down over the vast wild stretches—then retire to your cozy mountain inn. Skiing and maple-sugaring are two cold-weather diversions in the Whites.

Hiking: This chapter mentions some favorite White Mountains trails, but there are many more. Proper preparation being an absolute must, we enthusiastically refer hikers (for that matter, all readers) to the *AMC White Mountain Guide*. This little booklet has been ushering experts and novices through the wondrous Whites since 1907.

Weather: Summer temperatures average 66 degrees F, winter 17 degrees, with extremes of 97 and -32. If you're hiking, dress in layers even on hot summer days; the mountain ridges are colder, by about 5 degrees for every 1,000 feet in altitude, and the winds can compound that greatly (Mount Washington experiences hurricane-force winds on average every third day). Foliage peaks mid- to late September.

WHITE MOUNTAINS

■ HISTORY: THE MOUNTAIN VIEW

The Italian navigator Giovanni da Verrazzano, exploring the new world for France, saw the Whites in 1524 from the deck of the *Dauphine*. One hundred years later, the British Capt. Christopher Levett, who was surveying the Northeast coast, wrote, "there is no ship that arrives in New England, either to the West so farre as Cape Cod, or to the East so far as Monhiggen, but they see this Mountaine the first land." (Monhegan, off Maine's coast, is actually west of Provincetown on Cape Cod, so perhaps Levett's compass was defective.

In the mid-17th century, Darby Field, an adventurer and interpreter from Exeter, climbed the largest of these peaks, which the Abenakis called "Agiocochook" (Aa-ja-chook) and Jeremy Belknap renamed Mount Washington. Field's eager reports of loose diamonds and "muscovy glass" (isinglass) were thinly veiled attempts to coax fellow opportunists to the region.

By the late 1700s, European settlers had discovered the principal notches through the mountains (the Abenakis had known them for generations). In 1771, Timothy Nash, tracking a moose, climbed a tree for a better view and saw a V-shaped cleft through the mountains and beyond it a meandering valley. It was not the only passage through the Whites. To the east of "the Notch," as Nash's find became known, was Evans (later Pinkham) Notch. To the west was Franconia. Still farther west lay Kinsman Notch, a quiet valley different from the deep gorges to the east. In time, these passages through the Whites would become the destination of this country's first tourists.

The first log taverns, crude but convivial, were established by the legendary Crawford family. Between 1790 and 1840, the Notch became "Crawford's Notch," and the scene changed from bucolic to frenetic. From 1850 on, the railroads and grand hotels began to market the Whites in earnest. In 1869, the cog railroad engine Peppersass puffed up the side of Mount Washington. President Ulysses S. Grant nonchalantly puffed a cigar while riding the world's first such attraction.

If a single man can be credited with changing the appearance and fate of the White Mountains, he would be James Everell Henry, who clear-cut thousands of acres. "I never see the tree yit that didn't mean a damned sight more to me goin' under the saw than it did standin' on a mountain," he once proclaimed. By the time he died, in 1912, Henry was worth $12 million.

(following pages) Skiers in the Whites. (Peter Guttman)

THE HOMELY INN

We stood in front of a good substantial farm-house, of old date in that wild country. A sign over the door denoted it to be the White Mountain Post-Office, an establishment which distributes letters and newspapers to perhaps a score of persons, comprising the population of two or three townships among the hills. The broad and weighty antlers of a deer, "a stag of ten," were fastened at a corner of the house; a fox's bushy tail was nailed beneath them; and a huge black paw lay on the ground, newly severed and still bleeding—the trophy of a bear-hunt. Among several persons collected about the door-steps, the most remarkable was a sturdy mountaineer, of six feet two and corresponding bulk, with a heavy set of features, such as might be moulded on his own blacksmith's anvil, but yet indicative of mother-wit and rough humor. As we appeared, he uplifted a tin trumpet, four or five feet long, and blew a tremendous blast, either in honor of our arrival, or to awaken an echo from the opposite hill.

Ethan Crawford's guests were of such a motley description as to form quite a picturesque group, seldom seen together, except at some place like this, at once the pleasure-house of fashionable tourists, and the homely inn of country travellers.

—*Nathaniel Hawthorne, "Sketches from Memory," in* The Great Stone Face and Other Tales of the White Mountains, *1882*

The Crawford Notch House, as illustrated in a book published in 1840. The Crawford family built the inn in 1823. (New Hampshire Historical Society)

WHITE MOUNTAINS

The voracious tree cutting of J. E. Henry and others spurred the creation of advocacy groups like the Society for the Protection of New Hampshire Forests (SPNHF) and the Appalachian Mountain Club (AMC). In a shrewd political move, Philip W. Ayres of the SPNHF "put together a coalition that included loggers and pulp manufacturers, nature lovers, hotel owners, political leaders, and literary figures," as New Hampshire governor Sherman Adams, a former logging company president, later recalled. Ayres's objective was to save the White Mountains yet allow for their continued use by all.

In 1911, the Weeks Act created the White Mountain National Forest, under the auspices of the U.S. Department of Agriculture. Why Agriculture? Because trees, in addition to being recreational and wilderness resources, are valuable crops. Western advocacy groups like the Sierra Club and Wilderness Society have criticized this "fox-in-the-henhouse" coalition. Yet from the outset, the inclusion of all participants in forest activities seems to have reduced acrimony and fostered cooperation.

■ Geology of the Whites

The tallest mountains in the Granite State are not made of granite. Four hundred million years ago, the entire region lay at the bottom of a shallow sea. Thousands of feet of mud, silt, and sand accumulated, creating a vast bed called the "Littleton Formation." This sediment was transformed under great heat and folding pressure into gneiss, schist, and mica quartzite, the last a cousin to granite but not quite granite. Molten magma, cooling and crystallizing several miles down, formed Concord quartz monzonite, another granitic cousin. This new land lifted and eroded.

The North American and Eur-African continents collided, and then pulled apart. Volcanoes erupted in the gap, or moat. The Willey Range in Crawford Notch and the Moat Mountains south of Conway are remnants of these moat volcanoes.

Later, the earth's rising molten gorge intruded into existing rock. It cooled and crystallized. The peculiarly pink stone it evolved into is called Conway red granite, apparent everywhere, most pleasingly in the Webster Cliffs of Crawford Notch. Across the notch is Frankenstein Cliff, made of Mount Osceola granite.

During the last ice age, the Wisconsin Glaciers moved slowly but inexorably across northern New Hampshire, smoothing the jagged peaks and axe-cleft valleys. Mount Washington's glacial cirques (Crawford Notch, Tuckerman Ravine, and the Great Gulf to the north of Mount Washington) are what a glacier leaves behind

Painters Come to New Hampshire

Even before the grand resort hotels drew people to the White Mountains, the area attracted artists eager to document the grandeur of the American landscape, depict its relationship to the national character, and convey the spirituality of their surroundings. The formalism of their landscapes gave way to the proto-impressionistic works of the Barbizon School and to those of artists like Winslow Homer who rediscovered the human form as a fitting central subject.

Thomas Cole 1801–1848

When Thomas Cole visited the wild White Mountains in 1827, rough roads led only to log taverns in the notches. Later painters of the region depicted agrarian idylls, but Cole focuses on the treacherous wilderness that had destroyed the Willey family the year before (see page 245). Cole is credited with founding the Hudson River School, in which idealized nature becomes a vehicle for allegory. In later years, he created series of large paintings on a theme, often showing the same spot through ages of man's habitation. Though he visited the Whites only three times, 45 of his canvases depict local scenes.

View of the White Mountains *(1827), by Thomas Cole. (Wadsworth Atheneum, Hartford, Connecticut)*

WHITE MOUNTAINS

Jasper Cropsey 1823–1900

Jasper Cropsey was known for landscapes with brilliant autumn colors—so brilllant that British art critics accused the painter of exaggerating the colors. He disproved this by sending for some fall foliage and presenting it alongside his works. A native of Staten Island, as a young man Cropsey apprenticed himself to an architect; his training shows in his careful composition. Like others of the Hudson River School, he believed that nature was the earthly manifestation of God and that America's landscape was an expression of the country's character.

An Indian Summer Morning in the White Mountains *(1857), by Jasper Cropsey. (Currier Gallery of Art)*

Albert Bierstadt 1839–1902

One of 19th-century America's most celebrated artists, Albert Bierstadt was born in Germany but raised from the age of three in Massachusetts. The painter of enormous, spectacular canvases of the American West, he is best known for his works depicting the Rockies and Yosemite. But he created 86 paintings of the White Mountains between 1858 and 1873, and with his brothers Charles and Edward shot numerous stereo-scopic photographs. Moat Mountain, just west of Conway, was a favorite subject of painters. Visible in the foreground of Bierstadt's painting of the mountain are the domed cliffs of White Horse Ledge and Cathedral Ledge, also seen in Benjamin Champney's *Saco River, North Conway.*

Moat Mountain, Intervale, New Hampshire *(1862), by Albert Bierstadt. (Currier Gallery of Art)*

Winslow Homer 1836–1910

Winslow Homer created only four paintings during his visits to the Whites between 1868 and 1870, but all were significant. Unlike his contemporaries who depicted humans as ancillary to nature, Homer's central topic in *The Bridle Path* is the travelers themselves, survivors of the Civil War. Isolated within the scene, the woman's face carries an air of

The Bridle Path *(1868), by Winslow Homer. (Sterling and Francine Clark Art Institute, Williamstown, Massachusetts)*

dejection. As the art scholar Pamela Jane Sachant notes, the red, white, and blue sash on the horse, the black trim on the rider's dress, and the mountain laurel by the horse's ear suggest a common post-war tragedy. Does the kerchief-waving figure behind her symbolize her past, her deceased soldier-husband? Beyond her down the mountain lies her future—and there is only one path.

Charles Herbert Moore 1840–1930

Unlike many painters of the White Mountains, who tended to depict dramatic seasons and times of day—and somewhat in opposition to the title of *Mount Washington from Sunset Hill*—Moore chose a midafternoon view in late summer. Missing are the vibrant golds of sunset or autumn that made Cole, Cropsey, and Bierstadt so popular. What draws the eye instead is the delicate, almost etched detail of this image, all the more astonishing for the fact that Moore achieved it using watercolors. The point of view is from a popular hill in North Conway. Moore was the first director of the Fogg Art Museum at Harvard.

Mount Washington from Sunset Hill *(circa 1870), by Charles Herbert Moore. (New Hampshire Historical Society)*

George Inness 1825–1894

A restless man who traveled extensively around the United States and the world, George Inness changed his style in response to his journeys. Inness broke with other American landscape painters in the late 1870s, asserting that "A work of art does not appeal to the intellect. It does not appeal to the moral sense. Its aim is not to instruct, not to edify, but to awaken an emotion." He became a follower of the Barbizon School, and his paintings of forbidding weather are charged with feeling. Inness briefly had a studio at the North Conway Academy.

Saco Ford: Conway
Meadows *(1876),*
by George Inness.
(Mount Holyoke
College Art Museum,
South Hadley,
Massachusetts)

Benjamin Champney 1817–1907

If the White Mountain School of painters has a "grand old man," it is Benjamin
Crackbone Champney, a native of New Ipswich, New Hampshire, who began painting in the Conway area in the 1830s. Both the White Mountain and Hudson River
Schools idealized nature, emphasizing the minuteness of humans in contrast to earth's
majesty. *Saco River, North Conway* includes a trademark Champney image: a tall, slender birch and a rich foreground treatment to frame the scene and lend scale to the
foreboding cliffs beyond Conway.

Saco River, North
Conway *(1874),*
by Benjamin
Champney.
(New Hampshire
Historical Society)

Samuel Lancaster Gerry 1813–1891

Like most American landscape artists of his era, Samuel Lancaster Gerry created his paintings in a studio, from pencil or charcoal sketches made from nature. The availability of tin paint tubes and a growing vogue for "en plein air" painting brought artists with their canvases and easels out into nature. The large boulder portrayed in Gerry's *The Flume* was washed away in a storm in 1883. The painting, which was in the collection of the manager of the Profile and Flume Hotels, may have been hung to entice guests.

The Flume *(date unknown),* by Samuel Lancaster Gerry. *(New Hampshire Historical Society)*

after it passes through a V-shaped valley cut by a river. The sheer weight of the glacier, and the loose glacial till at the interface, scraped out the valleys it met, leaving the classic U of a cirque.

Touring ←🚗→ *If you're heading to the White Mountains from the seacoast, the shortest way north is via two-lane Route 16 to Conway. From there, you can either continue north through Pinkham Notch on Route 16 or turn left and head west to Lincoln along Route 112, the Kancamagus Highway. But most motorists choose faster I-93 to the west, which winds north through Franconia Notch above Lincoln.*

■ SOUTH OF THE NOTCHES

◆ PLYMOUTH *map page 231, C-4*

Plymouth sits in the southern foothills of the White Mountains, at the confluence of two important rivers: the Pemigewasset and the Baker, formerly the Asquamchumauke—the name changed when a force led by Thomas Baker destroyed the Abenaki village here in 1712.

Plymouth is a great walking town, with plenty to see. Most of its sights are within a mile or two of the common, on which stands a gracefully modeled statue of a Boy Scout. On the grounds of the nearby courthouse is a cannon that was captured by John Stark's troops at the Battle of Bennington. Cast on the barrel is a British crown, above the markings "GR" (George III, Rex) and royal munitions identification markings.

Close by to the east, Rounds Hall stands as the symbol of **Plymouth State College**, where Robert Frost taught education and psychology in 1911 at what was then called the New Hampshire Normal School. The Frosts shared a cottage with Ernest Silver, a generous man who was nonetheless put out by Elinor Frost's casual housekeeping. The cottage is near Rounds Hall on the corner of School Street and Highland Avenue. Frost, an inveterate walker, often ambled up Ward Hill north of the cottage. These walks inspired "Good Hours," an evocative portrait of a small town at evening.

◆ WATERVILLE VALLEY *map page 231, D-3*

Head north past the Lakes region on I-93, and you'll soon arrive at Exit 28 to Route 49 east and Waterville Valley. There's a state visitors center off the exit on the right,

The Old Man of the Mountain.

WHITE MOUNTAINS

and beyond it the winding way to a beautiful valley encircled by the Sandwich Range and the White Mountains. In winter, Route 49 is the only way in or out of the area; Tripoli Road, to the northwest, is usually knee-deep in snow at that time of year. From partially paved Tripoli Road, easy hiking trails lead to picturesque East Pond and Little East Pond. For tougher hikes, try the **Mount Osceola Trail,** accessible from a parking area on Tripoli Road; or take the **Livermore Trail** at Livermore Road to see the daunting gravel-slides of the triangular peaks known as the **Tripyramids.** An eastern spur of the ridge is aptly named the Fool Killer, in honor of hikers who have attempted it only to find themselves lost in dense brush and unable to reach the summit.

The **Welch-Dickey Trail,** one of the finest features of Waterville Valley, is 5 miles in from the exit. It encircles two little peaks with great views of the Mad River Valley. The 4-mile loop takes about three hours to complete and is relatively easy, with just a little scrambling up one or two granite ledges. A shorter path winds to ledges leading up to Mount Dickey. In the autumn, this spot offers a view into a salad bowl of reds, yellows, and deep greens. To reach the trailhead, turn left off Route 49, go over Sixmile Bridge onto Upper Mad River Road and past some condominiums, and take the third right onto Orris Road. If Orris is not marked, just follow the signs to the Welch-Dickey parking lot.

At **Waterville Valley Ski Area**, one of the top resorts in New England, more than four dozen trails wind through 255 acres on Mount Tecumseh, named for the Shawnee leader. A 3-mile run is a joy for intermediate skiers. Snowboarders have the run of the mountain and three other areas, and there are miles of cross-country trails. In summer you can go mountain biking. *1 Ski Area Road, at the end of Route 49; 800-468-2553.*

Black Bear Lodge, a year-round resort, is surrounded by 773,000 acres of White Mountain National Forest wilderness. You can golf, ski, play tennis, hike, bike, skate, and even shop nearby. *3 Village Road; 800-349-2327 or 603-236-4501.*

◆ LINCOLN *map page 231, C-2*

North of Waterville Valley is Lincoln, a town that owes its existence to J.E. Henry's logging activities. Lincoln is a long commercial strip that offers things parents of young children appreciate: a train to ride, restaurants that welcome the sippy-cup crowd, ice cream, video stores, a big ski area, and the largest variety of accommodations on the stretch of the interstate below the notches.

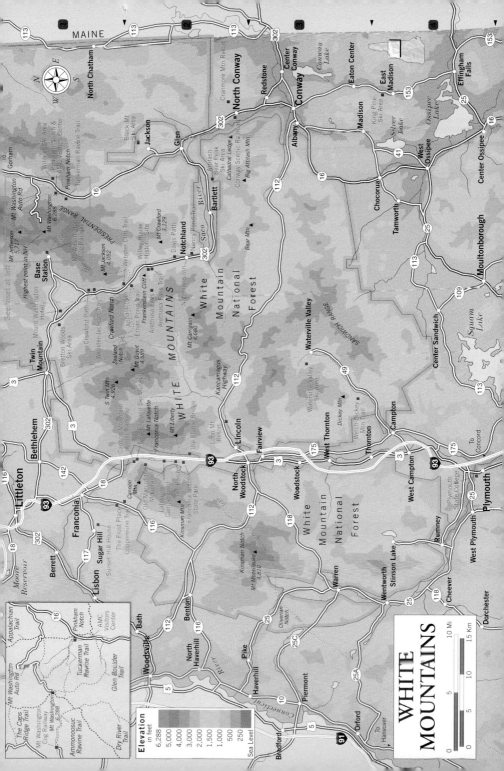

MAINE

113 113 113 302 153

North Chatham

North Conway

Cranmore Mtn. Resort
Redstone
Center Conway
Conway
Conway Lake
Eaton Center
East Madison
Effingham Falls

Jackson
Beck Mt. Ski Area
Wildcat Mtn. Ski Area & AMC Valley Center
Pinkham Notch
Tuckerman Ravine Trail
Glen

Albany
Madison
King Pine Ski Area
Silver Lake
Ossipee Lake
153
16

Presidential Range
Mt Jefferson 5,717
Mt Washington 6,288
Highest point in NH
Mt Washington Auto Rd

West Ossipee
Chocorua
Tamworth
Center Ossipee
Moultonborough

Base Station
Mt Washington Cog Railway
Mt Washington Hotel

Mt Jackson 4,052
Mt Crawford 3,129
Willey House Historic Site
Davis Path
Bartlett
Attitash Bear Peak Ski Area
Cathedral Ledge
Conway Scenic Railroad
Big Attitash Mtn

Saco River

Notchland

White Mountain National Forest

25
113
109

Twin Mountain

Bretton Woods Ski Area
Crawford Path
Webster-Jackson Trail
Zealand Notch
Mt Guyot 4,589
Appalachian Trail
Ethan Pond Trail
Frankenstein Cliff
Arethusa Falls
Frankenstein Trail
Nancy Pond Trail
Notchland Inn
Webster Cliff Trail

Bear Mtn

Center Sandwich
Squam Lake

Bethlehem

S Twin Mtn 4,902
Mt Field
Crawford Notch
Mt Carrigan 4,680

Waterville Valley

Sandwich Range

Kancamagus Highway

Campton

Littleton
Franconia
Bretton Woods Ski Area
Cannon Mountain Aerial Tramway
Mt Lafayette
Franconia Notch
Mt Liberty
The Flume Bridge
Loon Mt Resort

Lincoln
Fairview

West Thornton
Waterville Valley Ski Area
Welch-Dickey Mtn Trail
Dickey Mtn
Thornton

93
3
175
175
93

North Woodstock

Woodstock

West Campton
Rumney

West Plymouth
Plymouth State College
Plymouth

Sugar Hill
The Frost Place
Coppermine Trail
Old Man of the Mountain
Kinsman Notch
Lost River
Lafayette Campground
Franconia Notch State Park

116
142
116
118
25

Berrett
Moore Reservoir

Lisbon
Sunset Hill House

116
117

Bath
112
116
Benton

Kinsman Notch
Mt Moosilauke 4,810
Oliverian Notch

White Mountain National Forest

Warren
Wentworth
Stinson Lake

Cheever
Dorchester

Appalachian Trail
Pinkham Notch
AMC Visitors Center
Mt Washington Auto Rd
Tuckerman Ravine Trail
Glen Boulder Trail
The Caps Ridge Trail
Mt Washington Cog Railway
Mt Washington 6,288
Ammonoosuc Ravine Trail
Dry River Trail

Woodsville
North Haverhill
Pike
Haverhill
Piermont

Connecticut River

Orford
To Hanover

Bradford
91

112
116
5
10
25C
25A
118
25

Elevation
in feet
6,288
5,000
4,000
3,000
2,000
1,500
1,000
500
250
Sea Level

WHITE MOUNTAINS

10 Mi
15 Km
0   5   10
0   5

From Hobo Junction, the **Hobo Railroad** train rolls along the Pemigewasset River from Lincoln to the miniature covered bridge at the Jack O'Lantern resort in West Thornton. A ride of about 90 minutes, it's a fine activity for kids too young for difficult trails. *Trains depart 11, 1, and 3 daily from Memorial Day to Labor Day; fall foliage trains at 11 and 1. Route 112 (Main Street); 603-745-2135.*

Loon Mountain is one of the busiest ski areas in New Hampshire. Purists I know eschew the "fashion-ski" slopes here for the more remote experiences Cannon, Attitash, and Wildcat provide. Summer activities include mountain biking, pony and horseback riding, and hiking. On summer weekends, the Old Mountain Man at the top of the gondola entertains visitors by spinning yarns about the great Pemi wilderness. During September's **Highland Games,** grown men play pipes, toss rocks and logs, and answer the question about what's under the kilt. *I-93 Exit 32, on the western end of the Kancamagus Highway, Lincoln; 603-745-8111.*

◆ Kʀɴᴄᴀᴍᴀɢᴜꜱ Hɪɢʜᴡᴀʏ *map page 231, C/F-2/3*

Lincoln is at the beginning of the Kancamagus Highway (Route 112), which runs east-west, south of the notches, making its way across the mountains for 37 miles to Route 16 south of Conway. The "Kanc" was named for the grandson of Bashaba Passaconaway (see page 35). Far less accepting of Europeans than his forebears, Kancamagus led a raid against Dover in 1686, and then disappeared, perhaps to Canada. He was known as the Fearless One, a title that may seem all the more fitting as you tackle the Kanc's switchbacks.

About 14 miles from Route 16, watch for signs on the south side of Route 112 for the **Sabbaday Falls picnic area.** Behind it, there's a path to a 40-foot waterfall that drops into a granite pothole. There are turnouts everywhere for views, trails, and swimming holes in the Swift River.

Touring ←🚗→ *As you head north on I-93 after passing Waterville Valley, Plymouth, and Lincoln, you're driving through Franconia Notch, the most westerly of three major passes, or "notches," through the mountains. Crawford and Pinkham are the other two passes. Together, the three notches form an irregular* N *underlined by the Kancamagus Highway. Interstate 93 through Franconia Notch forms the left vertical stroke of that* N; *Route 16 is the right vertical stroke, and Route 302, the diagonal, passes through Crawford Notch. A fourth pass, Kinsman Notch, a gentle valley west of Franconia, can be reached out of Woodstock on Route 112 to Route 116.*

Dazzling mountain views can be had from the Kancamagus Highway.

Wʜɪᴛᴇ Mᴏᴜɴᴛᴀɪɴꜱ

■ FRANCONIA NOTCH *map page 231, C-2*

> The Franconia Notch…is a pass about five miles in extent between one of the western walls of Lafayette and Mount Cannon. The valley is about half a mile wide; and the narrow district thus enclosed contains more objects of interest to the mass of travellers, than any other region of equal extent within the compass of the usual White Mountain tour. In the way of rock sculpture and waterfalls, it is a huge museum of curiosities.
>
> —Thomas Starr King, 1859
> *The White Hills: Their Legends, Landscapes and Poetry*

Unless you're driving a convertible, you won't be able to appreciate Franconia Notch from the car. The slopes on either side of Franconia Parkway are too steep. Pull over at one of several viewpoints. Mount Lafayette climbs behind you to the east, the cliffs of Cannon Mountain to the west, and I-93 winds north through the notch.

The Flume Gorge *map page 231, C-2*
The first natural curiosity you encounter in Franconia Notch is the Flume Gorge. The narrow 800-foot-long chasm was carved by Flume Creek, which sliced through 90-foot-tall granite cliffs. From the visitors center you can walk or take a shuttle bus to the gorge, where a boardwalk winds through the lush plant life that flourishes in the mist. The mile-long trail returns you to the visitors center. *Open May–Labor Day Parkway Exit 1; 603-745-8391.*

The Basin *map page 231, C-2*
Formed by the cascading waters of the Pemigewasset River, the Basin is a giant granite sink, the kind of natural oddity that has drawn reverential or merely curious humans for millennia. North of the Flume, the Basin is the jumping-off point for a short hike north along the west bank of the Pemigewasset River to the Lafayette Campground.

Lafayette Campground *map page 231, C-2*
Flanked by Mount Lafayette and the stark cliffs of Cannon, Lafayette Campground contains heavily wooded campsites. Hot showers, firewood, ice, and camping

WHITE MOUNTAINS

supplies are available at the lodge. Reservations are accepted, but more than half the sites are assigned on a first-come first-served basis. *For reservations at all 17 state parks, call 603-271-3628.*

Climbing Mount Lafayette *map page 231, C-2*
For an unforgettable experience, hike the tundralike trail along Franconia Ridge. Clamber out over the craggy monoliths that extend from the ridge, and you'll feel like an ant. The complete Franconia loop takes you from the parking lot up to the 5,260-foot peak, then along the ridgeline between the cliffs of Cannon and the deep, great bowl of the Pemigewasset Wilderness. The last descent is past the steep, sometimes slippery **Falling Waters Trail.** The loop can be done in a day if you leave at daybreak. I prefer to spend the night in the AMC Greenleaf Hut below Lafayette, so I can spend the second day on the ridge. This requires climbing up the bridle path to the hut on day one, and down Falling Waters Trail the next. *For hut reservations, call the AMC Pinkham Notch Visitor Center; 603-466-2727.*

Cannon Mountain Aerial Tramway.

Old Man of the Mountain *map page 231, C-2*
The most famous feature of Franconia Notch, the Old Man of the Mountain, is a series of ledges on Cannon Mountain. When viewed from a pullover opposite Profile Lake, they appear to form a face. Surveyors discovered the Old Man in 1805, when the first road was built through the notch. "A work of Nature in her mood of majestic playfulness," waxed Nathaniel Hawthorne in his story "The Great Stone Face."

Tourists began traveling to see the Old Man and other natural wonders of the notch, at first by stagecoach and after 1850 by train. Accommodations could be found at the base of Cannon Mountain at the Profile Inn. After it burned in 1923, the hoteliers tried to sell their 6,000 acres to timber interests. A nationwide campaign to save the area raised over $200,000, and with matching state funds Franconia Notch State Park was founded in 1928.

Cannon Hikes *map page 231, C-2*
On the west side of the parkway are several wonderful and colorfully named trails: Hi-Cannon, Cascade Brook, Fishin' Jimmy, and Lonesome Lake. Hike at dawn or dusk, and you may hear a loon. At the top of Cannon, you will encounter people dressed in shorts, T-shirts, and street shoes emerging from the Cannon tramway.

Cannon Mountain *map page 231, C-2*
Because the Cannon ski area is owned and operated by the state of New Hampshire, development is minimal and lift tickets are reasonably priced. Cannon is famous for its expert terrain, but the more than 40 slopes and trails here include some gentle ones. *Franconia Notch Parkway; 603-823-8000.*

At the base of the mountain is **Echo Lake Beach**, open daily in summer for swimming and boating (canoes and paddleboats can also be rented). *Tram Valley Station at Parkway Exit 2. Skier services and other lifts at Exit 3; 603-823-5563.*

Cannon Mountain Aerial Tramway *map page 231, C-2*
The first aerial tramway in North America opened on Cannon Mountain in 1938. Today's tram holds 80 riders, who take in remarkable views while suspended over Franconia, a marvelously surreal experience. *Franconia Parkway, Exit 2; 603-823-8800.*

New England Ski Museum *map page 231, C-2*
This museum takes you back to the days when boots and bindings looked like boots

The Flume Gorge.

and bindings. Norwegian immigrants formed the first ski club in Berlin in the 1870s, and a German doctor skied Mount Washington in 1899, but most Americans considered skiing an exotic foreign sport until about 1911, when the first Dartmouth Winter Carnival established a skiing competition. In the 1930s, experts from Europe arrived in New Hampshire to help build ski areas. The Marquis degli Albizzi and Duke Dimitri of Leuchtenberg designed trails in Franconia and Waterville Valley, and a slew of European pros taught skiing around the state. Peckett's Inn in Sugar Hill hosted the first skiing school in America. The museum's artifacts, especially the collection of early skiing posters and movies, can induce a nostalgic glow on the coldest day. *Open Memorial Day–Columbus Day and Dec.–Mar. Franconia Parkway, Exit 2, next to Cannon tramway base; 800-639-4181 or 603-823-7177.*

■ FRANCONIA AREA *map page 231, C-1*

At the west end of the Kancamagus Highway past Lincoln (Exit 32 off I-93) is North Woodstock, a resort town at the opening to Kinsman Notch. Most visitors never see this vast area to the west of Franconia Notch. Take Route 112 west out of North Woodstock, then head north on Route 116, over the "back side" of Cannon Mountain, up to Franconia.

The fastest way into this area on the "upper west side" of Cannon Mountain is to take I-93 north through Franconia Notch and Parkway Exit 3 to 18 west. A left on Route 116 takes you directly south into the notch, and a left on Route 117 takes you to Sugar Hill.

The Frost Place *map page 231, C-1*
Robert Frost made his home near Franconia from 1915 to 1920. The Frost Place is now a poetry center dedicated to his memory and the Festival of Poetry in August. *Open Memorial Day–Columbus Day. Take Parkway Exit 38 and go south for 1 or 2 miles on Route 116; follow signs to the Frost Place; 603-823-5510.*

Coppermine Trail to Bridal Veil Falls *map page 231, C-1/2*
This trail takes you to one of the most beautiful falls in the White Mountains—high and wild, with long strands of white, watery lace flowing down an angled bluff. The trail begins on Coppermine Road, on the east side of Route 116 about a mile

The Old Man of the Mountain rock formation gets some "facelift" maintenance.

south of the Franconia airport. Park and hike on the road about a half-mile to where the trail turns left on an old road (you'll see signs for the path). About a mile later, the trail joins Coppermine Brook and follows along the north side. Then it crosses to the south side on a bridge, passes the Coppermine Shelter, and ends at the base of the falls. This 2.5-mile hike takes a little under two hours.

Sugar Hill *map page 231, B-1*

The town is named for the maple trees that provide the sweet, brown liquid so loved on pancakes and waffles. The delightful **Sugar Hill Historical Museum** surveys two centuries of northern New Hampshire history. *Open mid-June–mid-Oct. Main Street (Route 117); 603-823-5336.*

Sunset Hill House, an inn that dates back to 1880, was the servants' quarters of a hotel of the same name. At the height of its popularity in 1910, Sunset Hill House—a large Victorian-style grand resort hotel north of Kinsman Notch—could accommodate 300 guests. In 1974, the main hotel was torn down. It lasted much longer than the many other grand resorts in the Whites, which closed their doors when the automobile and changing tastes made shorter stays more popular. *Sunset Hill Road, Sugar Hill; 800-786-4455 or 603-823-5522.*

Also in Sugar Hill is the **Homestead Inn,** one of the oldest family-run establishments in America. Heirlooms—dishes, glasses, furniture, silver—dating from the inn's opening in 1802 conjure up the past. A guest book on display in the parlor bears the name of every visitor since 1880. *Route 117 and Sunset Hill Road; 800-823-5564 or 603-823-5564.*

White Mountain Tour Service

Arthur Jolin, who lives in Gorham, arranges tours of historic covered bridges and moose territories. Arthur entertains his customers with a lifetime of local lore. His fees are flexible, depending upon the job, but the average charge is $35 an hour. *603-466-2127.*

Touring ←🚐→ *To reach the Crawford Notch area, get off I-93 at Exit 35, drive about 12 miles north on Route 3, and turn south on Route 302. Several trails to Mount Washington begin in Crawford Notch, including the Crawford Trail, the oldest continuously maintained footpath in the United States. The Mount Washington Cog Railway is another route up; off Route 302, take Base Road to Marshfield Base Station.*

WHITE MOUNTAINS

■ CRAWFORD NOTCH *map page 231, D-1*

Crawford Notch, the diagonal of the N the White Mountains notches form, is famous for the Mount Washington Hotel, Frankenstein Cliff, the domed rock called Elephant Head, and fine hikes up the steep slopes that surround it. "The mountains here are abruptly torn apart, forming a very narrow valley, through which flows the Saco," wrote Rev. Benjamin J. Willey of the 3-mile-long notch in his 1855 *White Mountain Reader.*

Mount Washington Hotel *map page 231, D-1*
Winston Churchill, Joan Crawford, Thomas Edison, and Babe Ruth are among the guests who have checked in at this Spanish Revival–style hotel that has the look of an ocean liner. The place has seen a lot of activity since it opened in 1902, from Prohibition-era parties in the speakeasy (known today as the Cave) to the Bretton Woods Conference of 1944, which launched the International Monetary Fund. Gazing at forest views from the colonnaded veranda is just one of many present-day pleasures this grande dame offers. *Route 302, Bretton Woods; 800-258-0330 or 603-278-1000.*

(above) The Mount Washington Hotel.

WHITE MOUNTAINS

Maple Sugaring

During the fight for independence, pouring maple sugar over flapjacks was a revolutionary act. Benjamin Franklin encouraged using maple sugar as a substitute for white sugar from the West Indies, the purchase of which benefited the king of England. Processing maple syrup became a vibrant industry and remains so to this day. New Hampshire is responsible for about two percent of the world's annual production of seven million gallons.

Maple sugaring time runs from mid-March to mid-May, depending on how long the sap is running, which has a lot to do with temperature. "A good crop depends on a pressure differential in the tree that will help the flow of sap," says Bruce Bascom of Bascom Maple Farms, a syrup broker. "That means below freezing temperatures at night and warmer temperatures (40 to 45 degrees) during the day. After more than two nights warmer than 32 degrees, the harvest is done."

You can learn more about the industry and techniques involved in harvesting maple sap on the last weekend in March, **Maple Weekend,** when many of the state's producers receive visitors. For more information about this event, call *603-225-3757.*

Some producers run sleigh rides up into the "sugar bush," a term for all the trees harvested, and some let kids make that most New England of delicacies, sugar on snow. Doughnuts and pickles are usually provided to clear the palate between tastings of the sweet syrups.

No matter where you go sugaring, you'll be introduced to the major steps of syrup manufacturing. These include sap gathering (in many places now done with clear tubing that runs from tree to tree and then downhill to the sugar house) and incessant boiling—it takes 50 gallons of sap to make a gallon of syrup, which means lots of boiling and, for the workers, not very much sleep for six weeks.

The Rocks Christmas Tree Farm hosts the **Maple Syrup Festival,** at which participants get hands-on experience with the entire process, from tree identification to tapping to boiling. Many local inns have special packages that include lodging and the event. *Take I-93 Exit 40, head east on Route 302 for a half-mile, and then turn right and follow the signs; 603-444-6228.*

Other producers around the state include:

Christie's Maple Farm. You can visit the Maple Museum and taste syrup samples for free at this family-run operation. *246 Portland Street, Lancaster; 800-788-2188 or 603-788-4188.*

Fadden's Sugar House. You don't even need to trek to the farm to sample syrup from Fadden's, which sets up a portable sugar house right downtown. *Main Street, North Woodstock; 603-745-2406.*

Parker's Maple Barn. Parker's boils its sap over a wood fire (most places use oil or gas burners), giving the syrup a smoky flavor. *Mason Road south of Milford off Route 101A, Mason; 800-832-2308 or 603-878-2308.*

Polly's Pancake Parlor/Hildex Maple Sugar Farm. Some folks say Polly's serves the best pancakes in America. The restaurant, in business since 1938, is open daily from mid-May to mid-October and on weekends from April to mid-May and mid-October through November. *Route 117, Sugar Hill; 603-823-5575.*

Sugar Shack. If you can't make it up to the Whites, head on over to this farm near Portsmouth that's open year-round from Wednesday to Saturday and on Sunday during sugaring season. *314 Route 4, Barrington; 800-576-2753.*

Collecting sap on a cold day in early spring. (Peter Guttman)

Bretton Woods Ski Area *map page 231, D-1*

The ski area is south and across Route 302 from the Mount Washington Hotel, which owns it. The steepest vertical drop is 1,500 feet, and about a quarter of the six-dozen trails are expert level. You can ski at night on several trails. *Route 302, Bretton Woods; 603-278-3320.*

The Gateway

Pull over at the little railroad station on the right a few miles south of the Mount Washington Hotel. That's **Crawford Depot**, an information center for hikers and other visitors. To the south, you'll see a tall gray rock on the east side of Route 302, poking its head out of the greenery surrounding it. One of the best-known icons of the White Mountains, the bluff is called **Elephant Head**, for obvious reasons.

The Gateway to Crawford Notch is south of Elephant Head. Try to imagine it as it was 330 years ago, a cleft in the wild unforgiving mountains, promising trade and connection with Canada. A painting by Thomas Cole shows just such a view, from the south, before the notch's 22-foot width was blasted open to accommodate trains. Three historic trails begin within hailing distance of the railroad station, and there are many more through the notch's southern reaches.

Webster Jackson Trail to Elephant Head *map page 231, D-1*

To hike to the top of Elephant Head, head east up the Webster-Jackson Trail, which you can access a tenth of a mile south of Crawford Depot. Look for a short spur trail to Elephant Head, another tenth of a mile farther (perhaps 15-20 minutes of moderate uphill hiking), for some of the best views of the northern notch.

Crawford Path *map page 231, D-1*

Abel and Ethan Crawford forged this path in 1819, making it easier for visitors to explore Mount Washington. It was widened into a bridle path by Abel's grandson, Thomas Jefferson Crawford, in 1840. *The trailhead is at the junction of Mount Clinton Road and Route 302, north of Crawford Depot.*

Willey House Historic Site *map page 231, D/E-2*

The summer of 1826 had been unnaturally dry, and when torrential rains finally came on August 26, the soil could not absorb the water fast enough. It is said that the Willey

(opposite) Silver Cascade is one of many Crawford Notch falls.

family fled their house and ran to the base of the mountain behind them to escape the flooding Saco River. A massive slide down the mountain killed the family of seven and two hired men. A large boulder that diverted the slide saved the house itself. There is an interpretive exhibit at the site. *603-374-0999.*

Ethan Pond Trail *map page 231, D-2*
The 2-mile trail leads to the shores of the pond named for Ethan Allen Crawford, the "giant of the mountains." It begins opposite the Webster Cliff Trail on Route 302, about a mile south of the Willey House site, taking hikers along the Appalachian Trail and through an area heavily logged in the late 1800s (for a long time afterward it was known as the Desolation Area). Today, it's as wooded as any site in the White Mountains.

Webster Cliff Trail *map page 231, D-1/2*
Mount Webster forms the east wall of the notch, providing wonderful views from its red granite cliffs. It takes about two hours of hiking to reach the first open ledge. The trail then follows these ledges, which have great views of the southwestern notch to the summit of Mount Webster.

Arethusa Falls *map page 231, D-2*
The state's tallest waterfall, named for a mythological nymph who was transformed into a fountain, is on Bemis Brook. The trailhead is at the Arethusa Falls parking lot, on the west side of Route 302 south of Dry River Campground. The hike to the falls, a winding route down a rippled cliff, is not difficult. To make it much more so, continue up and around to steep **Frankenstein Cliff**, named not for the monster but for the German-born artist George L. Frankenstein (1825-1911), a cofounder of the Cincinnati Art Museum.

Notchland Inn *map page 231, E-2*
In 1840, Dr. Samuel Bemis, a Boston dentist and early photographer, took the first daguerreotype landscape, a view of Mount Crawford House, which he later purchased. He built what is now the Notchland Inn as a summer home. Gustav Stickley, a founder of the Arts and Crafts movement, designed the home's front parlor fireplace. The Davis Path, which ascends Mount Crawford and links to other trails

leading to the summit of Mount Washington, starts across the road from the inn. *Route 302, Hart's Location; 800-866-6131 or 603-374-6131.*

Davis Path *map page 231, E-2*
Building the Davis Path was daunting, and Mount Resolution was named for the effort. Nathaniel P.T. Davis, Ethan Crawford's brother-in-law, created this third bridle path up to Mount Washington in 1844. It crosses over the Saco River on a suspension footbridge and ascends the steep ridge to the summit of Mount Crawford. From there, the path continues north over Mount Resolution to the "giant stairs," one of Davis's major obstacles. *The trailhead is north of the Notchland Inn on the east side of Route 302.*

Nancy Pond Trail *map page 231, E-2*
Almost 7 miles south of the Willey House site and 3 miles north of Sawyer Rock picnic area, a trail leads past a beautiful cascade, through a moss-carpeted virgin spruce forest, and up to a high mountain pond. Its namesake, Nancy Barton, along with the Willey family, was fodder for 19th-century tragic-romantic conceptions of the notch. On a cold night in 1778, she set out from Jefferson, where she had been working on a farm. Her fiancé had absconded with her dowry, and pursuing him through the notch she succumbed to the cold. Her frozen body was found next to the brook that bears her name. It takes about two hours to get to the base of the cascades also named for Nancy. From there the trail to the pond becomes steeper and the footing can be treacherous in the root-bound spruce forest.

Attitash Mountain and Bear Peak *map page 231, E-2*
Attitash Mountain and Bear Peak are considered among the state's finest ski areas. The narrow trails appeal more to experienced skiers than to beginners. In summer, you can hike, ride a water slide, and swim in the pool. *Route 302, east of Bartlett 3 miles; 603-374-2368 or 603-374-0946.*

Touring ←🚗→ *Route 16 runs through Pinkham Notch. If you're driving north from the seacoast, this is the road to take. If you're in Crawford Notch, follow Route 302 south through the notch, through the town of Bartlett to Glen, and past the cockamamie Storyland kiddie playground. South of Glen, Route 302/16 leads to Intervale and North Conway. North of Glen, Route 16 is the way to Pinkham Notch (about 12 miles).*

WEATHER IN THE WHITES

"Will anyone believe us?" thought Sal Pagliuca one day in April 1934. He'd been hanging off a rope in howling winds, banging a foot of ice off the Mount Washington Observatory's anemometer, an instrument that measures wind velocity. The reading was incredible: 231 miles per hour, three times hurricane-force winds, and the fastest wind speed ever recorded on earth.

The U.S. Weather Service tested the anemometer and confirmed Pagliuca's reading, but some scientists remain skeptical that winds can reach such a velocity on Mount Washington, which is barely over 6,000 feet. Many mountains in the West rise to 13,000 feet and above, yet no such speeds have been recorded at them.

One possible explanation is that Mount Washington is the nexus of three storm paths that moisture-laden winds follow to New England: north up to the Atlantic coast, northeast up the Ohio River Valley, and east over the Great Lakes. As the winds roar up Mount Washington, they pick up speed and their temperature drops 5.4 degrees for every 1,000 feet they rise. The wind-chill factor was so low one day that no chart existed to calculate the combination of minus-41-degree temperature and 110-mile-per-hour winds.

It's not comforting when you approach the mountaintop and encounter the weather-beaten U.S. Forest Service sign that relays this ominous message:

STOP

THE AREA AHEAD HAS THE WORST WEATHER IN AMERICA. MANY HAVE DIED THERE FROM EXPOSURE, EVEN IN THE SUMMER. TURN BACK NOW IF THE WEATHER IS BAD.

What you may think is snow at the summit, hanging sideways from power lines and telephone wires—and what was hanging from Pagliuca's anemometer that day—is rime ice, fog that turns to ice just as it touches a surface.

If you hike in the Whites, dress appropriately, with rain gear and wool or polypropylene sweaters, hats, and gloves, even on warm days. Bring a map and compass (study them before you go), water, food, and energy snacks. And, most important, tell someone where you're going and when you expect to return.

The North Conway Village Green is far from green after a 30-inch snowfall.

■ THE CONWAYS TO PINKHAM NOTCH *map page 231, E/F-2/3*

Pinkham Notch is named for Daniel Pinkham, who constructed the second road through this eastern notch in 1824. (Capt. John Evans created the first one 50 years earlier.) North Conway, a shopping megalopolis, is another town the logging industry built. Like Lincoln, it attracts so much traffic you could easily forget you're in the mountains. North Conway's 100-plus outlet stores lure some, displease many.

Conway Scenic Railroad *map page 231, F-2*
The Conway Scenic Railroad is a far cry from the steam trains in the Whites. For one thing, the era is post-steam. Twin FP-9 diesels depart the North Conway train station for a round-trip of five hours through Crawford Notch, across the Frankenstein Trestle and Willey Brook Bridge. *Open Apr.–Dec. (months vary depending on excursion). Route 16, North Conway; 603-356-5251.*

(following pages) A misty dawn unfolds over Conway Lake.

Cathedral Ledge

Across the Saco River to the west of North Conway (follow River Road west, north of North Conway) are the Moat Mountains, remnants of the moat volcanoes created by the separation of the Eur-African and American tectonic plates. A common subject for landscape painters, the three Moat Mountains, and the dramatic White Horse and Cathedral Ledges in front of them, can be seen from Route 16. A road winds to the top of Cathedral Ledge.

AMC Pinkham Notch Visitor Center *map page 231, A-1 and E-1*

Run by the Appalachian Mountain Club, this is the base camp for popular trails to Mount Washington's summit. The center's huge three-dimensional model of the mountain is an invaluable aid to hikers. The Joe Dodge Lodge accommodates more than a hundred guests with double beds or bunks, and the well-stocked library has a great view of Wildcat Ridge. A scale outside the facility has convinced many a hiker to jettison a cherished bottle of wine or video camera before embarking. *Route 16, about 15 miles north of North Conway; 603-466-2727.*

Tuckerman Ravine *map page 231, A-1 and E-1*

Tuckerman Ravine is one of the White Mountain region's snowiest spots, making it a popular destination for skiers. A short hike along the Tuckerman Ravine Trail from the AMC Pinkham Notch Visitor Center leads to the headwall, where many have tried, and some have died, trying to beat the 1939 skiing record of six minutes and 39 seconds. One of many trails to Mount Washington's summit begins here.

Wildcat Ski Area *map page 231, E-1*

Wildcat has more than 225 acres of world-class terrain, offers spring skiing, and enjoys the longest ski season in New Hampshire. The weather is often cold, but this is one of the best-loved slopes in the Whites. *Route 16, about a mile north of the AMC Pinkham Notch Visitor Center, Jackson; 800-255-6439.*

Touring ←🚗→ *Most people who hike Mount Washington start from trailheads in Crawford Notch or from the AMC Pinkham Notch Visitors Center. If you're not hiking, you can drive a mile or so north of the visitors center on Route 16 to the Mount Washington Auto Road, which winds its way to the summit. Or you can hop aboard the Mount Washington Cog Railway to reach the peak.*

WHITE MOUNTAINS

■ MOUNT WASHINGTON   *map page 231, A-1 and E-1*

Mount Washington is a broad, massive mountain with great ravines cut into its steep sides, leaving buttress ridges that reach up through the timberline and support the great upper plateau.

—*AMC White Mountain Guide*

The Abenakis, keenly aware how treacherous Mount Washington could be, called it Agiocochook, or "place of the storm spirit." Since Darby Field climbed the mountain in 1642, more than 125 people have died here, most of hypothermia. Others have perished in accidents involving avalanches (10), skiing (5), falling (25), drowning (6), the cog railway (9), carriages (1), murders (1), plane crashes (5), and slideboard mishaps (4). A slideboard was a three-foot sled with an unreliable hand-brake. It was once the fastest but also the most dangerous way down the cog rails—the record descent took a little more than two-and-a-half minutes.

People cannot resist attempting to scale the summit—and haul the rest of civilization with them. Over the years, there have been five hotels, a newspaper, a daily radio broadcast, a weather observatory, various restaurants, the Mount Washington Museum, a huge parking lot, and a U.S. Post Office at the top. Most of the buildings (minus the

The summit of Mount Washington on a typical winter day. Wind-chill factor: minus-60 degrees Fahrenheit.

WHITE MOUNTAINS

lodgings) are still there, in a structure of concrete reinforced to withstand hurricane-force winds that on average howl by once every three days.

◆ MOUNTAIN ECOLOGY

The blunt dome of Mount Washington is an environment of brutal extremes and extreme beauty. Its deep ravines harbor huge rock slides, veil-like waterfalls, and sheer drops (particularly on the eastern Huntington Ravine and Tuckerman faces).

The broad slopes above the treeline on the plateau below the summit are described as "lawns," for the alpine sedges that wave thickly in the frigid breeze. What looks like a barren rockpile above these lawns supports many plant species, some found only in the 7.5 square miles of alpine environment in the White Mountains.

Along the upper approach is an alpine garden with low vegetation more commonly found in the arctic circle, like Greenland sandwort and Lapland rosebay. The rare dwarf cinquefoil, a rock-hugging plant with tiny yellow flowers, and a number of other species can be found only on Mount Washington and the Franconia Ridge.

Plants survive in this zone by staying low, out of the killing wind and close to the sun-warmed rock. Lichens of many colors, from silver to green to black, inhabit the boulder field below the inhospitable summit. Black spruce hugs the ground here as a mat. Other plants grow curled and furred leaves to retain moisture.

◆ HIKING AND CLIMBING THE MOUNTAIN

Trails and AMC Huts *map page 231, A-1*
If you're looking to climb Mount Washington, there are three great day-hikes to the summit. The most popular is the **Tuckerman Ravine Trail,** which starts at the AMC Pinkham Notch Visitor Center on Route 16 north of North Conway. In Crawford Notch, the **Ammonoosuc Ravine Trail** to the Crawford Path begins near the Mount Washington Cog Railway base station. This hike takes you to the beautiful Lakes of the Clouds area, a high mountain pond below the summit, near an AMC hut of that name. The **Caps Ridge Trail** starts high, off Jefferson Notch Road. *Take the Base Road off Route 302 in Fabyan.*

Mount Washington is best appreciated on a hike of several days. One of the best is the three-day trip up the Southern Presidential range along the Webster Cliff Trail and Crawford Path, with a stop at Mizpah Springs and Lakes of the Clouds Huts before you get to Washington. Strolling out of Mizpah Springs Hut after a hearty meal,

I saw the full moon rise one frosty night in August. We had made it from Mizpah to the summit of Washington that day, and though my legs felt like rubber bands, there was no other place on earth I would rather have been.

A coal-fired steam engine powers Cog Railway cars.

The eight **AMC huts** in the White Mountains are a marvelous resource for hikers, but they book up fast. Day-hikers find energy snacks, water, and a convivial atmosphere of fellow hikers and hut "croo," a charismatic group of twenty-something staffers with abundant energy, good humor, and basic but hearty culinary skills. Overnighters are fed, watered, and bedded down, so their packs are lighter, an added advantage. *Reservations essential; 603-466-2727.*

Mount Washington Cog Railway *map page 231, A-1 and E-1*

The Mount Washington Cog Railway, built in 1869, was the first mountain-climbing railway in the world (the second was erected in Switzerland in 1871) and is a National Historic Engineering Landmark. The first locomotive to climb the track and trestles built by Sylvester Marsh was Peppersass (these days known as Old Peppersass), and even today the passenger car is pushed up the slope by a curiously canted coal-fired steam engine. Near the treeline, the train passes over a 30-foot trestle called Jacob's Ladder. The round trip takes three hours, including a 20-minute stop at the windy summit. *Operates May–Oct. West side of Mount Washington, Route 302 to Base Road to Marshfield Base Station; 800-922-8825 or 603-278-5404.*

Mount Washington Auto Road *map page 231, A1 and E1*

The Mount Washington Auto Road, which ascends Chandler Ridge on the east side of the mountain, climbs 4,600 feet in 8 miles. You can drive your car to the summit and paste a "This Car Climbed Mount Washington" bumper sticker on it. You can also ascend by van (they call them stages) or in winter on a Sno-Cat. The Auto Road is open from mid-May to mid-October, weather permitting.

WHITE MOUNTAINS

GREAT NORTH WOODS

■ **Area Overview**

"I don't know about great," says John Harrigan, editor of three north-country newspapers, public radio contributor, and columnist. "But we're certainly north. And, by god, these are woods."

The Great North Woods is a recently minted term intended to define the region north of the White Mountains as separate from them. But this is not how locals refer to the place they live. They just call this wild land the north country. Everything else is "from away," or "down below."

Even well-traveled Graniteers think of the north country as terra incognita. Winter grips the rough highlands for seven months, followed by mud season, then bugs. Wild beasts are so common that hosts caution their dinner guests to "brake for moose" on the way home. The prevalence of black bear, coyote, ruffed grouse, and loon; the silence of the forest; the goofy volcanic carbuncles; and a certain human eccentricity set Coos County apart from all other regions. The north country is as wild and free as this state gets.

Weather: Summer temperatures average 63.3 degrees F, winter 11.8 degrees, with extremes of 93 and -46 and as many as 60 days of subzero weather. The North Woods has the state's highest annual precipitation (49.07 inches), so bringing raingear is a good idea in three seasons. Pack boots during mud season (April and May) and your warmest clothes when the Frost King is enthroned. Fog steams off the lakes during autumn mornings, and foliage peaks in mid-September.

■ About the Great North Woods

The topographical differences north of the White Mountains' famous notches are immediately obvious. The surface of the land changes from granite to gravel, the trees become softwood-dominant (spruce, fir, and tamarack), the place names more Algonquian than English. Even pronunciation changes: the town of Berlin (BUR-lun) is downstream on the Androscoggin from Milan (MY-lun) and upstream from Gorham (GOR-em). On the Maine border lies Umbagog (um-BAY-gog) Lake, in the county of Coos ("like co-operate," writes John Harrigan). It comes from the Abenaki word for evergreen, a recognition of the fact that here begins the great northeastern softwood forest.

■ North Woods History

The area known as the Great North Woods was not settled in earnest until after the fourth of the French and Indian Wars ended in 1763. During these wars between France and England, which began in 1689, both sides sought to use Native American allies to discourage and disrupt settlement. Native Americans had reasons of their own to fight—not the least of which was to take captives for ransom and adoption. The British had ties to the Iroquois, and the French in Quebec allied with Huron and Abenaki refugees, who joined French soldiers (and sometimes Jesuit priests) from St. Francis, in Quebec, on raids to the south.

English settlers who weren't killed were often kidnapped and taken to St. Francis. What little we know about the area's native groups during this period comes from the accounts of kidnap victims who later returned to English settlements. Among the captives were children given to Indian families who had lost their own offspring. Some adoptees found their treatment so humane they refused to return when ransomed.

To counter these raids and protect isolated settlements, governors Shirley of Massachusetts and Wentworth of New Hampshire formed militias that fought alongside regular British army units. The most famous of the militias was known as Rogers' Rangers. Under Robert Rogers, these soldiers raided the town of St. Francis in 1759. (See page 39 for more about Rogers.) After killing many people and burning the town they retreated, half starving and in rags, through what is now the North Woods. When the survivors arrived in Portsmouth, they spoke of the wild land along the northern Connecticut and Androscoggin Rivers. Settlers began moving in to clear the forests for farms, but the area wasn't as suitable for farming as was southern New Hampshire. As a result, subsistence farming gave way to more profitable logging.

◆ LOGGING AND GEORGE VAN DYKE

The industry that defined this land was born of trees and rivers—and the tough men who knew and exploited them. George Van Dyke was the lumber king of the north, a river-hog, as log drivers were called, most comfortable barking orders from a boat on the Connecticut during a log drive. Born into poverty, he did not own a pair of shoes until the age of 11. He came to own much of the north country, logged it tirelessly, amassed a fortune of $20 million, and died in an auto accident at the site of a logjam on the Connecticut in 1909.

As Robert E. Pike describes him in *Tall Trees, Tough Men,* an informal history of New England logging, "George was not a tall man, but he took a size 19½ collar and was very wide and thick. His powerful voice could be heard right across the Connecticut." The logs were floated to the Connecticut and the Androscoggin via smaller rivers fitted with "driving dams," logjams with large openings through which timbers can be driven.

A New Hampshire log drive, circa 1860. (Montshire Museum of Science, Norwich, Vermont)

DRIVING DAMS AND DAREDEVIL LOGGERS

The driving dams were so called because they were equipped with a plank gate in the middle, which was raised vertically in order to let logs be driven through. This operation was known as sluicing. The gateway, along with the attendant log apron below, was called the sluice. On the drive, when the last logs were being sluiced through a dam, there were always half a dozen dare-devils who would jump onto logs and ride them down through the sluice and the white, rock-toothed water below, while yelling like fiends. It was always dangerous, it was sometimes fatal, but it was magnificent to look at.

Dan Bosse was tending out below Errol dam one day when a New York tourist and his wife stopped to watch. "How can you ever stand on a log like that!" marveled the lady.

"Oh!" said Dan, "that ain't anything!" and just to show off, he went up above the dam and rode a log down through the sluice. It struck a rock head-on and for a few moments Dan was running up and down that log as if he had a swarm of bees in his pants. But he didn't fall off.

"My God!" said the woman. "What are you—some kind of a squirrel?"

— from *Tall Trees, Tough Men,* by Robert E. Pike

W.W. Norton & Company (1967)

Some waterways, like the Dead Diamond, Hall's, and Indian Streams, are still accessible over logging roads owned and maintained by major paper companies like Champion, Mead, and International Paper. For years these forest lands have been accessible to the public, though whether they will continue to be so as they change hands remains in question.

◆ INDIAN STREAM REPUBLIC

One of the more curious of New Hampshire's border disputes occurred in the 1830s. Canada and the United States were unable to agree on their border, and violent disagreements took place in the area of Hall's Stream (the current border) and Indian Stream. Frustrated by the inability of the two governments to settle the controversy and fueled by their staunch belief in self-determination, locals established the independent Indian Stream Republic in 1832.

Sharon Francis of the Connecticut River Valley Joint Commission believes the Republic expresses something important about the soul of the north country that resonates throughout the state. "Texas has the Alamo, and it represents something deep-seated in the psyche of Texans. We don't have such a building, but we do have the memory of the Indian Stream Republic."

The republic's constitution guaranteed the right of religious freedom, life, liberty, property, and happiness. The necessities of life—including books—could not be attached. In 1835, the New Hampshire militia marched in and put an end to the new governing party, but the spirit of self-determination survives. As recently as the late 1980s, locals were again threatening to secede over a proposal by the Army Corps of Engineers to build a dam.

In an essay on the Web site of the *Coos County Democrat,* a paper he once published, John Harrigan describes what sets north country folks apart from their fellow citizens to the south:

"Residents revel in Mud Season and scoff at a foot-deep snowstorm. Most of the land is privately owned and virtually all of it is unposted, open for use and enjoyment by the public at large. The air and the water are clean and the region remains a place of great beauty. The less government, the best government, remains the ethic of the land. It is, many will tell you, the last great free place."

North country people speak from the heart, if a bit bluntly sometimes, and from a pure memory that has persisted through the generations. To the residents of Pittsburg, the Indian Stream Republic is not a dusty historical footnote, but a lasting expression of principle.

Touring ←🚗→ *To drive into the north country from down below, take I-93 through Franconia Notch or Route 302 through Crawford Notch. Both connect to Route 3, the main route along the east bank of the Connecticut River, the border with Vermont. Farther east, Route 16 passes through Pinkham Notch to wind along the west bank of the Androscoggin River.*

Several east-west roads traverse the north country. From south to north, they are: Route 2 between Lancaster and Gorham, Route 110 between Berlin and Groveton, and Route 26 between Errol and Colebrook. All three are spectacularly beautiful, but my favorite is Route 26. Traveling east-west through Dixville Notch, it passes through primeval forests and a dramatic geological display before heading past a grand resort hotel on a little lake and on to busy little Colebrook.

GREAT NORTH WOODS

■ I-93 NORTH OF FRANCONIA NOTCH

◆ LITTLETON *map page 263, A-6*

North of Franconia Notch on I-93 lies Littleton (pop. 6,000), a town with a success story that is the envy of many struggling north country villages. In the 19th century, Littleton factories churned out tools, furniture, fabrics, whiskey, carriages, and the Kilburn stereoscope, which provided three-dimensional views of popular tourist attractions like the White Mountains. Traveling salesmen stayed in style at the four-story Thayer's White Mountain Hotel. Now called **Thayer's Inn,** this white-columned hotel has been in continuous operation since 1850. *111 Main Street; 800-634-8179.*

The 20th century saw the development of new concerns like the Saranac Glove Company, whose deerskin gloves are said to have warmed Admiral Richard E. Byrd's hands on his excursion to the South Pole. In the 1950s, New England's largest hydroelectric dam, the 190,000-kilowatt Moore Station, was built on the Connecticut River where 15-mile falls once challenged George Van Dyke's river drives.

By the mid-20th century, most industry had left the area, but when I-93 was extended through the notch in the early 1960s, a steady stream of tourists and commercial traffic eased Littleton's transition from a manufacturing economy into one based on tourism.

A walking tour of Main Street provides a great introduction to the north country. The octagonal stone tower of the Queen Anne–style town hall (built in 1895 at Main and Union streets) is visible from anywhere on Main Street. To sample local comfort food like roast turkey and tuna-pea wiggle, stop in at the **Littleton Diner,** a classic parlor-car diner at 145 Main Street.

The **Chamber of Commerce** has walking tour brochures. *125 Main Street; 603-444-3996.*

◆ WEEKS STATE PARK *map page 263, B-5*

This 450-acre estate atop Prospect Mountain commands sweeping north country views. It was once the home of Lancaster native and New Hampshire congressman John Wingate Weeks, who in 1911 helped enact the Weeks Act, which established the White Mountain National Forest. Near the mansion on the summit is a stone tower with terrific views of New Hampshire and Vermont. *Route 3, about 6 miles north of Whitefield; 603-788-4004.*

◆ **LANCASTER** *map page 263, B-5*

Lancaster is a major crossroads (Routes 2, 3, and 135 meet here) in the flat and fertile valley east of the Connecticut River and west of the Kilkenny Range. Though the town lacks the charm of Littleton, it's a pretty place in late summer, with green parks and well-built homes that hark back to the boom days of sawmills and log drives.

Lancaster was home not only to conservationist John Wingate Weeks but also to lumberman George Van Dyke. For most of his life Van Dyke lived with his mother in a house on Mechanic Street where the Siwooganock Bank now sits. Other native sons are honored in four parks along Main Street. Cross Park, across from the Post Office, is dedicated to Col. Edward Cross, who fought at the Bloody Lane at Antietam during the Civil War and died with New Hampshire's Fifth Brigade at Gettysburg.

Northeast of here is the little town of **Lost Nation**, so named because it could not keep a minister, and was therefore considered spiritually lost. To the east looms the Kilkenny Range, where Lancasterians established a quarry.

GREAT
NORTH WOODS

The Presidential Range looms over the Washington Valley in this view from Prospect Mountain in Weeks State Park.

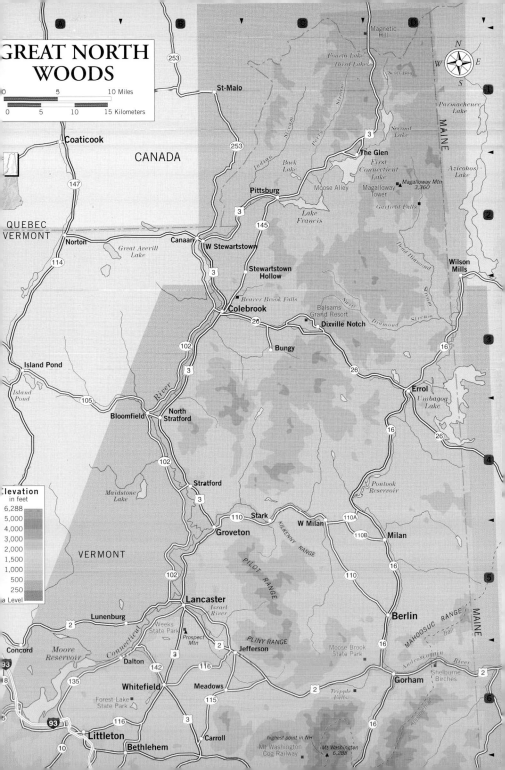

■ Route 16 North of Pinkham Notch

The Androscoggin River was an important waterway for the Abenakis, for the Jesuit missionaries who descended from Quebec and Montreal, and for early French fur traders, known as *voyageurs*. Lumberjacks later followed this route, driving logs to the mills at Berlin. Route 16 north out of Gorham toward Errol travels along the west bank of the Androscoggin and back through time.

◆ Gorham *map page 263, D-6*

This wide-open space is a pleasant respite for motorists or hikers on the Rattle River section of the Appalachian Trail. A cool mountain breeze sweeps off Pine Mountain and the Howker Ridge from the Northern Presidentials. A major crossroads for traffic headed north to Berlin and east or west between Maine and Lancaster, Gorham's Main Street can be quite busy in summer. Lined with restaurants and shops, it is a good place to pick up lunch. Everything from panini-style sandwiches to imported

(above) The Lancaster Covered Bridge spans the Israel River.
(opposite) Rider Ralph Shirley and his horse in Bethlehem.

NORTH WOODS   GREAT

Italian sodas and food items to chocolate truffles shipped up from Boston is sold here.

Summer **moose-watching tours** (603-752-6060) start downtown and head upriver. The ride isn't fancy—it's on a school bus—but the tour operators claim a 98 percent success rate in finding moose.

The **Appalachian Mountain Club** (603-466-2727) conducts a weekend whitewater canoeing seminar on the Androscoggin River that includes training, canoe rentals, lodging, breakfast, and dinner (no lunch).

◆ **BERLIN** *map page 263, D-5*

Route 16 heading out of Gorham curves along the river that powered the former factory town of Berlin. There's never been any attempt to prettify the gritty Pulp and Paper of America mill across the river, which at one time produced everything from kraft paper to artificial silk.

The area became a little North Woods melting pot. Northern and southern Italians lived in separate parts of town, French immigrants settled on the east side, Germans and Irish on the west, Norwegians in the north end, and Russians on the

Summer moose tours are popular in the North Woods.

GREAT
NORTH WOODS

hilly back streets. The architecture of local churches reflects this diversity; the mortared-fieldstone Episcopal Church dominates Main Street, and the onion-domed Eastern Orthodox Church is on Petrograd Street.

Berlin is trying to transform itself from "Paper City" into a tourist destination with events like the Festival du Bois (Festival of the Woods) and the Tour du Bois Pedal and Paddle Biathlon, whose participants bike through the woods and canoe and kayak down the Androscoggin.

The Lilac Festival in early July centers on the restored gardens at the Brown Company House, part of the **Northern Forest Heritage Park,** a re-created logging camp. Lumberjack competitions and demonstrations by blacksmiths are among the activities that take place at the park, where you can also tour a mill and take self-guided walks and drives. From July to early October, boat tours of the upper Androscoggin leave from the park. *Main Street, north end of town; 603-752-7202.*

North of Berlin on Route 16, beehive-shaped rock piers emerge from the Androscoggin. These were anchoring piers for booms that would corral logs floating downstream to the mills. It's easy to imagine men scuttling out on the booms, cant-dogs in hand, trying to free up the jams. At wayside pullovers all the way up to Errol you can enjoy the changing face of the river and the massive stands of spruce and fir trees on the opposite bank.

■ ROUTE 110 FROM BERLIN TO GROVETON

Touring ←🚗→ *Roadside oddities pop up along Route 110 west from Berlin to Groveston. From the balsam fir made of steel painted green outside Berlin (marking the local manufacturing facility of the Car Freshener company) to the peculiar peaks on Route 110, it's a unique drive. The flutey peaks are the remnants of volcanic carbuncles—intrusions of lava into other strata of rock that never quite reached the surface. Wind and water have exposed them to modern view.*

A historical marker on the north side of Route 110 near the village of Stark describes **Camp Stark,** where about 250 German and Austrian prisoners of war lived during the last years of World War II in an old Civilian Conservation Corps camp. While in detention they cut pulpwood in the surrounding forests. So many prisoners had fond memories of their experiences at Camp Stark they returned to New Hampshire for a reunion in the 1980s.

GREAT NORTH WOODS

The village of **Stark** contains a handful of buildings clustered around a covered bridge along the upper Ammonoosuc River. Each one is a New Hampshire classic. Under the bridge's roof and stuck into the latticework of its truss are four or five mailboxes, presumably placed there to make the postman's job a little easier during nasty northern weather.

■ ROUTE 26 THROUGH DIXVILLE NOTCH *map page 263, C-3*

◆ UMBAGOG LAKE *map page 263, D-3/4*

The tiny hamlet of **Errol** contains a few shops and restaurants. At the **Errol Restaurant,** on Main Street, you can dine on two local specialties, mooseburger and *poutine* (french fries with melted gravy and cheese).

A few miles east of town lies giant Umbagog Lake. Eight miles long and 3 miles wide, it straddles the border with Maine. Umbagog is the headwaters of the Androscoggin, the largest wetland complex in New Hampshire (17,000 acres). A unique feature is the **Floating Island National Natural Landmark,** a floating bog inhabited by many rare birds, including the palm warbler. Bits of the massive bog occasionally break off in a strong wind and wander the lake.

The best views of Umbagog Lake can be had across the border on Route 26 near Upton, Maine, but the best way to experience it is by boat; there's a launch up Route 16 from Errol on the lake's northern section. Patient paddlers might spot bald eagles, osprey, harriers, and loons. The state's largest loon population lives here.

You can rent canoes, kayaks, and boats and reserve campsites at Sargent Lake, 9 miles south of Errol on Route 26. *Umbagog Lake State Park, 603-482-7795; camping reservations, 603-271-3628. Lake Umbagog National Wildlife Refuge; 603-482-3415.*

◆ DIXVILLE NOTCH *map page 263, C-3*

Unlike the round-shouldered grand cirques of the Whites, Dixville is a rebelliously dramatic gorge, its spiky points crammed into nearly vertical slopes created by an upward thrusting of sedimentary layers below the earth's surface.

For a grand experience of Dixville Notch, head west out of Errol on Route 26. The road climbs up the Clear Stream Valley almost 12 miles into peaks that seem right

(opposite) A bald eagle nesting in Lake Umbagog National Wildlife Refuge.

GREAT NORTH WOODS

out of *The Flintstones*. Watch for the pullover on the right for Baby Flume. Though less dramatic than the Flume at Franconia Notch, it's less crowded and a great spot for a picnic. The tables are right at the edge of the gorge through which Flume Brook flows.

West of the Baby Flume pullover, be careful. You'll come to the top of the rise in Dixville Notch, and right as you're staring up at the spiky verticals of Table Rock, the road seems to disappear as it begins a precipitous descent into the valley beyond. Just when you've recovered your equilibrium, the sight of the **Balsams Grand Resort,** which dominates the shore of man-made Lake Gloriette, will take your breath away. Elegant and sparkling white, the original wooden hotel, built in 1866, stands proudly next to a soaring pinnacled structure, the first steel-and-concrete building erected in the United States. The addition must have been the toast of the north when it was completed in 1917. Like the Mount Washington Hotel, the Balsams maintains the gentility of the historic grand resort hotels. The golf course, built in 1912 on the slopes of Keazer Mountain, has superb views. Every four years the citizens of Dixville Notch gather after midnight in the Ballot Room to cast the first votes of the presidential primary. *Route 26; 603-255-3400.*

Cooks of the Balsams Resort display their delicacies. (Robert Holmes)

■ THE COHOS TRAIL

In 1978, Kim Robert Nilsen wrote an editorial for the *Coos County Democrat* that changed his life. After decades of tramping around secret places even most locals never see, he wondered why somebody hadn't put up a trail over the spine of Coos County. "It just made so much sense," says Nilsen. "The ridge that separates the Androscoggin drainage from the Connecticut passes through some of the most beautiful, pristine lands imaginable." After talking up the project, that "somebody" turned out to be Nilsen himself. His dream has taken decades to realize, and work is still in progress, but the Cohos Trail now stretches from the Davis trailhead in Crawford Notch to the Canadian border, passing through wilderness areas like the Montalban Whites, Jefferson Dome, the Kilkenny region, the Nash Stream Forest, Dixville Notch, and the Connecticut Lakes.

This is a wilderness trail for fit hikers with proper survival skills. Supplies are not readily available, particularly on the long stretch between Jefferson and Pittsburg, and rescue parties are not as well organized as they are in the White Mountains. This is as close to the wild as New Hampshire offers.

■ ROUTE 3 TO CONNECTICUT LAKES

◆ COLEBROOK *map page 263, B-3*

For its small size, Colebrook, a prime market for goods required in the north country, is a surprisingly busy town, with century-old storefronts crowding Main Street. The building housing Clarkeies Supermarket was a major vaudeville venue. The second floor of the police station, off Main Street, contains an impressive collection of local memorabilia.

◆ THE BUNGY *map page 263, C-3*

The Bungy (BUN-gee with a hard "g") is a wondrous high-level plain ringed by mountain peaks. Moose love to graze in the wetland here. There are two theories about how the Bungy got its name. In the Easton Valley, south of the White Mountains, when a low moaning wind comes through the notches, the locals say "The Bungy Jar is blowing." Others claim that *bungy* means "the long way" in Abenaki and referred to their preference for taking this longer west-to-east route around the White Mountains to traveling through their spooky and dangerous notches. To get to the Bungy, go east on Titus Hill Road out of Colebrook, take a right on Marshall Hill Road, and a left onto Bungy Road. You'll be traveling in a circle around Blueberry Swamp, and you may see a moose or bear.

◆ **PITTSBURG** *map page 263, C-2*

North from Colebrook on Route 3 is Pittsburg, the state's northernmost town and the largest one in the area. "Pittsburg has the feel of a frontier town," observes Kim Nilsen. "It's not a classic New England charmer with white steepled churches and aging stone walls. Rather, it fits like an old worn pair of shoes that you like and won't part with."

Some of Pittsburg's former farms and homes lie at the bottom of man-made Lake Francis. The Murphy Dam, which created Lake Francis, was built soon after the 1936 flood, during the height of the Depression, when dams and make-work projects seemed like a good idea to Gov. Francis Murphy.

The Trading Post Country Store in Pittsburg is a popular stop for snowmobilers.

◆ MOOSE ALLEY *map page 263, C-2*

What inspires our fascination with *Alces alces americana?* Weighing an average of 1,000 pounds, with faces like warthogs and pendulous dewlaps, moose are hardly cuddly. Yet most of us have fond feelings for these hulking, awkward-looking beasts.

Avid moose-spotters congregate along the winding reaches of Moose Alley, a stretch of Route 3 north of Pittsburg. It's common at dusk, but certain that before dawn, say 6 a.m., a moose will be spotted at one well-known hollow a few miles north of the Timberland Lodge sign.

Moose is an Algonquian word for "eaters of twigs," an apt name, as moose eat about 50 pounds of wet forage daily. Especially fond of water lilies, they will wade into swampy ponds to snag some. Active all day, they are most likely to be seen at low muddy spots called "wallows." The residual salt from winter plows draws them.

A grown moose stands more than 6 feet high at the shoulder, its antlers can span six feet, and it can run up to 35 miles an hour. Do not, as one hapless fellow in Moose Alley did, try to walk up to them in the wallow to say hello.

◆ FAR NORTH LODGING AND CAMPING

Accommodations in this farthest-north of north country regions are simple—hunting or fishing lodges. Cozy places filled with stuffed trophies include The Glen on First Connecticut Lake and the Tall Timbers Lodge on Back Lake. Rooms at most places are spartan, but clean and comfortable. But, the Balsams excepted, you're not in the North Woods for a five-star experience. You're here for the smell of fir needles, the cry of the loon, the tug of a fat salmon on the line, and the delicious shock of cold water in the pool at the base of Garfield Falls.

Camping in the region ranges from comfortable, at Lake Francis State Park, which has a bathhouse and campsites with fire rings, to primitive, at Deer Mountain State Park, between Second and Third Lakes, served by outhouses and a spring. *Both state parks; 603-538-6965.*

■ CONNECTICUT LAKES

North of Pittsburg lies the kingdom of water, the center of the universe for fishers in pursuit of salmon, lake trout, and brookies. The miles of wilderness in the Connecticut Lakes region delight and awe hikers, birders, and nature-lovers of all stripes.

Signs like this one along Moose Alley show who's boss.

◆ **First Connecticut Lake** *map page 263, D-2*

First Connecticut Lake is so deep (120 feet by some soundings, others read up to 160 feet) that cold-water species like rainbow trout and land-locked salmon live here. Watch for Ramblewood Campground and Magalloway Cabins, a favorite spot to photograph the lake and the angled slopes of Magalloway Mountain beyond the lake's far shore. *Magalloway Cabins; 603-538-6353.*

The Glen has many assets, not the least of which is its prime location on First Connecticut Lake, with Magalloway Mountain and Diamond Ridge looming beyond. But its special human resource is Betty Falton, who has been running this lodge-and-cabins complex since 1961. Having driven all the logging roads and tramped the woods, she knows how to match a guest to the right experience. Her advice might include hiking Fourth Connecticut Lake, fishing Moose Falls Flowage, setting out to sight a nuthatch or loon, or searching for the elusive pond on the far side of Stub Hill.

"The north country is not for everybody, that's for certain," Betty says. "It's probably not for the lady that called me up once and asked, 'What do you people do at night?' I told her we might go see what the moose are up to, then go to bed. 'Well,' she asks me, 'isn't there any kind of summer theater, or music festivals?' I told her that there were not and that, no offense meant, she would most likely be miserable if she did come to visit." A gracious host and entertaining storyteller, Betty is eager to introduce guests to the north country she loves so dearly. *Open May–Oct. 77 The Glen Road, off Route 3, Pittsburg; 800-445-4536 or 603-538-6500.*

◆ MAGALLOWAY MOUNTAIN   *map page 263, D-2*

About 3 miles east of South Bay, on First Connecticut Lake, regal 3,360-foot Magalloway Mountain has the best views of the region. *Magalloway* is Algonquian for "the shoveler," according to Kim Nilsen. "It was an affectionate term for the now extinct woodland caribou, which would shovel the snow aside with its hooves and snout to get at the lichens it fed on."

Access is via a logging road 2.7 miles north of the Timberland sign on Route 3. About 5.5 miles along the logging road, make a right turn and follow the road 3 miles to a dirt parking area. Two routes lead to the top: the steeper **Coot Trail** (40 minutes) and the longer **Bobcat Trail** (an hour). It may require some scrambling over and around blown-down trees.

The views from the top of Magalloway Mountain take in Maine, Vermont, and Canada, as well as the network of local logging roads. Even if you're only going on a short trip in this area, purchase the *Connecticut Lakes Region Road and Trail Guide*. The definitive regional map, it's available at most local stores and lodges.

◆ FALLS ON DEAD DIAMOND STREAM   *map page 263, D-2*

One of the stunning features the road and trail guide can help you find is **Garfield Falls,** about 6.5 miles past the Magalloway Tower turnoff on the dirt Magalloway Road. From the road, hike about 10 minutes down a path lined with bunchberries, whose spade-shaped leaves and red berries add a splash of color to the green of spruce and ferns. You'll hear the falls first—an ominous whoosh—and then catch glimpses of water through leaves and needles. Just above the bottom of the trail is the best view of the gigantic rock mass that holds back the east branch of Dead Diamond Stream. The water rushes through a narrow chasm at the top of the rock, falls 40 feet into a deep pool, and immediately turns sharply to the left.

It's hard to believe that logs could have been driven around this outcropping, but driven they were, whisked along by springtime's roaring high water. Logs often poked into the bottom and piled up like pick-up sticks, requiring sweat, swearing,

and dynamite to free them. Men would sometimes be lowered on ropes to cut the key-log that held the jam. When the bottleneck was broken, the men weren't always hoisted back up in time. Their bodies might be found far downstream, stripped of everything except spiked boots.

Downstream from Garfield lie three more elusive falls. One is a Niagara-like horseshoe, the next passes through a nondescript headwall marked by a vertical rock, and the last has created a beautiful sculpture of worn stone with the texture of driftwood. To get to the last falls, continue on the road past the parking area for Garfield Falls. Immediately past Garfield, the road splits. Take the right fork. A half-mile later, take the left fork and park in the circular area at the end of the road. A logging road heads off to the south from here. Walk along this road for 2 miles (about 45 minutes). At the intersection with another logging road that continues right, go left less than a quarter-mile to a wooden bridge. On the opposite side, bushwhack upstream through the woods no more than 20 feet to find the falls. A few hundred yards downstream, the East Branch meets the West Branch, and 10 miles downstream from here the Swift Diamond meets the Dead Diamond to become the Magalloway River.

◆ FOURTH CONNECTICUT LAKE   *map page 263, D-1*

Barely south of the U.S.-Canadian border and 22 miles north of Pittsburg is the valley that contains Fourth Connecticut Lake. It's hard to believe this tiny 2.5-acre pond is the source of the mighty Connecticut River, but it is. This jewel supports unusual flora—a floating bog and insect-eating plants like the pitcher plant, sundew, and bladderwort. The Nature Conservancy maintains a 1.7-mile trail that heads west from the Border Crossing Station (sign in first) at the parking lot on the east side of Route 3. *Nature Conservancy; 603-224-5853.*

■ ROUTE 145

Touring ←🚗→ *Route 145 is possibly one of the most fascinating drives in the state. Its best features can be seen on the southerly route, from Pittsburg to Colebrook. On either side of this tortuous road, deep cavities drop away to reveal dairy farms and vistas that stretch all the way to Vermont and Canada.*

Just south of the 45th parallel marker, turn right on West Road and drive 1.5 miles to a dirt road on the left. A short hike (just over a mile) takes you to the white-cedar Hurlbert Swamp. Be sure to bring insect repellent—though some areas are bug-free, in most places bug-juice is a necessity. South of the West Road turnoff, Route 145 continues along on its swooping, swerving way. A few miles later, you reach Stewartstown Hollow.

◆ **STEWARTSTOWN HOLLOW** *map page 263, B/C-3*

Writer John Harrigan's theory of "How Stewartstown Hollow Got Hollow" begins 12,000 years ago, when billions of gallons of glacial melt ran smack-dab up against an ice dam that blocked the water's passage through the gorge north of Beaver Brook Falls. The ancient river raged back in shock from the ice in a massive whirlpool and dug a hole deep into the terrain, dumping tons of fine silt in the process.

Moose love to scuff their hooves in the lush silt-grown grasses of the muddy wallow off the road to your left, in back. Shortly before you reach the hollow, a sign on the left marks the road to the grave of Metallak, the last of the Coashaukees, the "lone Indian of the Magalloway." A guide for travelers and hunters in the area, Metallak died in the 1840s, reputedly at the age of 120, blind and a ward of the state. Gifts of tobacco, fishing lures, shiny pebbles, dream catchers, and medicine wheels cover his grave, which is in a cemetery up Creampoke Road about a half-mile, then right on North Hill Road for a tenth of a mile. Metallak's gravestone is on the far left.

◆ **BEAVER BROOK FALLS** *map page 263, B/C-2/3*

South of the hollow is Beaver Brook Falls. A long green lawn slopes downward from the road to the base of the falls, and a rock cliff angles backward from the base to the top, creating a curious optical illusion. You can see Beaver Brook Falls from the roadside pullover, but you'll want to walk down the lawn, over the little bridge to the base of the falls, and have a picnic. "It's always a popular spot," says John Harrigan, "but nothing like the day a few years back when a photographer and his model decided this would be the perfect spot for a nude study." He was a meticulous photographer, and it took him a long time to set up the shot, by which time half of Coos County had shown up.

(previous pages) Morning fog on First Connecticut Lake.

(following pages) The rising sun silhouettes anglers on First Connecticut Lake.

PRACTICAL INFORMATION

■ AREA CODE AND TIME ZONE

The area code for New Hampshire is 603. The state is in the Eastern time zone.

■ METRIC CONVERSIONS

1 foot = .305 meters
1 mile = 1.6 kilometers
Centigrade = Fahrenheit temperature minus 32, divided by 1.8

■ CLIMATE AND CLOTHING

An overview of the four seasons in New Hampshire, begins on page 25, and the first page of each regional chapter of this book includes information about local weather conditions. At any time of year, even July, if you're planning a trip to the mountains or seacoast, pack a wool or polypropylene sweater and a windbreaker. When dining out, casual dress is the norm in most restaurants; only at the few fancy establishments will you need to dress up.

■ GETTING THERE AND AROUND

◆ BY AIR

Manchester Airport (MHT), the state's main airport, is served by several major carriers or their affiliates. MHT is a popular alternative to congested Logan airport. *1 Airport Road, off I-293 Exit 2; 603-624-6539, www.flymanchester.com*

Logan International (BOS), Boston's airport, is the major facility closest to southern New Hampshire. Many major airlines serve Logan. *Harborside Drive off Route 1A; 800-235-6426, www.massport.com/logan*

◆ BY CAR

The main routes into New Hampshire include I-93 from Massachusetts and Vermont,

I-95 from Massachusetts and Maine, and I-89 from Vermont. I-93 is New Hampshire's main north-south highway. The main east-west roads through the state are Route 101 through Manchester, the slower Route 4 through Concord, and Route 2 from Gorham to Lancaster. Regional chapters contain additional touring information.

There are self-service gas stations throughout New Hampshire, though stations in less populated regions may have attendants who provide full service (pumping gas, checking tires and oil, washing windows). The speed limit on most interstate highways is 65 miles per hour. In congested areas the speed limit is often lowered to 55 mph. To drive in New Hampshire you must be at least 16 years old and have a valid driver's license from your home state or country. Unless signs at an intersection note otherwise, you can make a right turn at a red light after coming to a complete stop. Left turns are permitted onto adjoining one-way streets after you have come to a stop.

◆ By Bus

C&J Transportation. *800-258-7111 or 603-430-1100, www.trailways.com*

Peter Pan Trailways. *800-343-9999 or 603-430-1100, www.trailways.com*

Greyhound. *800-229-9424 or 402-330-8552, www.greyhound.com*

Concord Trailways and Dartmouth Coach. *800-639-3317 or 603-228-3300, www.concordtrailways.com*

■ Food and Lodging

Seacoast: Cuisine on the seacoast predictably favors seafood—lobster stew, haddock sandwiches, mussels with traditional or contemporary broths. Places to stay range from chain properties to historic inns and rental cottages and condominiums.

Merrimack Valley: Dining options are plentiful, from four-star restaurants in historic homes to hip little bistros and wine bars. Larger cities in the Merrimack Valley have chain properties, and bed-and-breakfast inns can be found there and elsewhere.

Monadnock Region: Here you will find comfort food—from pot roast to osso buco—that harks back to the days when drovers would stop at local inns in search of hearty fare. You can spend the night in centuries-old inns, bed-and-breakfasts in Colonial-style homes, and, in cities like Keene, chain motels and motor lodges.

GETTING THERE AND AROUND

Lakes Region: Restaurant options around Lake Winnipesaukee and other mid-state lakes range from folksy diners to upscale establishments in remodeled barns and boathouses. Accommodations include smallish bed-and-breakfasts, family resorts, motor lodges, and grand manors. Lakeside accommodations are typically more expensive than cabins.

Sunapee & the Upper Valley: The best dining in this area is in the upper Connecticut River Valley; chefs at the region's finest restaurants whip up contemporary variations on traditional New England cuisine. You can spend your nights in lakeside cottages, bed-and-breakfasts, and luxurious inns. Chain motels can be found along I-89 and in the Lebanon-Hanover area.

White Mountains: As in the Monadnock region, cuisine in the mountains tends toward comfort food, though you can dine on fine contemporary fare at upscale lodgings. The Appalachian Mountain Club (AMC) operates a network of huts for hikers. Lincoln, North Conway, and other large towns have chain properties, and many smaller towns have bed-and-breakfast inns and boutique hotels.

Great North Woods: How you eat in the north country depends partly on where you stay. At the Balsams resort hotel, dinner is a veritable Continental event, but if you're camping at a state park (or eating at a local diner), the fare might be franks and beans. The best towns for restaurants are Pittsburg and Colebrook. There are no chain motels this far north, just lodges, bed-and-breakfasts, and cabins.

◆ HOTEL AND MOTEL CHAINS

Best Western. *800-528-1234, www.bestwestern.com*
Days Inn. *800-441-1618, www.daysinn.com*
Hampton Inn. *800-426-7866, www.hamptoninn.com*
Hilton Hotels. *800-445-8667, www.hilton.com*
Hyatt Hotels & Resorts. *800-233-1234, www.hyatt.com*
La Quinta. *800-531-5900, www.laquinta.com*
Loews Hotels. *800-235-6397, www.loewshotels.com*
Marriott Hotels. *800-228-9290, www.marriott.com*
Quality Inns. *800-228-5151, www.hotelchoice.com*
Radisson. *800-333-3333, www.radisson.com*
Ramada Inn. *800-272-6232, www.ramada.com*

Renaissance Hotels *800-468-3571, www.marriott.com*
Sheraton. *800-325-3535, www.starwood.com*
Westin Hotels. *800-228-3000, www.westin.com*

■ OFFICIAL TOURIST INFORMATION

New Hampshire Division of Travel & Tourism Development
603-271-2665, www.visitnh.gov

Greater Manchester Chamber of Commerce
603-666-6600, www.manchester-chamber.org

Greater Concord Chamber of Commerce
603-224-2508, www.concordnhchamber.com

Greater Portsmouth Chamber of Commerce
603-436-3988, www.portcity.org

■ CAMPING

Camping options in New Hampshire range from hike-in sites to car camping and RV camping sites. You can make reservations and access a directory of campgrounds at the Web site of the state park system. *603-271-3628; www.nhparks.state.nh.us*

The U.S. Forest Service regulates camping in the White Mountains National Forest. To read the backcountry camping rules, click on "Recreation" on the White Mountains National Forest Web site. *518-885-3639 or 877-444-6777, www.fs.fed.us/r9/white*

■ USEFUL WEB SITES

Appalachian Mountain Club. Information about huts, visitors centers, and camping sites, plus a link to the New Hampshire AMC chapter's page; *www.outdoors.org*

Currier Gallery of Art. In-depth look at Manchester's regional art museum; *www.currier.org*

Great North Woods. Local site with everything from maps to moose info; *www.greatnorthwoods.org*

Lake Winnipesaukee Home Page. Facts, history, and links to other Web sites covering the region; *www.winnipesaukee.com*

New Hampshire Historical Society. News about the society's museum, exhibits, and upcoming events; *www.nhhistory.org*

New London–Lake Sunapee Region Chamber of Commerce. Directory of events, history, seasons, and attractions; *www.newlondonareanh.com*

SeacoastNH.com. Informative, entertaining site with historical, dining, lodging, and events info, plus a photo gallery; *www.seacoastnh.com*

Society for the Protection of New Hampshire Forests. Directions to forest areas of the statewide land conservation group and downloadable trail maps; *www.spnhf.org*

White Mountains Chamber of Commerce. Helpful commercial site if you're planning a trip to the Whites; *www.visitwhitemountains.com*

Yankee **Magazine.** Lodging, dining, and other tips, plus articles about regional history and culture; *www.newengland.com*

■ SKI AREAS

Attitash Bear Peak. *Route 302, 3 miles east of Bartlett (map page 231, E-2); 603-374-2368, www.attitash.com*

Balsams. *Route 26, Dixville Notch (map page 263, C-3); 603-255-3951 or 800-255-0600, www.thebalsams.com*

Black Mountain. *Five Mile Circuit Road, Jackson (map page 231, F-2); 603-383-4490 or 800-698-4490, www.blackmt.com*

Bretton Woods Ski Area. *Route 302, Bretton Woods (map page 231, D-1); 603-278-3320, www.brettonwoods.com*

Cannon Mountain. *Franconia Notch Parkway (map page 231, C-1); 603-823-8800, www.cannonmt.com*

Cranmore Mountain Resort. *1 Skimobile Rd., east of Route 302, North Conway (map page 231, F-2); 800-786-6754, www.cranmore.com*

Dartmouth Skiway. *Off Route 10, Lyme Center (map page 195, B-2); 603-795-2143, www.dartmouth.edu/~skiway*

Gunstock Mountain. *Route 11A, Gilford (map page 165, D-3); 800-486-7862, www.gunstock.com*

King Pine Ski Area. *Route 153, East Madison (map page 231, F-4); 603-367-8896 or 800-367-8897, www.purityspring.com*

Loon Mountain. *Route 112 off I-93 Exit 32, Lincoln (map page 231, C-2); 603-745-8111, www.loonmtn.com*

Mount Sunapee Ski Area. *Route 103, Newbury (map page 195, C-5); 603-763-2356, www.mtsunapee.com*

Pats Peak. *Route 114, Henniker (map page 93, A-3); 603-428-3245, www.patspeak.com*

Ragged Mountain Resort. *Off Route 104, Danbury (map page 195, D-4); 603-768-3971, www.ragged-mt.com*

Waterville Valley. *1 Ski Area Road, off Route 49, Waterville Valley (map page 231, D-3); 800-468-2553, www.waterville.com*

Wildcat. *Route 16, Jackson (map page 231, E-1); 603-466-3326 or 800-255-6439, www.skiwildcat.com*

INDEX

COMPASS AMERICAN GUIDES

Alaska (3rd Edition)
376 pages; 0-679-00838-1

American Southwest (3rd Edition)
368 pages; 0-679-00646-X

Arizona (5th Edition)
292 pages; 0-679-00432-7

Boston (3rd Edition)
328 pages; 0-676-90132-8

Chicago (3rd Edition)
288 pages; 0-679-00841-1

Coastal California (2nd Edition)
400 pages; 0-679-00439-4

Colorado (6th Edition)
304 pages; 1-4000-1204-X

Florida (2nd Edition)
384 pages; 0-676-90494-7

Georgia (2nd Edition)
312 pages; 0-676-90137-9

Gulf South: Louisiana, Alabama,
Mississippi (1st Edition)
352 pages; 0-679-00533-1

Hawaii (5th Edition)
368 pages; 0-679-00839-X

Idaho (2nd Edition)
288 pages; 0-679-00231-6

Kentucky (1st Edition)
324 pages; 0-679-00537-4

Las Vegas (7th Edition)
304 pages; 0-676-90138-7

Maine (3rd Edition)
320 pages; 0-679-00436-X

Manhattan (4th Edition)
352 pages; 0-676-90495-5

Michigan (1st Edition)
320 pages; 0-679-00534-X

Minnesota (2nd Edition)
352 pages; 0-679-00437-8

Montana (5th Edition)
304 pages; 0-676-90133-6

Nevada (1st Edition)
344 pages; 0-679-00535-8

New Mexico (4th Edition)
336 pages; 0-679-00438-6

New Orleans (4th Edition)
304 pages; 0-679-00647-8

North Carolina (3rd Edition)
352 pages; 0-676-90498-X

Oregon (4th Edition)
304 pages; 0-676-90140-9

Pacific Northwest (3rd Edition)
376 pages; 0-676-90496-3

Pennsylvania (1st Edition)
336 pages; 0-679-00182-4

San Francisco (5th Edition)
336 pages; 0-679-00229-4

Santa Fe (3rd Edition)
272 pages; 0-679-00286-3

South Carolina (3rd Edition)
328 pages; 0-679-00509-9

South Dakota (2nd Edition)
312 pages; 1-878867-47-4

Southern New England (1st Edition)
384 pages; 0-679-00184-0

Tennessee (1st Edition)
320 pages; 0-679-00536-6

Texas (2nd Edition)
336 pages; 1-878867-98-9

Utah (5th Edition)
352 pages; 0-679-00645-1

Vermont (2nd Edition)
336 pages; 0-676-90139-5

Virginia (3rd Edition)
312 pages; 0-679-00282-0

Washington (3rd Edition)
336 pages; 0-676-90497-1

Wine Country (3rd Edition)
312 pages; 0-679-00434-3

Wisconsin (3rd Edition)
308 pages; 0-679-00433-5

Wyoming (4th Edition)
368 pages; 0-676-90499-8

ACKNOWLEDGMENTS

If a story belongs to those who tell it, then this book belongs to too many to list here. You know who you are, and I thank you all deeply. Special thanks to the following: Chris Burt, whose big idea this was, and editors Kit Duane and Danny Mangin. Wise counselors: Judson Hale, Peter Randall, John Harrigan, Gary Samson, Kim Robert Nilsen. Keepers of the flame: Ursula Wright, Sarah Hartwell and Barbara Krieger, John Frisbee, Art Bryan, William Copeley, Michelle Stahl, Ellen Derby, Eileen O'Brian, Alan Rumrill, Bill Driscoll, Linda Walton, Sharon Francis, Carl Schmidt, Ron Raiselis, Nick Brown, Karen E. Bartlett, Diane Rogers, Christine L. Fipphen, J. Denis Robinson, Thomas Hyman, Laura Gowing, Linda Coleman, Kathy Ritter, Hope Jordan, Joan Chamberlain. Experts: Brownie Gengras, Dr. Robert Goodby, Martha Pinello, Victoria Bunker, Mayor Robert Baines, David Scannell, Eric Aldridge, Bill Boynton, Carol Stephens, David Anderson, Mike Bergeron, Rob Burbank, Tom Durkiss, Professor John Burger, Nancy and Cayenne Harrigan. Storytellers: Betty Falton, Gail Weston, Nancy Coffey Heffernan and Ann Page Stecker, Eva Speare, Peter Marchand, Niall Palmer, Alonzo Fogg, Fred Anderson, Robert E. Pike, William Cronon, Mike Dickerman, Eric Pinder, Bill Bryson, John T. B. Mudge, Bryant F. Tolles Jr., James L. Garvin, Colin Calloway, Daniel Doan. Thanks to Ed and Claudia, Paul and Jane, Joe and Ruth, Katy and Steve, Mike and Beverly, and so many more. And finally, to Jeremy Belknap, patriot, minister, gazetteer, and guide, whose cherubic smile, beaming from the frontispiece of his 19th-century book, kept me in the spirit. He told this story first, and some say best. But he was wrong about the black flies.

—Jeff Binder

All photographs in this book are by Thomas Mark Szelog unless otherwise credited below.

COMPASS AMERICAN GUIDES ACKNOWLEDGES the following institutions and individuals for the use of their photographs and/or illustrations: Douglas Armsden, p. 74; Association for the Preservation of Virginia Antiquities, p. 29 (right); Barbara Appleyard, p. 136–137; Boston Athenaeum, p. 163; Canterbury Shaker Village Archives, p. 120; City of Montreal, Records Management and Archives, p. 28; Clark Historical Library, Central Michigan University, p. 40; Currier Gallery of Art, pp. 110 (contribution, Box Funds), 111 (purchased with funds provided by the John H. Morison Acquisition Fund and Ronald Bourgeault), 127 (gift of Dr. and Mrs. Huntington Breed II and many Friends of the Currier), 223 (Currier Funds), 224 (Currier Funds); Dartmouth College Library, pp. 48, 97, 203; Denver Public Library, p. 29 (left); Frye's Measure Mill, p. 128; Peter Guttman, pp.

122–123, 156–157, 218–219; Robert Holmes, pp. 77, 152-153, 201; Hood Museum of Art, Dartmouth College, pp. 91 (purchased through the Julia L. Whittier Fund), 202 (commissioned by the Trustees of Dartmouth College), 206 (gift of the artist through the Friends of the Library); John Carter Brown Library at Brown University, p. 36; Library of Congress Prints and Photographs Division, pp. 31 (right), 45, 46, 47, 73, 133; Maine State Museum, Augusta, Maine, p. 138; Manchester Historic Association, pp. 31 (left), 32 (bottom), 112; Mariners' Museum, Newport News, Virginia, p. 75; Montshire Museum of Science, Norwich, Vermont (photo by Bill Gove), p. 258; Mount Holyoke College Art Museum, South Hadley, Massachusetts, p. 226 (gift of Ellen W. Ayer); Museum of the American Numismatic Association, p. 44; NASA, p. 33 (left), 49; National Museum American Art, Washington, D.C./Art Resource, New York, p. 63; New Hampshire Historical Society, pp. 32 (top), 37, 41, 66, 100, 117, 130, 162, 166, 220, 225, 226, 227; Old Print Barn, Meredith, New Hampshire, p. 161; Portsmouth Athenaeum, p. 30; Claudia Rippee, p. 17; Segway LLC, p. 33 (right); Shelburne Museum, Shelburne, Vermont (photo by Ken Burris), p. 192; Sterling and Francine Clark Art Institute, Williamstown, Massachusetts, p. 224; U.S. Department of the Interior, National Park Service, Saint-Gaudens National Historic Site, pp. 209, 210; Wadsworth Atheneum, Hartford, Connecticut, p. 222; Wolfeboro Historical Society, p. 164; Yankee Publishing, p. 151.

COMPASS AMERICAN GUIDES ALSO ACKNOWLEDGES the following: Henry Holt and Company, LLC, and the Random House Group Limited for the excerpts from "Birches," "New Hampshire," and "Mending Wall" from THE POETRY OF ROBERT FROST, edited by Edward Connery Lathem, the Estate of Robert Frost, and Jonathan Cape as publisher. Copyright 1923, 1939, 1969 by Henry Holt and Co.; copyright 1944, 1951, 1958 by Robert Frost; copyright 1967 by Lesley Frost Ballantine. Reprinted by permission of Henry Holt and Company, LLC and The Random House Group Limited.

The excerpt from Susan Warner's 1882 novel *Nobody* appears in *A Tourist's New England: Travel Fiction, 1820-1920*, edited by Dona Brown; Hanover, New Hampshire: University Press of New England, 1999.

The publisher would also like to thank Lisa Oppenheimer for her essay on New Hampshire's presidential primary, Ellen Klages and Kristin Moehlmann for proofreading the manuscript, and Grael Norton for fact-checking and keyboarding.

■ About the Author

Debi Binder

Jeff Binder sojourned in big cities and backwater towns before he found his niche in the Granite State. For the past 25 years, he has written for clients in New York, Chicago, Washington, D.C., and Boston. But he's never lived more than a few miles from the Merrimack River, in towns that defined its history: Windham, Merrimack, Manchester, Allenstown, and Bow. Jeff began his career writing lingerie ads and has since produced everything from magazine articles to keynote speeches, corporate histories, video and Web scripts, and annual reports. An avid traveler and reader of history, he is, like his wife Debi, an enthusiastic hiker and a fairly decent cook. On a hot day in mid-July, you will find him, Debi, and their dog Chloe camped out on a secluded sandbar on the Merrimack River's upper reaches.

■ About the Photographer

Thomas Mark Szelog, a native of Manchester, New Hampshire, specializes in photographing wildlife, nature, and environmental subjects for clients that include the National Geographic Society, the National Wildlife Federation, the National Audubon Society, the Concord Group Insurance Company, and Patagonia Clothing. He is also a contributing photographer to Maine-based *Down East* magazine. Isolation, weather, and wildlife are Tom's companions when he photographs the natural world; ocean, forests, rivers, and mountains are his studio. Tom has earned national recognition for preserving wildlife and the environment through the art of photography. Tom, whose photography is also featured in the *Maine* Compass guide, presently lives with his wife, Lee Ann, in Marshall Point Lighthouse in Port Clyde, Maine.